SKETCHBOOK
1946-1949

Other books by Max Frisch

MONTAUK

SKETCHBOOK 1966–1971

A WILDERNESS OF MIRRORS

HOMO FABER

I'M NOT STILLER

MAX FRISCH

SKETCHBOOK
1946-1949

Translated by
Geoffrey Skelton

NEW YORK AND LONDON
A HELEN AND KURT WOLFF BOOK
HARCOURT BRACE JOVANOVICH

The quotations from Bertolt Brecht's poems on pages 151, 152–54, 203, and 204 are from *Selected Poems* ("The Return," "To Posterity," and "The Mask of Evil") by Bertolt Brecht, translated by H. R. Hays, copyright © 1947 by Bertolt Brecht and H. R. Hays, copyright © 1975 by Stefan S. Brecht and H. R. Hays, reprinted by permission of Harcourt Brace Jovanovich, Inc., and Ann Elmo; and *Poems 1913–1956* ("1940, VIII") by Bertolt Brecht, translated by Sammy McLean, copyright © 1961 by Suhrkamp Verlag Frankfurt am Main, translation copyright © 1976 by Eyre Methuen Ltd, reprinted by permission of Suhrkamp Verlag and Eyre Methuen Ltd.

Library of Congress Cataloging in Publication Data

Frisch, Max, 1911–
Sketchbook 1946–1949.

Translation of Tagebuch 1946–1949.
"A Helen and Kurt Wolff book."
I. Title.
PT2611.R814Z5213   838'.9'1209 [B]   76–54706
ISBN 0–15–182893–8

First edition
B C D E

For Constanze

Contents

1946

1947

1948

1949

The reader—always assuming there is one, that there is somebody who is interested in following these sketches and jottings of
a youngish contemporary whose claim to attention lies not in his
person but only in his contemporaneity, perhaps too in his special
position as one who has been spared, who stands outside national
camps—the reader would do this book a great favor were he not
to dip into its pages according to whim or chance, but to follow
the order as presented; the separate stones of a mosaic—and that
is what this book is at any rate intended to be—can seldom stand
up by themselves.

Zurich, Christmas 1949

1946

Zurich, Café de la Terrasse

Yesterday, on my way to the office, I came on a crush of people, already spilling over the sidewalk onto the road, all with necks outstretched; from the unseen center an occasional laugh—

Till a policeman arrived.

He asked what was going on and, since we did not know, burrowed into the crowd, not roughly, but with all the authority of his office. Can't have this, he kept saying, can't have this; probably because of the traffic—

And then:

A young man was standing there, large, pale, rather poor to judge by his clothing, but seemingly no beggar. Cheerful, uninhibited as a child. Beside him lay an open suitcase, and this case, as I could now see, was full of marionettes. He had just taken one out and was holding it by the strings in such a way that the little wooden manikin just skimmed over the paving stones. Not bothered by the policeman, who seemed for a moment taken aback:

"What are you doing?"

The young man, not a bit disconcerted, went on showing us how the separate joints could be manipulated, and for a moment the policeman, who had the amiable face of a beekeeper, watched too, his thumbs in his belt, smiling.

"What are you doing?"

The young man, his eyes on the puppet, smiling because everybody could see the answer:

"Jesus Christ."

The policeman:

"Can't have this . . . Not here . . . Can't do that . . ."

Marion and the marionettes

Andorra is a small country, very small indeed, and just for this very reason the people living there are odd people, as distrustful as they are ambitious, suspicious of everything, even when it comes out of their own valleys. An Andorran intelligent enough to be aware how very small his country is suffers throughout his life the fear of losing his sense of proportion. It is an understandable fear, praiseworthy and courageous too. To some extent it is the only way in which an Andorran can show that he is intelligent. The Andorran arms: a castle, inside it a tiny captive snake, seeking with its poisonous fangs to seize its own tail. A smart coat of arms and an honest one, suggesting the relationship between Andorran and Andorran, disagreeable as it usually is in small countries.

The lack of trust—

The Andorran fear of appearing provincial when he takes a fellow Andorran seriously; nothing is more provincial than this fear itself.

Marion had carved the puppets when he was ill. Because he was ill; time on his hands. He carved them out of linden wood, since of all woods this least tends to splinter; it is not hard, not stubborn, it has no knots to impede the knife. The danger, when the knife strikes a knot, is that it suddenly slips, and everything is ruined, a nose gone. Linden wood is amenable, dependable, with its brightness, the regularity of its annual rings: a wood to be prized.

When he knocked a third nail in the wall to hang up the puppet, which was his third, the nurse asked him what he intended to do with them, what play they were intended for. . . .

That was the question.

She took the puppet in her hand:

"He looks like Jesus Christ."

Yes, Marion thought, but what about the others?

Pontius Pilate—

Judas—

At the start Marion gave performances for the poor in the village. Not that he ever asked himself why there were poor people as well as others, whether that was just or not. He did not do it out of pity. He was happy just to give pleasure, which in turn gave him pleasure. He was without pretension, ambition, or ulterior motive. . . .

One day a man on vacation discovered him.

A gentleman with a monocle—

Cesario, Andorra's voice of judgment.

One would need to describe the touching and compassionate scene in which Marion tried to explain to his old mother what a letter from Cesario meant. He read it to her. It was an invitation. He read it out again. And the mother shivered, as she always did, poor thing, the whole day long:

"What is the gentleman's name?"

Ah, the limitations of fame! . . .

But there it was, whether his mother understood or not. Marion journeyed to the city, Marion who believed every word that was said to him. He stood at the open carriage window and kept on waving as the wind ruffled his hair and the smoke settled down over the fields of his home—amber clouds, for the morning was sunny. And so Marion journeyed to the city: with Jesus in his suitcase.

In the café, where Cesario kept him waiting of course, he showed his puppets to a waitress. Others joined them; they were intrigued, and Marion had to show them how a puppet can be made to walk—

Until that policeman arrived:

"You can't do that."

Why not?

Cesario was embarrassed; he removed his monocle from his eye and wiped it, giving the impression that without his monocle he could not speak, and Marion's question went unanswered.

His astonishment at seeing how everyone behaved a bit differently when others were at the table. He did not know what to make of people, and in the following weeks had the feeling of playing chess in a dream: every time he went to grasp a piece, it changed color—

Marion wrote in a letter:

"I often feel they are just trying to get a rise out of me. They say nasty things about an artist I don't know, call him an im-

postor and so on, and in the same week, when I go to the café,
I meet them again. They drink and smoke and talk finely, intelligently, seriously. What can a person like me say, in order not
to sit silent all the time? So I say some nasty things about this
artist, whom I know only from their own words. Then I ask a
strange man sitting there whether he knows this impostor. The
stranger is the artist himself, and now I am the impostor."

His growing urge to stop doing as they did; he would say
what he thought, as openly as possible, whoever was sitting
at the table. His mistake was to imagine that by doing this he
would force the others to do likewise. . . .

A certain rich Andorran woman was said, when she died, to
have had a very kind heart. This meant that, having no other
work or obligations, she had done much good, donations, etc. . . .
Marion had known this woman.
"Certainly," he thought to himself, "she had attacks of bad
conscience. But perhaps—who knows?—she should be given credit
for that much; I have met few rich people who have gone even
that far."
Did he say so?
And to whom?
And never mind who was sitting at the table?

Once, when they were already stacking up the chairs and
Marion was still sitting there head in elbows, lost in an emotional
deluge, a waitress took pity on him.
It was not very pleasant—
Next morning he saw them hanging on the wall: Moses, the
Three Kings, Jesus in linden wood.
Only Judas was still missing.
As if he did not know him.

A party at Cesario's.
Somebody played a sonata superbly and was obliged to give
an encore, and after he made his final bow, smiling, there was
a long silence; the ladies sat there in long dresses, the men in
black. They were moved. Then a door opened, a sliding door,

and they went into another room, where sandwiches were laid out, wine or beer, and tea for the ladies—

Marion was hungry.

"Ah," said Madame Trebor, putting down her cup, "so you are a poet?"

Marion blushed.

"You are a poet—and in the same breath you call yourself a poor devil. That I do not understand."

"Not everybody can live in a palace like this—"

"You mean, because you have nothing? If that is true, Marion, I envy you. You can do what we cannot: think the truth, even tell it."

Marion shrugged his shoulders:

"People who live on such carpets," he replied, "think poverty very stimulating, no doubt."

She blinked through the smoke of her cigarette:

"You see," she said, "so many people say they have nothing, and boast about it just as you do, but there is something they all have: and that is anxiety over things they would like to have —just like the rich, though without money. They are poor devils, if you like— But then they are not poets. Marion. A poet, I always thought, *should* have nothing at all—not even anxiety."

She smiled, looking straight at him:

"What do we need them for otherwise?"

A fairy queen eating sandwiches . . .

When the moment came, Marion was already in bed, the light turned out: it was the moment when he decided to stop fearing. He had to get up again. He put on his coat—it was already past midnight—and then to Madame Trebor he wrote all the things he had heard about her when she had not been present—

They did not meet again.

Everything has its consequences; there are friendships that last for years because one believes oneself admired by the other, a form of reassurance paid for by a return of admiration: one frank word and it is gone. And it was all Marion's fault; for every truthful word has its consequences.

Some of them may even be good—

For example, a marriage goes up in smoke, along with a house

9

and seven rooms, kitchen with refrigerator: in exchange for it one receives another love, which had long been lying in wait like a seed beneath a stone—something possible which, suddenly exposed to the sun, begins to live. . . .

Marion had a dog—this is important. It was a creature that was simply what it was. A small dog, sniffing in zigzags across the street; suddenly it would shoot off . . . and Marion would wait. . . . One day even this dog will disappoint him. Marion would not yet believe it, if someone were to tell him. It is a dog of indistinguishable race, without breeding, without dignity or class or any pretensions at all in that direction. That is why Marion chose it; a mongrel without a pedigree, a brownish ball which was always on the point of being run over. How could such a dog ever disappoint him? When it does happen, it will not be due to anything in the dog; the fault will be Marion's, and it will happen.

At the beginning of February the first signs of insanity appeared: the people Marion saw no longer seemed to him to be activated from within; their gestures, their whole behavior hung on strings, and they moved according to the whim of whoever happened to touch these strings; Marion saw a world of strings. He dreamed of strings. . . .

That was the beginning of February.

He felt the urge to play with the strings. He wanted in fact to convince himself that it wasn't true, that business of the strings. He gave up a whole day to it, visited once again all the people he knew—Cesario, for instance, who, being the educated man he was, always knew exactly what he was saying. He was talking about medieval puppet plays—

Marion listened.

"Incidentally, you can see a connection when you think of classical masks; even the ancient Greeks—"

Marion nodded. And Cesario was as friendly as on the day he first discovered the puppet player—indeed, he even ordered him another drink.

And Marion?

He had nodded: trustful and, as always—

Nothing more.

"A good lad, a clever lad. Didn't I see it at the very first glance? A boy with talent, but so modest, always so modest!"

While Marion was thinking:

"If Cesario believes in me—and how unjust I was when I recently called him an empty prattler!—if Cesario believes in my puppets, Cesario the incorruptible, the man whose judgment, as everybody knows, is severe but just, yes, just—"

Marion was in a sort of trance.

He had wanted to play; he had wanted to convince himself that it wasn't true, that business of the strings—

But it was true.

It was true even of himself.

Now in every mirror he saw Judas—

That evening he strangled the dog. It was found later in the wardrobe, the dog, and he had hanged himself in the adjoining lavatory, while people sat on the blue sofa clapping their hands at the little Moses, the Three Kings, the linden-wood Jesus, and the Pontius Pilate.

Cesario, when he heard of it in the café, was shocked and declared himself ready to attend the funeral and even, if desired, to speak at the graveside, although he did not in fact find Marion's reasons for hanging himself very convincing; it was a regrettable business, certainly, and sad, but not an inescapable necessity, therefore no tragedy in the classical sense. It was rather the story of an avoidable error which had arisen out of Marion's obvious belief that a man's truth lay in his words or in his pen. Marion had deemed it falsehood when people spoke now one way, now another; one of the two, he had thought, must have been a lie.

That had bewildered him.

He had hanged himself out of bewilderment—

Café de la Terrasse

All around me the surging city, busy at work, the hooting of cars, the hollow rumble from the bridges—and here this budding island of stillness and leisure, the first of the day, and all around me bells are ringing, a humming over the streets and squares, the avenues, the roofs with washing fluttering in the breeze, the lake. It is Saturday. It is eleven o'clock, the hour I love best: everything within us is still awake, gay but not overexuberant, almost playful, like the rippling light on the little marble table beneath the trees, sober, without the urgency of growing despair, without the evening shadows of melancholy—

Age between thirty and forty.

Café de la Terrasse

The point of keeping a diary:

We live on a conveyer belt and have no hope of ever catching up with ourselves and improving a moment in our life. We are Then, even when we spurn it, just as much as Now—

Time does not change us.

It just unfolds us.

By not suppressing them, but writing them down, one acknowledges one's thoughts, which belong at best only to the moment and the place that produce them. One has no hope that two days hence, when one thinks the opposite, one will be wiser. One is what one is. One uses one's pen like the needle of a seismograph: we do not so much write as get written. To write is to read one's own self, and it is seldom an undiluted pleasure. There are shocks all along the way. You think you are a cheerful person but, catching sight of yourself in a chance windowpane, realize you are a grouch. And, when you read yourself, a moralist too. There is nothing that can be done about it. All we can do, by bringing to light and recording the zigzag course of our successive thoughts, is to recognize our own nature, its confusion or its hidden unity, its inescapability, its truth, which we cannot directly attest, not on the strength of a single moment—

And time?

It would according to this be simply a magic device which separates out our nature and makes it visible by laying out life, an omnipresence of all possibilities, as a series. That alone is what makes it seem transitory, and that is why we always tend to suppose that time, the one-thing-after-another, is not actual, but apparent: it is an aid to visualization, a means of showing us one after another things that are in fact interlocked, forming a whole which we can no more grasp than we can see the separate colors that constitute light, until its rays are broken down and dissected.

Consciousness as the intervening prism which breaks down our life into serial form, and dreams as the other lens which reconstitutes it in its original form. Fiction, which in this sense attempts to emulate dreams— :

Later, while trying to read a newspaper, I am led by an advertisement to feel that clairvoyants might be significant in this connection—

Years ago in Zurich there lived a well-known professor, whose lectures I once attended. He had been a lawyer, a sober and self-possessed man. One day he disappeared. An accident, a crime? The analytical powers of the police (in a sense one of the tools of their trade) failed completely, as did the tracking powers of their dogs. Days and weeks went by without result. During this time a clairvoyant was appearing evening after evening in a cabaret, a man we considered to be, like all his kind, a harmless fraud. This man was now sent for, led into the study of the professor, whom he had not known, and asked what he could say about the room's occupant. The man, with hair like a lion's mane, went, so we were told, into a trance, exactly as in the cabaret. When the police then questioned him, he admitted that he could give no precise information. I can just see how those police faces fell! Only one thing he could see: water. Yes, and the man who had occupied this room was lying not very deep, hardly a meter, beneath it, among some reeds. But where? That he was unable to say, and so our clairvoyant was set free to return to his cabaret. The shores of the lake were searched in places where reeds grew. Nothing was found in the Obersee. To cover all eventualities they also searched the Greifensee: the professor, who had shot himself, lay scarcely a meter below the surface, among the reeds—

And another instance:

It is said that Strindberg was also clairvoyant. His wife tells how once in a fit of mad jealousy he made what she considered to be groundless accusations against her. He described in exact detail how, the day before, she had allowed a strange man to accompany her; he knew exactly which streets they walked in, the corners at which they had stopped: he could tell her everything. Only, not a word of it was true. He could not be persuaded out of his jealousy: for him it was true. It was several months later when his wife realized to her amazement that, in the company of a man, she was taking the route that Strindberg had formerly described to her. The streets were the same exactly, even the corners at which they stopped—

These cases have one feature in common:

The clairvoyant sees a picture, but not the place and not the time, and when he talks about it, he can easily make a mistake, as Strindberg also did when he took as a fact what was only a possibility. He did not see serially, and this seems to me particularly remarkable. What he saw was not history, but the present moment, the omnipresence of all possibilities, which we cannot perceive consciously. And it is clear that in order to see the whole the clairvoyant has to bypass consciousness, which always divides our being into time and place: he needs to go into a trance.

That acts of clairvoyance occurred in earlier times to a greater degree, above all more frequently, as we are often told, should not in itself seem surprising: they were times in which consciousness was less developed.

A nice expression: "In the dim and distant ages." Thus do the sagas begin which are not history but reflections of our being. They do not take place in time, but precede it. The active consciousness that divides and dissects did not yet exist, and for that reason we call the prehistoric ages dim. In contrast to our own times, which we label dark. We are like people gazing into the light; to everything outside the light of our consciousness we are blind. So we go stumbling onward. We lack clear-sightedness, clairvoyance. If need be, or more likely just to amuse ourselves, we can still find it in a cabaret, where it excites people, although they do not believe in it, neither laundresses nor lawyers; they sit confronting their own souls as if it were so much hocus-pocus, and when they come out they buy themselves a newspaper, read what has happened, and wonder where it comes from—

Basel, March 1946

An hour up beside the cathedral; birds on the deserted benches, the cool and elegant stillness of the old square, its house fronts bathed in a thin morning sunshine; the sudden feeling of a strange city; the Rhine stretching out in a silver arc, the bridges, chimneys through the haze, the heartening suggestion of a Flemish sky—

How very small our country is!

Our longing for the world, our desire for big, flat horizons, for masts and jetties, for grass-covered dunes, for reflecting canals, for clouds over an open sea; our desire for water binding us to all the coasts of this earth; our nostalgia for foreign lands—

Munich, April 1946

Munich must have been a splendid city. One can still feel it; the islands of green everywhere, the avenues and the parks, one imagines golden falls, gay and light, evenings after a summer storm, the smell of soil and wet leaves. It has a large spirit, a joy in living redolent of the South; an almost Italian lightness must once have played about its buildings—

A curious sight:

A conqueror on horseback, still riding toward the emptiness of a vanished room, proud and upright on a pedestal of misery, surrounded by burnt-out shells of buildings, outer walls whose windows are as empty and black as the eye sockets of a human skull; he too has not yet taken it in. Through a doorway beneath budding trees protrudes a frozen avalanche of rubble; it is an enchanting baroque doorway, and it looks like a mouth in the act of vomiting, suddenly out of nowhere vomiting forth the contents of a palace. Above it, the crumbling wings of an angel, solitary like all beautiful things, grotesque; the surrounding silence, bathed in bright sunshine, of something that has ceased to be, of finality. "Death is so permanent."

A girl lying with a colored man on the banks of the river Isar. He is half asleep, relaxed, plantlike. And the little blonde bends over him, bemused, as if there were four walls around them—

Even the great church, the Liebfrauenkirche, is an open space, filled with the flutter of birds. In the middle stands a single column, like a guest, like a returning wanderer looking around; somewhere one can see the beginnings of an arch, the shreds of a painting catching the sun. The roof is a black skeleton. And from here too one can see right through to the other side: there are chimneys still standing, high on an upper floor a bathtub, a wall with faded wallpaper and the black ornaments of fire, tongues of soot, windows full of distant skies and moving clouds, of springtime. Often it is possible to see right across one street into the next, even if it is through a web of red rust; the remains of a fallen ceiling. Hardly a house in the way of the view; only when one looks straight down a street does it give the impression of what it once was, leading me to think here is a street that has survived. But even here I find, as I walk on, gaping holes on both sides. The picture is the same almost wherever I go: a city, but spacious and sparse as an autumn wood. If it had been an earthquake, a blind act of Nature, one would find it just as difficult to understand; but at least one could accept it without trying to understand—

Odeonsplatz:

A cripple selling the first toys, monkeys of stuffed cloth which can be made to turn somersaults on the human hand . . .

Tomorrow is Easter.

Thou shalt not make unto thee any graven image

It is remarkable that the persons we love most are those we can least describe. We simply love them. And that is exactly what love is, and what is so wonderful about it: that it keeps us in a state of suspense, prepared to follow a person in all his possible manifestations. We know that every person who is loved feels transformed, unfolded, and he unfolds everything, the most intimate as well as the most familiar, to the one who loves him as well as to himself. Much he seems to see as if for the first time, because love has freed it from its imagery. That is the exciting, the unpredictable, the truly gripping thing about love: that we never come to the end of the person we love: because we love them; and as long as we love them. Just think of poets when they are in love: they look for comparisons as if they were drunk, they seize on everything in the universe, on flowers and animals, on clouds, stars, and oceans. Why? Because the person one loves is as ungraspable as the universe, as God's infinite space, he is boundless, full of possibilities, full of secrets—

Only when one loves can one bear it.

Why do we travel?
This too because it brings us into contact with people who do not claim to know us through and through; so that once again we can sense the possibilities life has to offer us—

They are few enough in any case.

Once we feel we know the other, love is at an end every time, but the cause of that, and the consequence of it, are perhaps not quite as we have always imagined. It is not because we know the other that we cease to love, but vice versa: because our love has come to an end, because its power is expended, that person is finished for us. He must be. We can do no more. We withdraw from him our willingness to participate in further manifestations. We refuse him the right that belongs to all living things to remain ungraspable, and then we are both surprised and disappointed that the relationship has ceased to exist.

"You are not," says he or she who has been disappointed, "what I took you for."

And what was that?
For a mystery—which after all is what a human being is—for an exciting puzzle of which one has become tired. And so one creates for oneself an image. That is the loveless act, the betrayal.

It has been argued that the miracle of prophecy can to some extent be explained by the fact that the future happening is presented by the prophet in words that create an image, and it is this image that finally causes, induces, makes possible, or at least facilitates the happening.

The nonsense of telling fortunes by cards.
Judgments based on handwriting.
The oracles of the ancient Greeks.

17

Regarded thus, do we really divest prophecy of its miraculous quality? There still remains that miracle of the word, which made history:

"In the beginning was the Word."

Cassandra, with her premonitions, her plausible, her disregarded warnings—was she always entirely innocent of the catastrophes she foretold?

Whose images she created?

Some fixed idea in the minds of our friends, our parents, our teachers—that too can prey on one like the oracle of old. Half a lifetime is spent with the unspoken question: will it happen or will it not? The question at least is branded on our foreheads, and one does not dispose of an oracle except by bringing it to fulfillment. The fulfillment does not, however, have to be direct; its influence can still be seen when one does the opposite, when one decides *not* to be what others think one is. One becomes the opposite, but becomes so because of others.

A teacher once told my mother that she would never learn to knit. My mother told us time and again of that declaration, which she had never forgotten and never pardoned. She became a dedicated and very accomplished knitter, and the many socks and caps, the gloves, the pullovers that eventually came my way I owe ultimately to that one exasperating oracle! . . .

To a certain degree we are really the person that others have seen in us, friends as well as foes. And it works both ways: we ourselves are the author of others; in some mysterious and inescapable way we are responsible for the face they show us, responsible not for the disposition itself, but for the development of that disposition. It is we ourselves who stand in the way of a friend whose settled habits cause us concern, for the reason that our opinion that he is settled in his habits is a further link in the chain that binds and is slowly strangling him. We would like him to change—oh yes, we wish the same of whole nations! But all the same we are by no means prepared to give up our preconceived ideas about them. We ourselves are the last to change those. We think of ourselves as mirrors, and only very seldom do we realize to what extent the other person is himself the reflection of our own set image, our creation, our victim—

Between Nuremberg and Würzburg

The end of a dream:

Our lake at home, ocean-going ships that, I maintain, come from Munich, a sort of flood which obviously began while I was away and is rising still, but in such a way that it does not lift up the ships; only their masts show above the surface, a line of moving flags, and I wonder how the passengers manage to stay alive. But nobody can tell me anything. I am trying to get to Küsnacht on account of our children. Reeds everywhere, a whirlpool full of ants, a spinning mass, and later we are climbing a mountain in frantic haste, the reddish rock crumbling beneath our feet wherever we tread. They are bricks, and in ever-increasing numbers they hurtle down the slope to fall into the sea—

I wake up completely exhausted.

Outside, as far as I can distinguish through the boarded window, another ruined railroad station—

Moonlight.

The Andorran Jew

In Andorra there lived a young man who was believed to be a Jew. It will be necessary to describe his presumed background, his daily contacts with the Andorrans, who see the Jewishness in him: the fixed image that meets him everywhere. Their distrust, for instance, of his depth of feeling—something that, as even an Andorran knows, no Jew can possibly have. A Jew has to rely on the sharpness of his wits, which get all the sharper because of it. Or his attitude toward money, an important matter in Andorra as elsewhere: he knew, he could feel what they were all silently thinking; he examined himself to see whether it was true that he was always thinking of money, examined himself until he discovered that it was so, he really was always thinking of money. He admitted it; he stood by it; and the Andorrans exchanged meaning glances, not speaking, hardly even drawing in the corners of their lips. As regards national loyalties, he knew exactly what they were thinking: whenever he spoke of his "native land" they turned their eyes away, as from a coin lying in the dirt. For Andorrans knew that a Jew either adopted or paid for

19

his native land—he was not born to it as they were. However good his intentions, it was like speaking into a mask of cotton wool when he talked of Andorran affairs. Eventually he realized that he was lacking in tact, indeed he was told so quite openly when once, upset by their attitude, he lost his temper with them. Once and for all, patriotism was their business, not his. He was not expected to love his native country; on the contrary, his obstinate efforts and overtures only served to increase their suspicions: he was trying to curry favor, seeking an advantage for his own purposes, they thought, even when they themselves could not see what those purposes could be. And so it went on, until one day he realized, with the acuteness of his restless, analytical mind, that he really did not love his native country, and least of all the epithet itself, which always caused embarrassment whenever he used it. Obviously they were right. Obviously he could never love anything, not as Andorrans understood the word: the heat of passion, which he certainly had, was modified by the coldness of his intellect, and this they saw as the secret, ever-ready weapon of his revengeful feelings; he lacked sensitivity, solidarity, he lacked—undeniably—the warmth of trust. His company was stimulating, certainly, but not agreeable, not reassuring. He could not become like all the others, and so, having tried in vain not to make himself conspicuous, he began to wear his otherness with a certain air of defiance, of pride, concealing a watchful hostility which he—since he himself did not find it congenial—tended to sweeten with a busy show of courtesy; even when he bowed, it was a kind of reproach—as though his environment were to blame for the fact that he was a Jew—

Most of the Andorrans did him no harm.

And so no good either.

However, there were some Andorrans of a more liberal and more progressive spirit, as they called it. They acknowledged humanitarian principles: they respected Jews, they pointed out, precisely because of their Jewish qualities, their acute minds and so on. They stood by him right up to his death, which was cruel, so cruel and revolting that even these Andorrans, who had not come to realize that the whole of life is cruel, were horrified. That is to say, they did not actually grieve for him or, to be quite frank, even miss him—they were simply angry with the people who had killed him and the way in which it was done—that in particular.

It was talked about for a long time afterward.

Until one day something came to light that the dead man himself could not have known: he had been a foundling, whose parents were later discovered, as much an Andorran as any of us—

The case is no longer talked about.

But the Andorrans, each time they looked in a mirror, were horrified to see that they themselves had the features of Judas, every one of them.

Thou shalt not, it is said, make unto thee any graven image of God. The same commandment should apply when God is taken to mean the living part of every human being, the part that cannot be grasped. It is a sin that, however much it is committed against us, we almost continually commit ourselves—

Except when we love.

Frankfurt, May 1946

When one is in Frankfurt, especially in the old city, and recalls what it was like in Munich, the difference is that one can visualize Munich, but not Frankfurt. A signpost shows where Goethe's birthplace once stood. The impression is due to the fact that one is no longer walking at the former street level: the ruins do not stand upright, but lie submerged in their own rubble, and frequently I am reminded of the mountains at home, where narrow goat tracks lead over mounds of scree and nothing remains standing but the bizarre towers of a weathered ridge. Here a waste pipe projects up into a blue sky, three joints indicating where the floors once were. One trudges around, hands in pockets, not really knowing where to look. It is all as one knows it from pictures; but here now it is, and at times one is astonished to experience no further awakening. This is the reality: the grass growing in the houses, the dandelions in the churches, and suddenly one can see how it might all continue to grow, how a forest might creep over our cities, slowly, inexorably, a sprouting unhelped by human hands, a silence of thistles and moss, an earth without history, only the twittering of birds, spring, summer, and fall, the breathing of years which there is no one to count—

In a park, as I awake and open my eyes: the playing children who woke me, their frocks, their very thin faces, and the thought that they have never seen a city intact, then the thought that it is not their fault, theirs less than anyone's. These are times when the only certainty is the need for trust and active undertaking. Beyond the urgent duty to rescue them, as all other children, from starvation, there is above all the need not to see them as felons or outlaws, whoever their parents; we owe them more than pity; we must not for a single moment doubt them, or it will be our fault if it all happens again.

At the railroad station:
Refugees lying on all the steps, and one has the impression that they would not look up even were a miracle to take place in the middle of the square; so certain are they that none will happen. One could tell them that some country beyond the Caucasus was prepared to accept them and they would gather up their boxes, without really believing. Their life is unreal, a waiting without expectation, and they no longer cling to it: rather, life clings to them, ghostlike, an unseen beast which grows hungry and drags them through ruined railroad stations, day and night, in sunshine and rain; it breathes in the sleeping children as they lie on the rubble, their heads between bony arms, curled up like embryos in the womb, as if longing to return there.

On writing

Everything we write down in these times is basically nothing but a desperate act of self-defense, which leads inevitably to untruthfulness; for whoever tried to remain truthful to the bitter end would find no way back once he had entered chaos—unless he were able to change it.

In between there is only untruthfulness.

Harlaching, May 1946

For two weeks I have been staying with some young Germans whom I previously did not know even by name. Their hospitality, quite without ostentation, reminds me of former happy journeys and affirms anew the feeling that in matters of ̦hospitality all other countries seem to have more talent than my own. Perhaps it has something to do with the fact that in Switzerland we live so close to one another, but more particularly it is because we have been obliged to turn hospitality, one of life's finest impulses, into a business occupation. At any rate I feel freer and easier, more natural here than when I am staying with my own compatriots. It is only at mealtimes that one feels inhibited; it is noticeable how people immediately use up everything that comes into their hands; who knows what tomorrow will bring?

Yesterday again we stayed up half the night talking. And toward the end we were once more joined by the old gentleman from next door, who could not sleep. His striped pajamas and bare neck recall familiar pictures, and indeed, as I have now learned, he did spend six years in the concentration camp at Dachau. But he does not speak of that; rather, of the time before, the causes.

"All of us in the camp were agreed that it was not our sons' fault, never mind how much they were mixed up in it—"

To bed at three o'clock.

Today, when I want to go to town, I find myself suddenly confronted with a barbed-wire fence extending all around the building: an overnight surprise. A few prisoners in field gray, working under supervision, are just fastening the last rolls of wire, while guards with rifles look on. All sorts of varying rumors, indignation, and bitterness, but silence about the armored vehicles, the machine guns with their shining cartridge belts—

The young American officer:

"If somebody flies at my throat and I knock him down, I don't do it because I consider myself his instructor, because I think I can change him, or because I want to prove I have no faults of my own—I do it to stop him from strangling me."

———

Once again I have been searching for the man to whom I was to bring greetings and other things; the address I was given, quite exact, leads me up to a platform from which there are suddenly no more steps, and when one looks up, there are once more just blue sky and passing clouds. There is a smell of toilets, presumably no longer connected but still in use; the ruins are obviously still lived in. I knock at a door and, when no one answers, press the dusty latch, open it, and again find myself looking down on the street; a gully of rubble mixed with girders. After contemplating it, I pull the door shut and try at the next; there somebody actually does appear: an elderly gentleman who receives me with a courtesy that makes me forget the stink. Unfortunately he cannot help, does not even know the name—

Later, back to the river Isar.

The feeling that what one says of whole nations is never correct, and that views based on such generalizations cause more harm than good—where could one realize that more clearly than in the presence of a young woman expecting a child, in the proximity of a human being still entirely faceless? Unfortunately my shoes and my accent betray that I come from Switzerland, but all the same a conversation develops. In the course of it she spoke of France, where she spent two years with the army, talking of it as of a vacation, in tones of "That was the life." Since I remained silent, she stopped, and shortly afterward there followed some bitter words about the occupation troops, some of whom were just speeding by in a jeep, and about Americans in general, whom she called barbarians. When I did not agree with her, she seemed a bit alarmed; shortly afterward she got up and left abruptly without a greeting, as if I were an informer.

Out on a field in the Isar they are playing soccer, all stripped to the waist. Others are sitting on the banks in rows, like gulls. It is a weekday. Even time, it seems, is junk, ownerless as the helmet I found lying in a crater, along with rubble and rusty cans. Well, what of it? The helmet was empty, and the shape I was now holding in my hand is familiar: we know it from the hundred pictures we have seen hanging on newspaper stands for years on end, and for years on end have bought, with laughing, singing victors inside—

An old woman with one leg.

At last I get rid of the food cans which had been intended for a missing man, and hope that the donor, a refugee, would be satisfied.

On writing

What is important is what cannot be said, the white space between the words. The words themselves always express the incidentals, which is not what we really mean. What we are really concerned with can only, at best, be written about, and that means, quite literally, we write around it. We encompass it. We make statements which never contain the whole true experience: that cannot be described. All the statements can do is to encircle it, as tightly and closely as possible: the true, the inexpressible experience emerges at best as the tension between these statements.

What we are presumably striving to do is to state everything that is capable of expression; language is like a chisel, which pares away all that is not a mystery, and everything said implies a taking away. We should not be deterred by the fact that everything, once it is put into words, has an element of blankness in it. What one says is not life itself; yet we say it in the interests of life. Like the sculptor plying his chisel, language works by bringing the area of blankness in the things that can be said as close as possible to the central mystery, the living element. There is always the danger that in doing so one might destroy the mystery, just as there is the danger that one might leave off too soon, might leave it as an unshaped block, might not locate the mystery, grasp it, and free it from all the things that could still be said; in other words, that one might not get through to its final surface.

This surface at which all that it is possible to express becomes one with the mystery itself has no substance, it exists only in the mind and not in Nature, where there is also no dividing line between mountain and sky. Is it perhaps what one means by form?

A kind of sounding barrier—

———

En route, May 1946

This beautiful German countryside! Wave upon wave of fertile plains, hills with white clouds above, churches, trees, villages, the outlines of approaching mountains; here and there an airfield, the glitter of silver bombers ranged in long rows, at one spot a shelled tank lying aslant in a ditch, its gun pointing to the sky, elsewhere a twisted propeller in the middle of a field—

In Landsberg a state of alarm:

Our jeep has to stop, and we are inspected: guards with helmets and pistols, belts with gleaming bullets, a teeming mass of ragged people gesticulating; I do not understand their language. At the far end of the pretty little town there stands another armored car, its gun bared.

Then open fields once more, the road lined with trees which we have been following for hours, a rolling landscape of quiet hills, clouds, forests, and occasional army huts; a camp in a forest clearing, the earth gray and bare, uncultivated—it reminds me of a farm for silver foxes perhaps, everything fenced in and tidy and straight as a die, a chessboard of utter despair, people, washing on the line, children, barbed wire.

Bregenz:

French colors everywhere. An overabundance of flags, which never looks impressive, whatever their color. We arrive during a march-past with drummers, driving toward music both exciting and elegant, clear and full of passion, cheerful, transparent, jaunty, irresistible. At last the soldiers come into sight, emerging from a side street, faces full of the Mediterranean, skin like fine clay, eyes of velvet. They march to the square with its lining of linden trees, down the left side, down the right side, drums rolling, they halt, more drums, they swing their bugles, and every time they do so there is a flashing in the evening sun like knitting needles. I observe their white gaiters, their white belts, their white gloves; the Marseillaise on Lake Constance. And still more drums, still more fanfares, still more knitting needles, a wedding of operetta and barracks, superb, but improbable.

Café de la Terrasse

Only at times when we are unable to work does it become clear why we choose to work at all. Work is the only thing that preserves us from terror when—suddenly defenseless—we wake up in the morning. It alone gives us the strength to persevere in the labyrinth which surrounds us; it is Ariadne's thread.

Unable to work:

These are the times when one can hardly walk through the suburbs without being depressed by the sight of their formlessly spreading petrifaction. The way a person, someone who has nothing to do with us, eats or laughs; the way there is always in every streetcar someone who stands in the doorway when others want to get out, such things can make us despair of mankind, and a nearer fault, one of our own, deprives us entirely of the confidence that anything can ever succeed. We can no longer distinguish between large things and small things: both are simply beyond our power. The indiscriminateness of fear. We are crushed by all news of misery, of lawlessness, of falsehood, of injustice—

On the other hand:

When we manage to write even only one sentence whose form satisfies us, seeming to have nothing in common with all the chaos around us—how safe we feel against the undefined and shapeless things within us and in the world outside! All of a sudden human existence seems possible, no difficulties at all, we can bear the world, even the real one, in all its absurdity. We can bear it because of our absurd confidence that chaos can be controlled, can be grasped just as a sentence can be grasped. Form of any kind, once achieved, gives us a uniquely powerful sense of inner comfort.

Concerning Marion

After the puppet maker hanged himself some people dubbed him an aesthete, because he was so dependent on playacting, on form, in order to live—because he was living so close to chaos.

Postscript to my journey

Looking back on my various encounters, I have come to the conclusion that the gap between us was on the whole greater than I had expected or hoped for, yet at the same time it becomes more bridgeable when one sees on the other side a human face. Some individuals can make us forget all the obstacles between us; we are not a Swiss confronting a German; one is grateful that one speaks the same language and ashamed of ever having forgotten these individual persons even for a moment. The majority are admittedly people one might again be tempted to forget: they seek to justify themselves and, whether we like it or not, make judges of us, with the duty of finding them not guilty. And if we cannot bring ourselves to do that, if we stay silent or remind them of certain things which must not be forgotten, we find ourselves being reproached, silently or openly, for behaving like judges—

Compassion—can the purpose of it be to set aside the judgment? Or is not its real purpose to help us go beyond the judgment, without, however, setting it aside, and proceed to the second part of our task, which is to act? And how can an action that does not arise out of a judgment ever be of real help? Help means change in the sense indicated by an acknowledgment of guilt; both help and change to the extent that lies within our power—

Often I have the feeling that the only possible future lies actually in the hands of these desperate people themselves, but then the question arises to what extent self-disgust, as distressing to listen to as it is embarrassing, can ever be fruitful; to what extent is it the harbinger of a genuine acknowledgment of guilt, which desperate people feel but are not yet able to accept? For we all tend to push our recognition of guilt into some immeasurable region where we ourselves can cease to believe in it. And that is of course flight into a sublimation, which can never bring about change.

Primarily it is of course the state of distress itself that makes change increasingly difficult, even where it is possible. If I were dying of pneumonia and someone told me that my neighbor had died through some fault of mine, it is possible that I should hear what was said, should see the picture that was being held up before my eyes, but should fail to take it in. My own suffering restricts my consciousness to a single point—myself. Perhaps it is for that reason that conversation sometimes proves difficult: it is inhuman, one comes to realize, to expect a person to see beyond his own ruin. So long as he is in the grip of his personal distress, how can he come to acknowledge that other distress which his country has brought on half the world? But without this acknowledgment, which goes far beyond mere awareness, he will never change his manner of thinking. His country will never become one nation among others—in our opinion the true goal. For a country that thinks exclusively of itself there are only two alternatives: world dominion or distress. World dominion was aimed for, and now there is distress. The depressing thing is that it is precisely this distress that in turn stands in the way of a change in the manner of thinking.

What should be done?

The first thing is to provide food, which is, however, to some extent in short supply among the victors themselves. The other suggestion one would like to make is that young Germans be permitted to spend some time in other countries. Many have of course already been abroad; they know Normandy and the Caucasus, but not Europe as a whole; what they know they saw only as conquerors. Certainly it is not possible for them to gain a broader view, even if they wish to, by remaining in their own country; they lack not only information, but detachment as well; all they see is the occupying powers, whose mistakes they use as alibis for themselves; and hardly anyone now living in Germany fails to discern these seeming anomalies between cause and effect. On the other hand, it has been proved almost without exception that young Germans who have spent six months to a year in another country see many things differently, and it is quite certain that it is only Germans who can tell other Germans what these differences are.

Concerning Marion

Marion goes to an exhibition, inspects the paintings of an artist he knows, and then, on leaving the gallery, happens to meet the artist himself. It is the man they called an impostor. He invites Marion for a cup of coffee and they sit down beneath the familiar arcades, smoking and chatting about all sorts of things as people pass by. It is late afternoon, the last sunshine; the soft glow on the tiles, the smell of freshly ground coffee, it could all be so pleasant, so rewarding. But the artist knows that Marion has just been to the gallery, knows that Marion has been looking at his newest paintings, and the things about which they are cautiously silent are becoming embarrassingly louder between them. They can do nothing about it. Whether sipping their coffee and watching the street over their brown cups, whether smoking or laughing or talking of a bad ulcer, basically they are doing only one thing:

Keeping silent about the exhibition.

The impostor naturally assumes that Marion does not like his new paintings, and the continued silence gets on his nerves. Marion can feel this, even understand it, for he himself has often enough been in the same position, at this very same table, when people kept silent about his puppets. You think: Well, say something! It is not pleasant to give an adverse opinion. One is afraid of hurting the other person; and so to some extent one does hurt him, but all the same, Marion thinks, it is unavoidable and could in fact be done in such a way that one might be positive about some aspect of the work at least. That would scarcely be possible of course if one felt obliged to reject everything the impostor does, even his efforts and his aims. But even then, in view of what Marion had once said about his water colors, there were surely ways of conveying his present adverse opinion in an acceptable way.

"By the way," Marion might say, "I have just been looking at your new paintings—"

And at the same time he could offer a cigarette.

"Speaking for myself, I must admit that I prefer your little water colors. I don't know how you yourself think about that. I particularly remember a leaf—"

That would sound all right. If not exactly like angels' harps . . . But Marion only offers the cigarette, and what does *not* sound all right is the utter silence: it is not natural, in fact it is quite horrible. For the impostor it is not so much his fear of the familiar pain one feels at any adverse opinion (particularly when it is justified) that is so torturing; the torture comes, rather, from his feeling that Marion considers the bridge of their human relationship too frail to bear the load of even a trifling pain; it is a plant that can flourish only on a bower of praise. So once again the sudden frightening realization that one (this time the impostor) is more alone than one had just been thinking.

And now even the sun has disappeared—while Marion is talking about Madame Trebor. Why? Simply to drown the silence, his own silence; for the longer it lasts the less escapable is the further suspicion that Marion cannot frankly condemn the paintings he has just seen, because the approval he had once given to the other's earlier paintings is suddenly no longer valid. There is no little leaf that he would prefer. Though at the time he had praised it. He remembers the occasion very clearly; but it had been a lie, of which he had perhaps only now, in the moment when he should be building on it, become conscious; obviously there is nothing at all between them on which he could build without telling lies—

But then:

Why do they talk together about other things, about God and the world, as they sit there offering each other cigarettes? Why do they join in passing judgment on other people?

And another thing. Even silence becomes, whether we want it or not, a statement that is in fact astoundingly presumptuous: we conceal our opinion because we consider it to be a death sentence, so utterly unassailable that the poor impostor whose pictures displease us can have no hope of appealing to a higher court. Do we not overestimate the importance of our opinions? In any case, Marion thinks, it would have been better if he had spoken.

But how?

After a flight

A flight over the Alps, which left me after the slight initial thrill with a certain feeling of emptiness, is still occupying my thoughts.

It is fourteen years since my last flight, which took me from the Bosporus to Greece. My memories of that, buried beneath my own reminiscences of it, which one plays over and over again like a phonograph record until one can no longer recall the event but only one's words about it, occupied my mind at first, when we were hardly in the air. The droning of the engines, which becomes like silence and cuts us off in a curious way from all we are seeing, the soundless wings, swinging above the fields and the roofs, now and again a little air pocket, that is enough: one could, while still flying over one's own home, talk—and as if it were for the first time—about the Black Sea, the Dardanelles, about Troy and that hour above the open sea; behind the anecdotal numbness of most of our memories, everything is still there. . . .

View of the lake:
The little white sails seem to be standing on a plate of glass, the water no buoyant mass, one can see right through to the green mud beneath. There is altogether something X-ray-like about this view from above—I remember a sunken battleship we saw on that previous flight beneath the waters of the Dardanelles. This time it is the treacherous Nagelfluhkante—that steep underwater shelf that has been the sudden undoing of many a nonswimmer—whose outline one can clearly follow. Almost comical, those tidy little gardens whose occupants imagine themselves to be sitting beside a sheet of pure water; from above it can be seen that it is really a murky, nightmarish tangle of mud and creepers beside which we are living, as innocent and oblivious as we are of our subconscious selves. The same X-ray effect on land: pale ocher or black marks showing like secret writing beneath the plowed fields. Some, easy enough to decipher, are the beds of vanished streams, but others are enigmatic. In England, a colleague tells me, ancient settlements have been discovered, betrayed by thin patches in fields and woods, rather in the manner of a geometrical watermark.

The only thing that intermittently alarms me is the almost rash feeling of security. Even the slight bumping does not disturb it—rather the contrary, in fact; air as a tangible substance; the natural confidence of a swimmer; one almost regrets having to sit crouched in this cabin instead of climbing out along the broad wing. One sees its tidy rows of rivets. A solid fixed pipe, presumably the exhaust, metal flaps to catch fresh air: it is all exactly as one sees it in the hangar; without relevance to the time and place in which it finds itself, it is performing a calculated function, whether in a wind channel or over the Titlis. I tell myself: Well, of course. What else can this molded metal do? All the same, I keep looking at it; there is something provoking about its repose. The thought of jumping off with a parachute causes no apprehension, so exempted from normal human standards does one feel—

It is magnificent!

Yet there is something demonic about it too.

Above a little town that looks like one of our architectural models I involuntarily make the discovery that I could bring myself to bomb it. I should not even require patriotic fervor or years of provocation; all one requires is a little railroad station, a factory with a lot of chimneys, a little ship at a jetty—at once one feels the urge to spatter them with a stream of black and brown spurts. And then it is done: one sees the little ship keeling over on its side, the street teeming like an anthill when one stirs it with a stick, and maybe one will just catch sight of the factory chimney as it bends in the middle and sags down in a cloud of dust; one sees no blood, hears no dying cries, it is all quite clean, all devoid of human reality, it is almost funny. Though not without personal danger; I don't imagine it would be easy, for I can also visualize the puffs of white smoke which now begin to burst around us, the squadron of fighter planes suddenly appearing from behind and soundlessly growing larger with every breath, the first splinters in the windowpane, the whining as on a rifle range, followed by a delayed and scattered rattle. No, allowing for all that, what I mean is simply the difference between strewing bombs over a model lying there beneath the driving clouds, and standing down there on my own feet, opening my jackknife, and attacking a human being, an individual whose face I can see—perhaps a man scattering manure, a woman at her knitting, or a child standing in a pond and crying because its paper boat will no longer float. This I cannot imagine myself doing. But that—and here is where the difference lies—I am not at all sure.

How one loses one's sense of direction on the curves! Since, as far as we are concerned, centrifugal force has taken over to a certain extent from gravity, one has the feeling of remaining constantly in the same position, and it is the earth itself that is swaying on the balance, suddenly sinking out of sight on the left while the other window is full of forest and lake—

We are circling somewhere.

One becomes aware how small the area is that nourishes and forms humankind; there already the last meadows, the ice taking over. Two or three thousand meters up, and world history ends. We see rock basins that could just as well be on the moon. The favorable set of circumstances, perhaps the only one in the whole universe, which allowed the human race to emerge, lies over the hollows like a very thin veil. One tiny change in those circumstances—an increase of water, a thinning of air, a variation of temperature—would be enough. Our living space is not large. We nest in an accident whose precarious balance, when we happen to become conscious of it, oppresses yet at the same time inspires us. Human existence as either a joke or a miracle; the few millennia it may keep going are nothing in relation to the timelessness surrounding it, and yet it is more than this timelessness. What it means to belong to this moment—

To return to the bombs:

Without that divorce from living experience which technology has made possible for us in a variety of ways it would presumably be none too easy to set up such huge armies of willing and obedient soldiers. Irrespective of whether people are now better or not, we are not all of us cut out to be slaughterers. But almost all of us can become soldiers, can stand behind a gun, consult a watch, and pull a cord. It is curious that mere distance, measurable in meters, should have so much influence over us; that our imagination should not be strong enough to overcome it. Perhaps for short moments it can, but not for any sustained period. The way in which we soon stop concerning ourselves seriously with people we cannot see or hear or take heed of with our other sensory organs is also discernible in other ways: correspondence soon dries up, for instance, when there is little likelihood of a further meeting; for a while we keep going out of decency, pride, a wish to be well thought of, our sublime conviction that at least *our* minds and hearts are not limited by space. But it is certainly not true of the heart. That does of course extend beyond our senses, but it has its limits; it does not encompass the whole globe; we speak of living in times of peace when there is a war going on in China. Even when we can make use of nonhuman inventions, human experience, it is quite obvious, is confined more or less to those areas we can control by our own powers. Or with the help of some other living creature—for example, a horse. Even sailing belongs to the category of living experience, for, though wind is a nonhuman force, it is not we who release it: it is part of the natural surroundings which shape our physical being, and is thus different from the forces we gather from inactive natural substances, store up, and release at our own will. It is these things that bring us into situations and impose on us a rhythm that Nature did not intend for us, and so far, at any rate, we can see no signs of our own nature adapting to them; the familiar sense of emptiness on arriving somewhere, due to the fact that our experience, once a certain speed is exceeded, cannot keep pace; it becomes attenuated, more and more. We may still continue calling it experience, but in fact it is now only a thrill, a voyage through a vacuum, the intoxication of blotting oneself out, a sort of ecstasy at being able to dilute oneself to the point of traversing a whole continent without experiencing anything. Exactly a hundred years ago the first railroad train ran in our country—at a speed of thirty kilometers an hour. Obviously it could not stay at that. The sign that we have overstepped our natural tempo is a feeling of dissatisfaction; yet if another car overtakes us when we ourselves are already driving at a speed with which experience cannot keep pace, we nevertheless give more gas—in the hope of catching up with our lost experience. It is satanic promise that tempts us ever further into the vacuum. Even the jet fighter will never catch up with our heart. There is, it seems, a human standard that we cannot alter, but only lose. That it is now lost cannot be denied; the question is whether we can ever recover it, and how.

Politeness

When we now and again lose patience, say exactly what we think of another person, and then see him flinch, we like to tell ourselves that at least we have been honest. As we so readily say when we can no longer contain ourselves: To be quite frank! Then, when we have said it, we are satisfied: the main thing is we have been honest, and it is up to the other person to see what he can make of the slap in the face our virtue has given him.

What has in fact been achieved?

If I tell a neighbor he is a clod—it may perhaps (according to the circumstances) call for courage, but not on any account for love; any more than it would be love if I were to lie, to go up to him and say I admired him. Both actions, which we employ alternately, have one feature in common: they are not intended to help. They change nothing. One the contrary, all we are trying to do is to evade our responsibilities. . . .

One may well ask what Marion was trying to achieve with his truthfulness, which as a part of him, leaving the other person out of account, was no more significant than a beautiful nose. By being truthful, was he just trying to please himself or to be helpful? If wanting to be helpful, he should have taken care to ensure that his outbreaks of honesty were acceptable, that they could be understood and acted on. And that means:

He would have been polite.

Truthful people who cannot or have no wish to be polite should not really be surprised if the community turns its back on them. They have no reason to be proud of themselves, as they are inclined to be the more they feel excluded. They assume a halo to which they are not entitled. They are practicing a kind of truthfulness that is always at the expense of others—

Politeness, often despised as an empty gesture, turns out to be the attribute of a wise man. Without politeness, which is not the obverse of truthfulness but, rather, a loving form of truthfulness, we cannot be truthful and at the same time remain part of the community, which in turn can only exist if there is truthfulness—and, consequently, politeness.

Politeness meaning here of course not just a set of rules in which one can be drilled, but an inner attitude, a readiness that has now and again to be put to the test—

It is not something one has for all time.

The essential point, it seems to me, is that we must be able to imagine how a word or an action arising out of our own circumstances will affect the other person. One does not, however much one might feel like it, make jokes about corpses when the other person has just lost his mother, and that means that one is being considerate. On paying a visit one brings a bunch of flowers: the outward and visible proof that one is considerate of others, and all subsequent gestures serve a similar end. One helps the departing guest with his coat. Such things are of course mostly empty gestures, but all the same they remind us what real politeness could mean were it not merely a gesture but a deed, an actual achievement—

To give an example:

One feels it is not enough just to state one's opinion; one tries at the same time to frame it in a way that does not disconcert the other person, but helps him; one is holding the truth up for him, yes, but in such a way that he can slip into it.

Why, when there is so much understanding in the world, does it usually remain unfruitful? Perhaps because it is self-sufficient and seldom possesses the power to apply itself to others—

The power I mean is love.

The wise man, the truly polite man, is always loving. He loves the person whom he is trying to understand in order to help him, and not merely his understanding as such. That one can feel in his tone of voice. He does not look up at the stars as he speaks, but at people. One only needs to think of the Chinese sages.

It is not the clever who help—only the wise.

"Being polite in German is the same as lying."

A horrible saying if considered a mark of distinction; it is the admission of a man who knows no limits, who is no longer himself when he restrains himself and consequently, when he *is* himself, cannot be borne—

Mephistopheles incidentally gives the answer when he speaks those well-known words: You do not know, my friend, how rude you are. The important thing is not that he is rude, but above all that he does not know it, which means that he cannot be considerate of others. When he asks after our health, when he is polite, he himself feels he is lying. An honest admission, certainly, but here again it is just that same blundering about with a virtue at the expense of others. It is not enough, because it satisfies nobody but himself.

Our idea of an artist:

An introspective person cannot and should not be polite; introspection and politeness are irreconcilable; lack of restraint as evidence of genuineness; the artist as an outsider—and not because he wants a new form of human society, but simply because society has nothing to do with him in any particular, and so he does not even need to change it—

Full stop!

One may wonder whether this romantic idea was ever in fact valid, whether it was ever valid for whole peoples (Germans, for instance), whether it is valid for ourselves and our future. It was certainly not valid for the artists of ancient Greece, who were always conscious of their obligations to their city-state; or for Dante, punished with exile; or Goethe; or Gottfried Keller, who became a civil servant and wrote sermons for the Swiss day of repentance; or Gotthelf; or the modern French writers, who remain poets even when they occupy official positions.

The goal is a community that does not turn the spirit into an outsider, a martyr, or a court jester, and it is for this reason alone that we must remain outsiders in our own community, as long as it is not what it should be—

Polite toward persons. But not toward money.

Our pledge is to a community of the future—whereby, as far as the pledge is concerned, it is no matter whether we ourselves attain this community, or whether in fact it is ever attained; as long as we recognize it as such, the nearness or farness of a goal does not affect the direction in which we are going.

Café de la Terrasse

A report from Berlin: A dozen ragged prisoners, escorted by a Russian soldier, are marching along a street; presumably they have come from some distant camp, and the young Russian has been detailed to take them to work or, as it is called, on fatigue duty. Somewhere or other; they know nothing of what is to become of them; they are ghosts, nowadays to be seen everywhere. Then suddenly a woman, emerging by chance from a ruined building, utters a cry and runs across the street to throw her arms around one of the prisoners. The little column has to stop, and of course the soldier also understands what has happened. He goes up to the prisoner who is holding the sobbing woman and asks:

"Your wife?"

"Yes."

Then he asks the woman:

"Your husband?"

"Yes."

Then he points with his finger:

"Away—run. Run—away!"

They cannot believe it. They stay where they are. The Russian marches off with the other eleven, and then, a few hundred yards farther on, beckons a passer-by and forces him with his automatic to fall in—so that the dozen the state requires of him is again intact.

The theater

Today at a rehearsal, and since I was an hour too early, I withdrew into a box, as dark as a confessional. The stage, fortunately, was open and bare of scenery, and I did not know the play that was to be rehearsed. There is nothing—at times at least—so stimulating as nothingness. Just now and again a worker moved across the stage, a young man in brown overalls; he shook his head, stopped, and began telling off someone I could not see; the language coming to me from the stage was ordinary, everyday—not at all like written words. Shortly afterward an actress appeared and crossed the empty stage in coat and hat, eating an apple; she greeted the worker with a "Good morning." And that was all; silence again, an empty stage, now and again a rumble as a streetcar passed outside. This little scene, witnessed a thousand times out there in the street—why did it make such a different, so much stronger impression on me here? The two people who had just crossed the stage had a present being, a destiny. What it was I of course did not know, but all the same it was there, and, however veiled, it assumed a reality that filled the whole large space. I should mention that there was just an ordinary working light on stage, an ashy light devoid of magic or so-called atmosphere, and it was obvious that the whole effect came from the fact that, apart from this little scene, there was nothing to see; everything around it was wrapped in night; for the length of a few seconds there had been only this in view: a cursing stagehand and a young actress going yawning to her dressing room, two human beings who met in space, who could walk and stand, upright, who possessed sounding voices, and then it was all over, inconceivable as when a person dies, inconceivable that he had once been there, had stood before our very eyes, had spoken, ordinary, insignificant things, yet somehow exciting—

Something about this little occurrence strikes me as significant, reminds me too of what happens when we take an empty picture frame and test it against a bare wall. Perhaps it is a room in which we have been living for years, but now, for the first time, we notice the pattern on the wallpaper. It is the empty frame that makes us see it. Common sense may tell me that the pattern inside the frame cannot look any different from that throughout the room; and of course it is not different, not a whit; but it has become apparent, it is now there, it says something. Why do we frame pictures? Why, when they are not framed, do they make a different effect? Because then they no longer stand out against the accident of their surroundings; without frames they are suddenly no longer sure of themselves; they are no longer self-contained; one has the feeling that they have come apart, and one is rather disappointed: they seem worse all of a sudden, that is to say, worse than they really are. Their frame, when they have one, lifts them out of Nature; it forms a window into a completely different room, a window of the spirit where the painted flower is no longer a flower that fades, but the image of all flowers as such. The frame has moved it outside of time. To that extent there is a tremendous difference between the area inside a frame and the area outside, which is infinite. Certainly they would be poor painters indeed who looked to the frame to rescue them; I am not suggesting that things assume symbolic significance just because they are inside a frame; but they do, whether they want to or not, stake a claim to such significance. So what does a frame say to us? It is saying: Look this way, here you will find something worth seeing, something outside the vagaries of chance and time; here you will find the image that remains—not the flowers that fade, but the mental picture.

All this applies equally to the framework of the stage, and of course one could cite other examples to explain, at least in part, the exciting effect that even an empty stage has on one. Consider shopwindows, for instance: those that reveal the whole shop and do not attract us, and those that confine themselves to a modest peephole through which we see a single clock, a single bracelet, a single tie. We tend to regard objects as valuable just because they are rare. Some of these little windows are like small stages; we stop in front of them and enjoy gazing into another world which at any rate looks worth having. Applying this principle to the real stage, I might say that it is not thousands of fools I am watching on the stage, but one single fool whom I can love; not thousands of lovers whose love, presented en masse, looks repulsive, but two or three lovers whose declarations can be taken as seriously as our own. This is worth watching. I am seeing individual persons. I am not looking at millions of workers, which (such is human frailty) prevents my seeing them singly: I am seeing this single one, who stands for the millions and alone is real: I see a stagehand cursing and a young actress eating an apple and saying good morning. I see what I otherwise do not see: two human beings.

Café de la Terrasse

In all newspapers one sees pictures of Bikini. Several hours after the atom bomb went off the smoke still hangs there like a black cauliflower. With a certain sense of disappointment one reads that the cruisers and destroyers anchored before the atoll are still more or less intact, not turned into raspberry jam. The goats, this time standing in for mankind, are even alive still, chewing grass as if nothing had happened; the monkeys did not come through quite so well. None of this affects the basic feeling of joy this event has caused. In Hiroshima, where hundreds of

41

thousands of people died, such joy was not possible. But this time it was only a dress rehearsal. Even the palm trees are still standing. Doubtless one will soon be able to do better, however, and the progress that made Bikini possible will be in a position to take the final step: to create the deluge. That is the great thing. We can now do what we want, and the only question is: what *do* we want? At the end of our progress we stand where Adam and Eve once stood: all we are faced with now is the moral question. Perhaps we ought not to speak of joy; that sounds like either overconfidence or cynicism, and in fact we feel neither of these emotions as we look at these pictures. It is rather the stimulating alertness of a wanderer who suddenly finds himself standing before a clear and unmistakable signpost. We know now that we must decide; we feel that we once again have a choice, perhaps for the last time. A feeling of dignity; it is for us to decide whether mankind continues to exist or not.

The theater

When one speaks of frames one must of course speak of the raised platform, which is a part of that particular frame, indeed the most distinctive one. A stage without a raised platform would be a gateway, and that is precisely what it does not wish to be. It does not want to let us inside. It is a window, through which we may only look. In a proper window we call this a sill, and there are a whole number of devices that fulfill the same purpose —the pedestal, for instance, in all its forms. The object is always the same: to separate the picture from Nature. There is a statue by Rodin, the famous *Burghers of Calais,* which was designed without a pedestal. This was obviously an attempt to project into everyday life the idea these selfless burghers of Calais represented, as an example to mankind, and to do this by placing it on the same level—on the paving of a public square—as the living people who are being invited to heed the example. This is a special case which, by deliberately avoiding the use of a pedestal, shows how effective and important the device normally is. The temples of ancient Greece, as we know, also stand on pedestals of three, five, or seven steps. Now steps, one might protest, are made to be walked on, to negotiate height. But, as one finds out if one tries, these particular steps are far too steep; one can climb them, but not with the dignified bearing befitting an approach to a temple. And of course approach is the very opposite of what the pedestal is there to ensure. Its function is to separate the temple from us; and not only from us, but also from its site, from the accident of its surroundings; it takes no account of slopes, as we do, for instance, when building a house in the country. There our objective is to blend the house into its site, in such a way that it could stand only in that one place and nowhere else. In other words, we acknowledge the relationship and try to adapt ourselves to it. There is only one Greek temple from the great period that adapts itself to its terrain and makes play with height differences: the Erechtheum on the Acropolis. All the others make use of the stylobate, which rises above its site, separates the temple from all the accidents of a particular terrain, raises it above all earthly considerations and puts it on a different plane: the plane of the absolute.

Is this not always the aim?

Dramatists are forever trying to go beyond the confines of the stage; there is no lack of cases in which actors enter from the auditorium, or come right up to the footlights and speak directly to the front rows, as if there were no gap between, of which the stage itself is only a weak symbol. I am thinking of Thornton Wilder, in whose play, *The Skin of Our Teeth*, Sabina at one point turns to the audience and passionately appeals to them to put the seats on which they are sitting on the fire that will save mankind. Here, as in Rodin's statue, the aim is to provide an example for real life by putting the work of art on the same level as its viewers. One might wonder whether by eschewing detachment one enhances the effect of this example. Certainly, when we think of Sabina's appeal, we see that one achieves the ephemeral advantage of surprise; but how short-lived that is Wilder himself well knew, for after it he immediately brings the curtain down. As an exception it is tenable, but not as a rule. Every action transgressing the limits of the stage loses its power of magic. It opens the floodgates, which may be startling, but hardly has the effect of allowing the fictional form to flow into the chaos it is trying to control; on the contrary, chaos comes crashing into the world we have set apart as different, that is to say, the world of fiction, and the writer who attempts to tear down the stage sacrifices only himself.

To be fashionable?

In despair?

Perhaps it was not pure chance that made me use Sabina, who in her attempt to save mankind appeals to us across the footlights, as my example. Perhaps there is nothing literature can do when it recognizes its impotence, demonstrates its impotence, but go under with a final cry of warning.

From a newspaper

A man who has already spent two-thirds of his existence as a loyal and conscientious cashier is awakened in the night by a call of Nature. Returning, he spies an ax gleaming in a corner, and with it he slaughters his whole family, including grandparents and grandchildren. Reports state that the culprit could give no reason for his monstrous act; embezzlement is not suspected—

"Perhaps he had drunk too much."

"Perhaps . . ."

"Or it was embezzlement after all, only it hasn't yet been discovered."

"Let's hope so. . . ."

Our need for a reason: to assure ourselves that such an aberration, revealing as it does the unsureness of the human character, can never overtake people like us—

Why do we talk so much about Germany?

Beside the lake

Often in the mornings, when I am going to work, I get off my bicycle to allow myself a cigarette. I leave the bicycle unlocked, to prevent my staying too long in this place where the waters of the lake lap the stones at the edge. It is not in fact a park, but a storage area, and at times there are heaped-up cakes of black tar, mountains of pebbles, which men bring and then take away in lorries, leaving the place empty again; only the wooden sheds remain, the huge quarried stones, the lizards, the rusting metal, and of course the clump of birch trees, the untended grass, the lake, and the keep-off notices, which for years held me at bay; beyond them, open space. This spot, where one can also go swimming, has now become my daily refuge; whether I am returning home, exhausted by a dreary day, or once more going to the office, where work will be just as dreary as it was yesterday and the day before, I always feel full of confidence and hope as I head toward the water. One day, no doubt, a policeman will come along and ask me for my pass: we must keep things tidy! This is the last untouched stretch of bank in our area. Sometimes it smells bad. There are rotting shoes in the water, broken bits of crockery and glass, farther out the white contours of a broken toilet bowl glimmering beneath the surface; wood lice swarm beneath the sandstone blocks as I move them around. It is still summer, but the mornings are autumnal, the sun hazy, the banks bleached. Birch and beech trees droop over the lake, casting unreal violet shadows across the pale pebbles shimmering up through the cool green water. One could spend hours here watching. Water, whether it be a spring, a racing mountain stream, a river, or a tame and peaceful lake, is always striving down toward the vastness of the sea, and it never rests until it has become a part of this vastness, the watery vault of our planet. Perhaps this is what attracts one to water; among other things. Beneath a barge moored to a buoy the light is green; the water is in shadow, yet the sun, sinking down behind the barge, is lighting it from beneath; now and again one sees a swarm of little fishes in it, shadow-gray, suddenly divested of their camouflage. Back come the two swans, noiseless, upright, unhurried, dignified, and across the liquid surface float the vibrant sounds of the nearby city; the drone of a streetcar, the rumble of the bridges, the rattle of a crane, a constant, undefined activity. It has long since struck eight; one thinks of the hundreds of thousands of people now seated at their little desks, and my conscience, I know it, will smite me as soon as I remount my bicycle. But here at the water's edge I feel free, as if everything happening on land were behind me, not cluttering my path. I am fully aware of my negligence, which grows more reprehensible with every stroke of the clock; but the swans are more real, and the sudden swish of the waves too, the rippling reflection of the pebbles, the squawking of the gulls perched on the buoy. Often, as I sit here, I find myself wondering more and more why we do not simply get up and go.

But where?

It would be enough, if only one had the courage, to throw off that kind of hoping that simply implies postponement, a reason for not doing things now—that insidious promise of after-working-hours and weekends, those perpetual hopes of the next time, the next world—it would be enough to snuff out that kind of hoping in all the hundred thousand enslaved souls now sitting crouched over their desks; the shock would be great, but great too—and real—the change it would bring.

Money: mysterious the way in which we all accept its existence, though it is in fact a specter, less real than all the things we sacrifice for it. Yet almost all of us have the feeling that we are making a tremendous nonsense of our days on earth; two-thirds of all the work we do during a lifetime is unnecessary and there-fore ludicrous, all the more so because we do it with such solemn faces. It is work purely for its own sake. Looking at it from a materialistic point of view, one could perhaps call it organization; from a moral point of view, virtue. Virtue as a substitute for joy. The other substitute, since virtue by itself is seldom enough, is pleasure, which is equally an industry, equally part of the cycle. And all in order to keep our anxiety neuroses at bay through ceaseless activity. There is only one truly natural thing about this Babylonian enterprise that we call civilization: it always manages to exact its revenge.

Count Öderland

A woodcutter's hut; a young girl is standing by the stove, and her mother is putting plates on the table.

"The soup is ready. If father doesn't come, it will get cold, and then he will start grumbling."

"It's always the same. . . ."

"Father!"

"He has already heard you. Just dish it out."

The girl ladles out the soup, and after a short while her father is heard at the door, stamping his boots. The door opens and he appears, brushing the last traces of snow from his shoulders. After closing the door, he puts his ax down against the wall. He is the man who cuts down the trees and makes the wood which others turn into paper, and naturally he is very poor. The mother says grace.

The father is already eating his soup.

"Amen."

They eat in silence.

At last the father speaks. "Who is that fellow loitering around outside?"

"Where?"

"I asked who he was."

"Why do you always look at me?" the girl asks. "How should I know?"

"He hasn't come here after me."

"I don't know who you are talking about, I haven't seen a soul for weeks."

"There's no salt."

The mother fetches it.

"Yesterday when I was cutting the logs he was there, standing in the woods with his hands in his pockets, watching me. For hours on end, with the snow falling."

"What does he want?" the mother asks.

"That's just what I'd like to know. He'll ask me soon enough, I thought. I've plenty of time—"

"What does he look like?"

"He's got a leather briefcase—"

"A gentleman?"

"He's standing out there by the saw now."

The mother goes to the window, but it is already getting dark, and obviously she can see nothing. It is snowing. The father is gulping his soup noisily. The girl has stopped eating. She gazes over her plate into the distance as she says:

> "Thus is our life.
> Evening after evening.
> The clock ticks,
> and I cannot tell
> who is speaking here

47

out of nowhere,
through my lips;
I just hear it. . . ."

The father:
"What are you staring at now?"
The girl:

"They do not hear me,
my soul cries out in vain;
they will not believe
until it happens,
till all will see. . . ."

The father, as he continues to eat:
"She's thinking of her count again. Day in, day out, the same."
The girl:

"Thus is our life.
But one morning
when I bring in the logs
as ever and always,
when the daily round begins,
there he stands in the room,
suddenly,
Count Öderland!
There he stands with an ax in his hand,
and when my father scolds me,
as ever and always,
he splits him like a log.
Together we go out into the world.
And all who bar our way
are felled;
Count Öderland comes with an ax in his hand."

As she speaks, the door opens slowly and a stranger appears in the doorway, a man in hat and coat, and he really is carrying a briefcase. He stands there a long while in the half-light before he is noticed. And even then, as they exchange glances, it is some time before the father speaks:
"Are you looking for us?"
"If I am disturbing, tell me—"

"Who do you want?"

"We are just having supper," says the mother. "If you would like a plate of soup—"

"Thank you, yes, very much so."

"Fetch another plate."

The girl goes out and the stranger is shown a little bench on which he can sit down. He does so. He lays his hat aside, but retains the leather briefcase on his knee, as if it contains important documents which he must on no account lose. The father helps himself to more soup and goes on eating for some time before he says:

"You have been here quite a while."

"I saw you, yes, up there in the woods cutting down fir trees—"

Silence.

"It's a lonely place."

"Yes," the mother says. "A lot of people lose their way. Particularly in winter."

"I can believe that."

"If you're looking for the village, there's still a good way to walk. But now there's a track—I mean, you mustn't think we are trying to send you away. I don't know if it's the village you really want, but nobody has ever come to visit us, you see, never—"

"No?"

"Why should they?"

The father nods:

"There's nothing here worth having, my wife means. A saw, an old house which gets no sun for two months every winter, rabbits and chickens, yes, there's that—a kitchen, two rooms in the loft, and that's all."

"There's no shame," the mother says, "in being poor."

"Once somebody came—"

It is an old story, and the mother does not want it told. She is altogether irritated by the manner in which the father treats the stranger, and in consequence becomes even more polite:

"I'm sorry you're having to wait so long for the plate."

"I am happy to be here in the warm."

"The other plate—well, you see, we never need a fourth plate, so it is often out with the hens. The child has to wash it first, but it will soon be here. I'll put the soup back on the stove—"

49

She does so.

"Once somebody came," the father says. "That was nineteen years ago, when I was away in the war. He killed my father and then my mother. A madman, he was, didn't take a cent! Did it with an ax, I mean. My father was a woodcutter, the saw came later."

"Why must you bring that up again?"

"Nothing much else happens here."

The stranger:

"You needn't be afraid I am a murderer."

"I'm never afraid."

"I wish I could say the same. . . ."

At this moment the girl at last returns, carrying the washed plate; the mother takes it, wipes it again with her sleeve, and fills it with soup, asking the stranger if he wants it thick, though it is only potatoes.

"I have no right," the stranger says, "just to drop in like this, but I really am hungry."

"Then eat."

"Yes," he says, plate in hand, "it is not my usual habit—"

He is silent a while, as if reflecting what his usual habit might be. He begins to eat before he finds what he is looking for, and the girl cuts him a slice of bread, which he accepts with a word of thanks. As he continues to eat, the girl says:

"I am glad you have come at last."

He looks at her.

"Don't be surprised," the girl says, "nobody can hear us. You are the only one in this kitchen who can hear what I am thinking. Don't say anything to me! I am glad you have come at last, before I am old. Don't speak to me, but tomorrow, when the old round begins again, take me away from here."

Second Scene

In a prison cell—and it is on the very same day—stands the murderer who is awaiting the last day of his trial. His attorney, Dr. Hahn, is sitting on his bed, while he himself is looking through the small barred window, his hands behind his back.

"A life sentence?"

"If you won't reply to my question, how can I help you? I am not asking as your judge, remember that. I am your attorney. I am doing what I can."

"Life, then—"

The murderer walks three times backward and forward along the gray wall and then returns to the barred window. He is smoking a cigarette which the attorney has given him, blowing the smoke out in front of him.

"What were you thinking or feeling at the time when—I am speaking of last year, the fourth of February—you were sitting on the toilet?"

"Snow . . ."

"What do you mean?"

"Snow, I tell you! Nothing but snow, I mean, from morning till night . . ."

"We must keep to the point. Our last hearing is in one hour, time is precious."

"It is indeed."

Dr. Hahn looks at him, but sees only the back of his head, which is like most heads seen thus—you cannot guess the face that belongs to it. Even the judge's face, Dr. Hahn is thinking, could belong to the back of this particular head. But then he reminds himself that he must keep to the point and looks at his documents, self-possessed as always.

"Why on that evening, when you came from the place we have mentioned, did you pick up the ax?"

"You have been asking that for the past seven weeks."

"Try to remember."

"That is easily asked, dear Dr. Hahn."

"What were you thinking? What were you feeling? You went to the toilet, you state—"

"How many more times?"

"I am quoting from the documents."

"As the days pass, I fear, even that is no longer true—"

"How so?"

"If everything in your precious documents is true, it seems as if my whole life were spent in that place we have mentioned."

"Everything in these documents is what you yourself have stated, neither more nor less."

"I know."

"Well, then—"

"Maybe," says the murderer after reflecting a while, "it is true, more or less—"

"What?"

"That I spent my life in that way, more or less . . . I remember that I often did have that feeling. In the bank where I worked—"

"You have already said you always went in your working time. That made the jury laugh, and it's good to make the jury laugh. But it is not significant. Practically every employee does it."

"I also had the feeling, dear Dr. Hahn, that it was not significant . . . nor was it when I stood shaving in front of the mirror at home, or tied my shoelaces every morning, or went to my counter every morning, and—"

"What are you trying to say?"

"In the spring I should have been made chief clerk."

"We know that. . . ."

"But you are right, even that would have altered nothing. It just occurs to me; the chief clerks have a toilet of their own—and altogether, thinking of the bank, the whole organization was first-rate. . . . The janitor kept a diary in which he noted down when he last oiled the swing doors. I've seen that diary with my own eyes. There were no squeaking doors or anything like that there. To give them their due."

Dr. Hahn bites his lips, something he frequently does to show that he is keeping a grip on himself; he never changes his tone:

"To come back to our question—"

"Ah, yes," the murderer says. "What is significant."

"On the day in question you went into a bar, which you left after half an hour. You walked home, sober, and at nine o'clock went to bed—"

"One was often very tired."

"After some dreams which you can no longer remember you woke up, got dressed again, went back into the city, again on foot, and knocked at the door of the bank. When the janitor opened it, you told him you had to go to the toilet—"

"Yes, we can't get around that."

"Go on. . . ."

"Perhaps it would all have happened differently if I had understood more about money."

"How do you mean?"

"I know nothing about money," says the murderer. "Millions passed through my hands, coming in and going out, and it was always correct, but basically, you know, I understood nothing about it."

Dr. Hahn understands.

"You mean," he says more slowly, "if you had been cleverer, if you had risen further and earned more and so on, it would never have happened?"

The murderer is silent.

"That's a tricky line of argument! We must never forget, because our whole defense is based on it, that it was never a question of the money—"

"No."

"We must stick to that. I said so from the very first day. You could have embezzled a million without having to kill an old janitor with an ax. Murder it is, but not for the purposes of robbery, and that I shall make completely clear."

Pause.

"But that is not what I was getting at, Dr. Hahn. . . ."

"Then what was it?"

"I mean that if I had understood money, I should perhaps not have been so bored. You know, when one stands at the counter day after day—"

Dr. Hahn stops in his tracks:

"Are you suggesting telling the court that you killed that old janitor out of boredom?"

"You don't quite understand."

"No."

"Of course you don't." The murderer smiles. "Otherwise you would long ago have done the same—"

He throws down his cigarette and crushes it beneath his foot.

"If in an hour's time you speak like this in front of the jury, you will be accused of showing no remorse, not the slightest trace, and, as I'm always telling you, remorse is very important, particularly with juries."

The murderer frowns:

"Remorse . . ."

His foot is still grinding the cigarette butt he has thrown

down, and both are looking at this foot as the murderer continues:

"I don't understand why everybody is suddenly so concerned about this janitor—they never even noticed him when he held those well-oiled doors open for them."

"A man's a man."

"Yes—"

"It is no laughing matter."

"No—go out and tell the whole world that: a man's a man. Nothing else. But take care, good doctor, that you don't lose heart and in your desperation pick up a handy ax—"

A knock at the door.

"Come in."

It is a policeman, a man with the amiable face of a beekeeper, two old yet at the same time childlike eyes which are always watering slightly, as if he had a cold, and between them a bluish nose which would be like a soft fig to the touch; he speaks in a bass voice, hoarse but muted:

"Dr. Hahn."

"Our time is not yet up."

"A letter—"

"For me?"

"It's urgent. At least that's what it's marked."

"Thank you."

The policeman goes. Dr. Hahn tears open the envelope at once, after apparently recognizing the writing on it. He reads, while the murderer, back at the barred window, watches the snow falling.

"The hearing has been postponed—"

It is still snowing hard.

"Did you hear what I said?"

His next words, describing the surprise with yet another surprise, are spoken in that sudden tone of familiarity which is often the by-product of a startling event:

"The judge has been missing since the day before yesterday, without explanation or trace—"

He watches the back of the prisoner's head:

"Vanished without trace!"

As he reads the letter again the murderer at the window says, as if this news were no concern of his:

"You have no idea, Dr. Hahn, how familiar everything is when I look through this window—snow, and always these five bars in front! Why should I show remorse in front of the jury? That's what it was like at the bank, every single morning—"

Dr. Hahn collects his papers. The missing man's wife, from whom the letter has come, is expecting him urgently.

"We'll talk again on Monday."

Third Scene

The following morning the stranger awakes in the woodcutter's hut. He does at least remember that he ate in this kitchen on the previous evening. The leather briefcase is still there, and that comforts him, though he does not really know what is in it. The girl is at the stove, having just brought in the logs: perhaps it was this that woke him. He watches her for a long time, her strong cheekbones, which look somehow Mongolian, her fair hair, such as the women in Latvia have, her eyes, gray like water, and her two front teeth, which catch the eye at every smile, however restrained, owing to the rather large gap between. . . . The girl too watches him for a long time, expectantly; then she says:

"Take me away from here."

"Why . . . ?"

"Don't you see why?"

"Yes, I suppose so. . . ."

"It is dreary here. Sit in this kitchen for ten years, everything is the same. Nothing changes. In half an hour you know it all."

"I know what you mean. . . ."

He passes a hand across his forehead, as if to wake himself still further, then suddenly, afraid of being asked, puts the question himself:

"What is your name?"

"Inge."

"A nice name . . ."

"Why do you look at me like that?"

He had not meant to; he takes his eyes off her young face and looks at something else, perhaps the stove, where a fire is burning, or the little window, or the snow outside, which is still falling; after a while he says, almost without thinking:

"If I only knew—"

"Knew what?"

"What my own name is . . ."

He smiles quickly:

"Sometimes, previously, I had this feeling—it is about the only thing I can still remember—a stupid feeling of being expected somewhere or other, and having something quite specific to do."

"What was it?"

"I've no idea. . . ."

Inge laughs.

"But previously I did know," he says, though without regret for the lost knowledge. "Or at least I thought I knew, but I was never right, you know. Do what I would, whatever it was my duty to do, I could not rid myself of that stupid feeling . . . never really—"

The girl blows on the fire.

"Go on."

She crouches down before the stove until flames appear again, then puts on more logs, and her hair is tinged red by the fire.

"I was so afraid yesterday," the stranger says, "when I saw the woodcutter. But not on account of his ax. Afraid of any person I might meet, though least of all of you."

"My father is not as bad as he looks."

"You are a person who doesn't ask questions, that's what is so wonderful. But don't think I have fallen in love with you, Inge, just because you are very young and very beautiful. . . ."

"No, I'm not."

"Oh yes, you are," he says. "I didn't really want to go off to sleep, since I didn't want to forget you. It is dreadful when one forgets everything. I have a job, but there I am suddenly at the edge of the forest, a leather briefcase in my hand, and in a place I have never seen before, not even in pictures, and trembling at the sight of another person, because I don't know who I am. Do you understand that? What was behind me, all suddenly gone— nothing but a forest full of snow, trees and nothing but trees, and the thudding sound of an ax . . ."

At the window:

"And to think there is no further awakening—never again, never!"

She looks at the back of his head:

"I don't know what is the matter with you."

Later, putting a cigarette in his mouth in the unthinking way one does, he turns with a sudden smile:

"The plate in the chicken run?"

"How do you mean?"

"You see?" he says contentedly, even happily, "I am delighted to be able to remember anything."

Then he smokes his cigarette, and Inge watches like a child who has never smoked herself, full of admiration for his gestures, which give the impression of a gentleman, a man of the world: the white cigarette seems to give him back a certain confidence, a natural air of superiority. The admiration she radiates as, so young and earnest, she looks up at him, makes him smile:

"So your name is Inge?"

"Yes—"

"How do we come to know each other?"

"All people know each other. . . ."

"You think so?"

"When they know themselves."

"Maybe so, yes—"

He shakes the first ash off his cigarette, moving a little toward the stove, as if there were a carpet on the floor, and for a short moment the girl is standing alone, watching him.

"Seriously," he says, a shadow of concern returning to his face, "it does often seem as if—how shall I put it?—as if there are basically only three, four, or five people we keep meeting all our lives, always the same ones, and if one were to go right around the world there would always be a girl, a face like yours, young, earnest, shy, yet at the same time resolute, waiting, believing, demanding; there would always be a policeman to ask one's name and where one is going—and always, when one wants to go and keep going, there are bars in the way. . . ."

"There are what?"

"Bars and barriers, customs officials, cages, bars; like the tree trunks in the forest, which one would like to cut down, if only one had an ax—"

He suddenly laughs, throws down his cigarette, which is not yet finished, on the floor of the kitchen, keeps grinding it beneath his foot long after it has gone out, and then once more changes his tone, so that Inge is uncertain whether he is just teasing her like an uncle or whether he really means what he is saying.

"Once I was captain of a ship; it had three masts and a beak-like prow which I still remember well enough to draw, and we sailed to all the coasts of the earth, this way and that, and lived on fish and on fruit which we fetched from the shore; we went hunting, and when we had all we needed we sailed away . . . yes—and then—"

"And then?"

"Then, all of a sudden, it was a toy: this big—"

He indicates.

"You could hold it in your hand, this ship of mine of which I was the captain; you could stand it on a table or a buffet."

"Horrible!"

"Yes," he smiles maliciously, "but that was how it always was with me. . . ."

Then the father comes in; he says no word of greeting, but looks at the girl, asking silently and half reproachfully whether the soup is ready. Only when he sees the stranger does he say:

"There's the ax, if the gentleman would feel like . . . in this weather . . . There's enough wood, as I said yesterday—"

"Thank you."

"My name is Jens."

"How do you do?"

"And yours . . . ?"

The stranger stands there with the ax which has just been put in his hand, disconcerted both by the question and by the girl, who answers it for him, saying:

"Count Öderland."

"Count—"

"Why are you staring at me?" the stranger says. "Yesterday you said you were frightened of nobody."

"Count Öderland?"

The father slowly backs away from the stranger as he stands there with the ax in his hand, in such a way that the ax seems to stand out by itself and to take on (even for its bearer, who hardly dares to look at it) an ever-increasing significance—

Inge, at the stove, says:

"But one morning
    when I bring in the logs,
    when I go to feed the hens
    as ever and always,
    when the daily round begins;
    there he stands in the room,
    suddenly,
    Count Öderland!
    There he stands with an ax in his hand,
    and when my father scolds me,
    as ever and always,
    he splits him like a log.
    Together we go out into the world,
    and all who bar our way
    are felled.
    Count Öderland comes with an ax in his hand."

Perhaps she is even singing it; but the father, who has fallen to his knees, suddenly screams like an animal, holding his hands over his face—

Fourth Scene

We see the study of the missing judge. Two of the walls are covered with black file boxes, each adorned with a white label. In addition to the desk, which stands at an angle in the room, there is a cozy corner with a standing lamp and solidly upholstered chairs; a fine carpet is also not lacking. . . . Three people are in the room: the wife of the missing man, slim, elegant, and high-strung, and Dr. Hahn, who stands rather aloofly to one side smoking a cigarette, as if he were not listening over his shoulder to every word that is being spoken. The third person, standing in the middle of the room, is indeed a curious figure, an ugly little man with a theatrical mane of hair which one would rather not touch, and his hands, since the sleeves of his jacket are too short, look like flippers when he puts them on his hips or now and again raises them to his chin, as if to see whether he is properly shaved. With a smile that seems as unmotivated as his gestures he keeps saying:

"Aha . . . aha . . . aha . . ."

As he moves about, a few paces this way and that, the wife retreats, so that the distance between them always remains the same. His gait is something like a dancer's, at least as far as his short legs are concerned, though he holds his back upright and stiff. At last he comes to a halt before a wall, which he contemplates as if looking through a window. We see him from behind, flipper-hands on hips.

"So this was his study?"

"Yes."

"Aha . . ."

"As I told you."

"And these are all files?"

"Yes."

"Cases?"

"How do you mean?"

"I mean court cases—murder, assault, rape, blackmail, embezzlement, adultery—"

"Yes, yes," the lady says, "yes, yes."

He examines the labels:

"Very methodical, very methodical."

Then he moves on. . . .

"The fact that my husband was very methodical," the lady says with a thin smile, as if offended, "is nothing new: everybody in the town knows it."

"And what is that?"

"What?"

"Here on the buffet?"

"Oh," says the elegant, high-strung lady, "nothing special . . ."

"A ship?"

"A toy, a family heirloom, an ornament . . ."

"Aha."

"Such things are not unusual."

"A sort of Viking ship?"

"Perhaps . . ."

"With parchment sails."

Then he turns:

"What about the other rooms?"

The lady crosses the room; her gait is always swift, always

light-footed, and beneath the clinging dress one sees the movement of her thighs; she holds the upper part of her arms always
close to her slender body, and—for instance, when she smokes—
raises her long sleeves only from the elbow; a gold watch glitters
on her wrist; her mouth, even when she has stopped smoking,
looks as if she were still breathing out smoke, her full lips open,
slack, displaying a warm, moist brilliance. . . . She opens the
door, which is likewise surrounded by file boxes:

"This," she says, "was his bedroom—"

"Aha."

"Nothing has been touched."

"If I may—"

"Certainly."

The odd little man gives a slight bow as the lady holds open
the door for him, as if aware how his sudden proximity to her,
caused by the narrowness of the door, is difficult for her to bear.

"But perhaps you would prefer to be left alone—"

"If I may."

"But of course."

She closes the door.

Dr. Hahn and the wife look at each other like two people
with a secret understanding who at last find themselves un-
observed. They still say nothing; they are still conscious of the
door behind their backs. She goes to an armchair, sits down,
frowns, and takes another cigarette. Dr. Hahn, who has moved
close to her, takes a lighter from his pocket and flicks it on.

"You seriously think there is any point in this?"

"It is our duty, Elsa, to try everything, even a clairvoyant—"

"A clairvoyant from a cabaret show!"

"Where else can you find them?"

"Horrible, horrible . . ."

"Our own investigations, as you well know, have led to nothing.
So far. Tracker dogs have failed as utterly as our own brains."

"It's three days now since he disappeared—"

"If it were not for the snow—"

"I know, I know."

"No footprints, nothing, no scent, no person who has seen
him—"

A knock. They look at each other. Then:

61

"Come in."

It is the maidservant, who is wearing a white apron, a young girl with strong and strikingly high cheekbones which look almost Mongolian, and with them very fair hair and gray eyes the color of water, set wide toward the temples; the expression in them always contains the hint of a smile and a certain watchfulness, but, since it does not reveal what the brain behind is thinking, one tends in the end, for one's own peace of mind, to assume that the girl is thinking nothing at all, that she is just stupid. The lady says:

"What is it?"

"The mail, madam—"

When she speaks, one sees the two front teeth, conspicuous on account of the rather wide gap between them; her whole manner, as she remains standing there, is half shy, half insolent; maybe her eagerness to hear the latest news concerning the disappearance of her employer is natural, but she carries her curiosity around like a sacred right and does not move until the lady says sharply, without looking at her:

"Thank you."

She curtseys. And goes . . .

The lady is opening letters:

"I cannot bear that girl—"

"Why not?"

"Did you take a good look at her?"

"Well, yes."

She goes on opening letters.

"The servant problem," Dr. Hahn says, "it lies in the air like so much else nowadays. . . ."

He cuts himself a cigar.

"Nothing there?"

"Nothing," Elsa says, "nothing from him, nothing about him, just bills, invitations, circulars, regulations, testimonials, appeals against alcoholism, more invitations—"

He lights his cigar:

"It was Friday when I last saw him, as I told you, just after the hearing, but it was nothing special—he just gave me a lift in his car and we talked about the summing up for the jury—"

He puffs his cigar.

"And you didn't notice anything either—"

"I heard him getting dressed, of course," she says. "He was always very considerate, didn't turn on the light, knowing as he does exactly where everything is, his shoes, his ties—"

"What time was that?"

"Two o'clock, maybe three—"

"And you didn't ask him . . . well . . . why he was getting dressed, where he was going?"

"Why should I? To his study, I thought—as he so often did—"

"In the middle of the night?"

"Yes, if he had a lot of work to do—particularly before trials. Nothing unusual about that. He makes himself some black coffee, goes to his study, reads documents and things, and in the morning, when I come down to breakfast, he has already left. . . ."

"Yes."

"And then there had been so many things recently—other things. . . ."

"What do you mean?"

"Well, one doesn't actually enjoy asking one's husband where he spends his nights—"

To show his deep understanding, Dr. Hahn puts a hand on her hair, and this is enough to start her weeping; she makes no sound, but one can see by the shaking of her narrow shoulders that she is sobbing. Dr. Hahn continues stroking her hair:

"Don't . . . Don't . . ."

He puts down his cigar.

"Elsa . . ."

She takes his handkerchief.

"Do you think," she says, as her sobs gradually subside, "that he knew—about us . . . ?"

A knock.

After a moment of indecision, as both try to convince themselves that they have not heard a knock, there comes a second knock, and Elsa pushes the handkerchief into her sleeve. It is rage that brings her to her feet, and she marches determinedly toward the door:

"This is really the last straw—"

She opens the door through which that maidservant she cannot bear previously appeared, and the words she speaks are sharp and vindictive:

"All this shameless eavesdropping, how much longer do you expect me to put up with it? Inge? . . . Inge? Inge?"

Dr. Hahn says:

"Perhaps it was the other door—"

A third knock.

"Come in."

The clairvoyant, as he emerges from the bedroom, makes a bow exactly as before, and just as superfluous and theatrical. He rubs his flippers together:

"Pardon me—"

"That is quite all right."

"I see it is seven o'clock. Is that right? I have a performance at eight—"

"You have to go?"

"I'm sorry," he says, looking around for his coat, "but we have seen all there is to see—"

A silence filled with distrustful anticipation.

"Very methodical, very methodical—"

Then he puts on his coat, which has been draped over a chair, and the others are so full of unspoken questions that they make no move to help him, in spite of his struggles with the second sleeve.

"Mostly," he says, "mostly I see him here—behind these walls. . . ."

"Alive?"

"Oh, yes, certainly . . ."

Elsa sits down:

"Alive."

"Yes, very much so . . ."

"But?"

"I don't see where."

Dr. Hahn bites his lips, as he often does when he has to control himself during some ridiculous interrogation:

"Pity," he says politely, "a great pity."

The coat has now been donned.

"All I see, if you will allow me to say so—I see the judge. . . . But you mustn't be shocked by what I say; I have never set eyes on him—"

"Well?"

"How shall I put it . . . ?"

He feels his chin:

"Anyway, I see him with an ax in his right hand—"

Elsa looks at her lover:

"An ax?"

"Yes, that is very clear. . . ."

"An ax? But that is ridiculous! Karel with an ax in his hand? There isn't an ax anywhere in the house!"

"Perhaps that is why."

Elsa seems relieved:

"What is he doing with the ax?" she asks, smiling. "Cutting down trees?"

The clairvoyant takes up his hat:

"Let's hope so—"

So that is all—a cabaret performance, just as one might have expected, and although it might be lacking in taste, although it means that no progress has been made, Elsa feels almost relieved by this confirmation of the impossibility of seeing through walls. As she accompanies the clairvoyant out, she turns her amusement, which she is obliged to conceal, into an exquisite show of courtesy; for quite a while one can hear her talking out in the hall, though unable to distinguish her words. . . . Dr. Hahn, now alone in the room of his vanished friend, opens a little cabinet and takes out two glasses and a bottle of cognac, visibly of ancient vintage. But before he pours out the drinks he turns on the radio, which begins to play soft, indistinct music. When the standing lamp is switched on, we find ourselves in a cubbyhole as solid and cozy as anyone could wish.

A voice from the radio:

"On the third stroke it will be seven—ten—and thirty seconds. . . . You are listening to the home news—"

Elsa, returning with a silent conspiratorial smile, is now in an almost high-spirited mood, and again one is conscious of the movement of her hips beneath the close-fitting dress. As she arrives, he is just filling the glasses. She says nothing but, taking a cigarette between her full, slack lips, throws back her hair, and her relief gives her an almost magical air of youthfulness, a charm that has no further need of elegance; lucky, one feels, the man who can now sit down with this woman beneath the standing lamp. . . .

A voice from the radio:

"According to another report—"

Dr. Hahn hands her a glass of cognac.

"—a serious crime was committed yesterday at a border post. Three customs officials engaged in their normal duties were struck down and killed with an ax. No trace of the culprit has yet been found, but it is believed that he was riding a horse stolen from a farmer. . . ."

Fifth Scene

Inge has now let down her hair; as it flies in the wind, she is hardly recognizable; her gray eyes, set wide toward the temples above the strong cheekbones, sparkle as never before, and were it not for the two front teeth, one would never believe it is she laughing thus as she flings up her arms and cries:

"Glorious are we, and free!"

All are drunk, their bottles empty, these charcoal burners who char the wood, these casual laborers who dig the clay, boilermen who sweat over furnaces, workers who roll the tubes, women who bear the children, more and more charcoal burners and laborers and boilermen and men who live for tubes, and an ancient handyman who can no longer stand raises his empty glass and bawls through his almost toothless gums:

"Long live the Count!"

"Amen," they cry. "Amen."

"Long live the Countess!"

"Amen," they cry. "Amen."

The Count on horseback:

"And long live all who understand; the night is long, but life is short; cursed be dependence on leisure hours, the day is sacred, and each shall live while the sun shines; glorious is he, and free. . . ."

Cheers without end.

The Count smiles down from his horse:

"It is the last time, brothers, that we drink together—"

"No, no!"

"You mustn't say that, sir. You promised us it would always be like this."

"Why the last time?"

66

"I promised that the milk would flow as long as you did not ask from where it came; the honey too, so long as you did not ask. Gather it up, I said, and bring it here for us to eat. Drink your brandy to celebrate the day, even if it is the last drop you bring, the last drop in the whole village. And let no one ask what will happen next—"

"The last drop in the whole village," cries one of the charcoal burners with a laugh. "Here it is, Count, the last—"

And he throws down his empty glass.

"I promised to bring you joy, as long as you did not ask. And did you not have what I promised you?"

"From our own cellars, yes—"

"I ask: Did you not feel joy?"

His horse is shaking its mane; he has to pull hard on the reins to control it, to stop it from suddenly springing through the grumbling crowd, and again it is the old handyman who tries to rise to his feet:

"The Count is right," he babbles. "It was a week such as no one here has ever known before. . . . Say what you like: long live the Count!"

Silence.

"I kept my promise as long as you kept yours; I sent to our estates for food to eat as long as you lived; I sent for clothes such as you have never seen before, my brothers, for silk cloths for your wives and daughters—"

"That's what we agreed, it's true."

"I have seen no silk cloths," someone calls, "however much brandy I drank—"

"That's true too, Count, like our empty cellars and stalls!"

The Count on horseback:

"Why had you to go inquiring who I am? Why did you go to the neighboring village to find out whether I had kept my word there? Why do you spread rumors that I set the neighboring village on fire? Why do you not believe me? Why are men skulking among you who would like to throw a net over me?"

They are silent.

"They will not succeed."

The handyman:

"I don't understand a word of it. . . ."

The horse is the first to smell the smoke and can no longer be held back. As it rears up with skidding hoofs the Count can only call out the words:

"Douse your burning houses!"

An hour later, as they look back, they see the glowing clouds above the drunken village; flames wave on the roofs like red flags; their eyes inflamed by the smoke, the helpless charcoal burners and laborers and handymen stand watching.

"He's vanished."

"We've been betrayed and ruined."

Inge laughs:

"Why do you look back?"

"It is heaven turning the heath red."

"It is the heath turning the heavens red."

"What have I done?"

"Onward, friend, onward."

"I do not know what has happened—"

"The road is open, Count Öderland; glorious are you, and free!"

"Glorious am I, and free—but where, my soul, are you leading me?"

Sixth Scene

The murderer in his prison cell:

"I am lying on the bed the state provides for me, and don't know whether it is Monday or Friday. Why should I show remorse when I can't feel it? Maybe today happens to be Monday, and if I were released for having shown remorse, what would be different? When I look at these walls, I sometimes think we would only have to stand up and the walls would fall like dust from our shoulders. But where would I go? What should I have gained? My favorite day was always Friday. When one knew: tomorrow is Saturday. On Saturday one worked and knew: tomorrow is Sunday. Every Sunday there was a soccer match, but even the half-time pause was horrible, because you would then start thinking about the coming Monday, and on the way home you saw people buying their cakes and pastries. The best time, I really believe, was Friday, as it got on toward evening. Once somebody loved me. She was very young, just out of school, and, just like now, I didn't care then whether it was Monday or

Friday. Every evening there she was, waiting outside the entrance to the bank. That lasted almost a year. Then she got tired of me, for she was very much younger than I and had another boy friend, so I became jealous and vindictive, and that's something, in fact the only thing, I *do* regret. I shall never mention her name. Otherwise she'll be brought into court, and if I then start showing remorse, they'll misunderstand. A janitor is a human being; of course—who doubts it? But how much is a human being worth? At times during the trial, when I see all those people, and particularly the thirteen members of the jury, who have left their shops and their places of work to see justice done, then I feel comforted in a way: to see how much a human being means to them, once he's been murdered. It couldn't be expected while he was there opening doors. It didn't show. . . ."

He listens, then jumps up, leaving one foot on the floor, the other on the bed; behind him the gray wall and the barred window, through which the morning sun is shining. As he stands there listening, one can see the chain between the handcuffs on his wrists.

"Who's there? Who's there . . . ?"

The sound of keys and voices, muffled by the door, continues for quite a while. At last the door opens, revealing a man in an overcoat, and the murderer asks:

"Who are you?"

The man in the overcoat takes no notice of the murderer at all, but turns in the doorway and says:

"This way, gentlemen."

They enter with a certain amount of ceremony, as one motions another to precede him; some of them are wearing bowler hats, and one is even a general. Some twelve or thirteen people file in, so that the cell is very full, and the man who entered first says:

"Gentlemen, you have seen where the murder took place, you have seen the ax, and now you are standing in the murderer's cell. We have troubled you to come here so that you can satisfy yourselves personally as to whether the facts of the case, which are familiar to you from our government's last note, are correct or not. The murderer has been living in this cell for the past eight months. Except for the hours spent at the hearing, he has not left this cell. The only people who have spoken with him are his attorney, the trial judge, and the prison wardens, whom we shall also let you meet. The single window, as you see, looks out on the sky; it would be impossible to make signs down to the street outside, even if there were not anyway a wall in between; that too you will be given an opportunity to check."

A few in the group glance around them.

"I might also add that the murderer knows nothing about the incidents on the border, or about the events of the past week which have aroused such grave suspicions in the government of our neighboring state. Beyond the fact that all these crimes were committed with an ax, we see no evidence to suggest a conspiracy to interfere in the internal affairs of our neighbors; this charge, which jeopardizes the friendly relations between our two peoples, our government most emphatically rejects. It is grateful for the opportunity of meeting your large delegation, and in particular grateful to the gentlemen from the Ministry for Internal Affairs, the Ministry of Economics, and the Ministry of Defense. Gentlemen, I now invite you to put any questions you please to the prisoner in person."

The murderer continues to stand there motionless, his left foot on the floor, the other on the bed, just as when he first sprang up, the chain showing between the two handcuffs. They stand waiting for the questions. They are by no means comical figures—on the contrary; the only comical thing is the place in which they are searching for the evil.

Seventh Scene

It might be in Brittany, or perhaps somewhere in the south: through an open door one can see the sea, and a ship riding at anchor on it—the Viking ship we already know. As for the rest, it is a hotel lobby of the usual sort, with a board on which keys are hanging and a cabinet containing mail to be collected. Before this stands a desk clerk, a black book open before him, and examining this book is a policeman, who wrinkles his nose:

"Count Öderland?"

"And the Countess—yes."

"Been here three weeks? And no registration, no papers, nothing?"

"Of course he has papers. . . ."

"Where?"

"We are, as I already told you, a grand hotel—not a flophouse for hobos."

"You know you could be charged with an offense?"

"One can always be charged with an offense. . . . For God's sake, do you expect me to get things from our guests by force? Or what? On the very first evening I asked the Count to let me have the passports whenever it was convenient—"

"Whenever convenient."

"Hardly have people arrived, hardly had a moment to get their breath—"

"Three weeks not long enough to get their breath! Must have been a tiring journey—more like a gallop . . ."

Since the desk clerk does not laugh at his conciliatory jest, does not even smile, the policeman has no alternative but to take refuge once more in officialdom, and this time in a tone of finality:

"If the papers are not in our hands by tomorrow, by this time tomorrow at the latest—"

"But of course!" says the wrongdoer. "I'll ask the guests as soon as they return from the golf course, I really will, but you can't expect me to take the book up to the course, even if—"

The policeman, now without helmet:

"An ideal hotel!" he laughs, wiping the sweat from the inside of his helmet. "That would be the day—when anybody can come along and say, 'My name is Count Something-or-other,' and everything's fine: he can live for three weeks in the very best rooms, have his breakfast brought up to his bed—no papers, nothing, no signature . . . and everybody quite sure he isn't a hobo—"

"Hobos don't play golf."

"That would be the day too."

"To be honest with you," the desk clerk comforts him, more at ease now that he suddenly has a human being without a helmet opposite him, "we ourselves were a bit worried for a while, round about the second week—"

"Because of the papers?"

"No, because of the bill—"

"So he hasn't paid either?"

"When people have enough money to buy a yacht—we get to

71

know all sorts of things, standing here in the lobby all day—anyway, once he started playing golf, we stopped worrying; I've heard he plays very well, too. Whether he's a real count or not, or whether he's really married or not—all we care about is whether he can pay!"

"And all we care about is the papers and nothing else—not whether he can pay or not."

"Oh, papers . . . !"

The policeman gives a salute, having decided to leave before the conversation tears his official manner to shreds.

"Oh, for God's sake," the desk clerk protests in the face of this new threat, "how can people get here at all unless they've got papers? In these days! How is he to get through all the borders and checkpoints, how can a person without papers even put a foot on this doorstep? In these days! It's quite absurd!"

"There's something in that—yes. . . ."

"I should think so!"

"But absurd—no, I won't take that from anybody. All day long I hear nothing else, and I'm sick of it. . . . Did you read that story in the papers recently? That man who murdered the customs officials, because he had no papers—"

"Murdered?"

"With an ax."

"But that's terrible! Terrible!"

"I can understand it—"

Feminine laughter is heard, and they move apart, as if caught in an illicit conversation. Inge comes in with the Count, who as always is carrying his briefcase. Both are dressed in white summer clothes, and Inge has a hand on his arm. . . . The desk clerk bows:

"Good morning, sir, good morning, madam."

"Mail?"

"Sorry, sir, nothing."

"Still nothing . . ."

"The people who have come about the yacht left a message they were expecting you in the bar, sir."

The Count seems preoccupied:

"Still nothing," he murmurs. "The world seems really to have forgotten us. . . ."

"Sir, the people about the yacht left a message they were expecting you in the bar."

"Yes. Thank you . . ."

The desk clerk moves obligingly toward the door to the bar, then hesitates as he sees the Count has not moved.

"Before I forget," the Count begins slowly, in the relaxed tone of a man who is used to being listened to, "before I forget: you are a policeman, of course?"

"Yes, indeed."

"My husband is always saying he knows you."

"Me?"

"Seriously," the Count says, smiling, "but I cannot remember—"

"Nor can I."

"Weren't you once with us in Öderland?"

"Öderland?"

"You see," Inge says. "He has never even heard of it."

"You bear a very great resemblance to a man who once spent a long time in my service—"

"On our estate, he means."

"A beekeeper, I think."

"I?"

"Or perhaps a head groom?"

"Head groom?" the policeman says, and seems impressed by the mere words themselves. "That wouldn't be bad, I must say, something like a head groom. . . ."

He laughs uncertainly.

"You do not like being a policeman?"

"To tell the truth, sir, to tell the truth—"

"I understand."

Meanwhile the desk clerk, to save his prominent guests from having to spend too long with the policeman, has opened the sliding door that leads to the bar; music is heard, coming from a radio, a soft, indistinct music, and the people waiting in the bar, the people who have come about the yacht, are sitting in solid armchairs; they are smoking cigarettes and drinking cognac: Elsa and Dr. Hahn. . . . But the Count, a man of charm and easy affability, is still talking with this policeman who reminds him of a beekeeper.

"Why are you a policeman then?"

"People like us, sir, can't always pick and choose."

"Why not?"

"Yes—why not . . . ?"

"Life is short," the Count says with a little smile and in the manner of one using a very well-known quotation, "the night is long, cursed the dependence on leisure hours, the day is sacred while the sun shines, and each shall live while the sun shines, glorious is he, and free."

The policeman watches him in silence.

"Speaking seriously—"

The policeman nods. "You are quite right, sir. Even people of our sort would sooner be sailing around in a yacht—"

The Count looks at Inge:

"Then perhaps he should come with us, don't you think? As a deck hand or a cook or something."

Inge nods.

"That is, if you would like to?"

"Like to!"

"We shall be sailing tomorrow or the next day."

"Do you seriously mean that, sir?"

"Why not?"

The policeman, unprepared for this chance for which he has been waiting all his life, terrified by the mere thought that it really could happen, looks from the Count to the Countess; he would like to laugh, as if he knew they were only pulling his leg, but his laughter dies in his open mouth, and he can no longer pretend to himself that the moment is not real; dismayed by his own belief, outraged almost by its implications, he looks for snags:

"Well, if I only had some leave coming—"

"Nothing easier."

"And permission to leave the country—"

"Nothing easier."

"You think so?"

"Seriously, take an ax."

"Like that man in the papers, you mean . . ."

Inge interrupts:

"One shouldn't joke about these things—"

The policeman sticks to his guns:

"You're quite right, sir! Sometimes one gets ideas like that, even without the newspapers, but luckily you don't always have an ax handy—"

"I always do."

"Karel, please!"

"Here in my briefcase."

The policeman laughs.

"I could never kill a human being," says the Count, "but a customs official—yes, without a qualm—or a policeman. . . ."

The policeman laughs even more.

"Think it over till tomorrow—about the yacht. Whether you want to be a human being or just a policeman, whether you want to live or not. By this time tomorrow at the latest."

They go into the bar.

The music increases in volume, but remains indistinct, a lulling noise which gives one's words a sensual quality. One knows the feeling: when, however banal the words, one seems to be speaking from the profoundest depths of one's heart; the conversation moves as on a soft carpet. . . .

The policeman in the lobby outside:

"He's a joker."

"And the papers?" asks the wrongdoer. "Why didn't you demand his papers?"

"Beekeeper! Head groom!"

"I'm asking you about the papers—"

"When you think what you could do with your life—deck hand on a yacht sailing all around the world—and what in fact you are—here . . ."

"A policeman . . ."

"An asshole with a helmet, yes."

"Sh."

"But he's a real joker. . . ."

Meanwhile the guests have exchanged greetings in the way that strangers do when sharing life in a grand hotel; there is from the very start a certain sort of understanding, even if it is due simply to the fact that one is eating the same food. Yesterday, for example, there was lobster on the menu, and if it had been bad, all the guests would have had food poisoning at the same time, never mind where they came from. They belong together somehow. (The lobster, incidentally, was *not* bad.) There is much suffering in the world, for sure, but there are oases, and a touch of bad conscience, about which one does not speak, also has a binding effect. One knows that Fate will treat us all the same, whatever comes. Somehow we just all belong together, and show it in similarities of manner, so it is not surprising that one has a sense of somehow being already acquainted. . . .

They sit down.

Their conversation is about the yacht which can be seen outside at anchor, and it also concerns the contract the Count is to sign to make the yacht his own; having already taken his fountain pen from his pocket, the Count unscrews it and holds it in his hand as he talks about the South Seas, as if he had often been there:

"You do not know the South Seas?"

"No—"

"I think I have never seen anything in the whole world more beautiful. . . ."

Then, before he signs, he glances swiftly through the contract—incidentally, for the first time—and it remains doubtful whether he is in fact really reading the text; his gesture arises more from politeness than from genuine interest.

"There is perhaps a certain little difficulty," he says. "The sum asked, which we need not discuss further, we can only pay in our own currency, unfortunately—in Öderland dollars. . . . As for the permits the port authorities require, you need not worry about those; I shall get permission to leave—"

"Are you sure?"

"Oh, yes, once I have the yacht."

"They are very strict these days."

"Nothing easier," the Count says, smiling. "If you have no papers, you take an ax— Have you not read the newspapers?"

They look at him.

"I always have one with me."

"Karel, please!"

"I mean it," the Count says. "Where would one be without an ax? In these days! In this world of papers, in this world of borders and stamps, of laws and barriers and taxes—"

All this he says quite casually, as if telling an old joke, chatting as he signs the contract, which he does in the manner of a man who has signed very many documents; he screws the cap back on his pen, looks to see if the ink is dry. The ship that he has acquired with this signature is no longer in the harbor, where it could previously be seen riding at anchor, but is standing on the table, where the other man has meanwhile placed it. As the Count looks up, having put away his fountain pen, he sees the familiar Viking ship with its parchment sails. . . . He looks at it, silent, motionless; only his heavy breathing is perceptible.

A voice comes from the radio:

"On the third stroke it will be twelve—ten—and twenty seconds. . . . You are listening to the foreign news—"

Slowly he raises his eyes; he watches the two people seated opposite him, and at last he says:

"Dr. Hahn?"

"Yes—"

"So it's true." He turns to Inge. "I often suspected they were having an affair together."

Elsa cannot contain herself:

"You can talk, when you yourself are carrying on with the maidservant!"

Hahn grips her arm:

"That's not the point now."

"Then what is?"

The Count tells her:

"They want to arrest me—"

He takes up his leather briefcase:

"But they won't succeed."

Without any particular haste, he takes out an ax, in the way one might take out documents, calmly, bored even by the familiar action; for two or three minutes they watch him, as if unable to believe their eyes; then they spring to their feet, as if lifted up by their own cries—

Inge says:

"Why are you hesitating again?"

A voice from the radio says:

"A report from Haifa states that another ship carrying Jewish emigrants to Palestine was intercepted at the harbor entrance. The ship is now lying out at sea with a slight list. The news has given rise to further outbreaks of violence; Jewish terrorists have bombed a number of oil tanks; the fire, which has not yet been brought under control, is still spreading."

Dr. Hahn calls for the policeman—

The voice from the radio says:

"In a number of German cities, miners have gone on hunger strike; it has been resolved to speed up the supply of potatoes, as far as transport facilities allow; should there be further disturbances, the government will be forced to proclaim martial law."

Dr. Hahn calls for the policeman—

The voice from the radio says:

"From the United States it is reported that Negroes continue to organize protest meetings involving hundreds of thousands of people at a time; in a number of districts the threatening behavior of the Negroes is said already to have caused clashes in which blood has flowed."

Dr. Hahn calls for the policeman—

Inge:

> "Count Öderland goes around the world,
>   Count Öderland goes with an ax in his hand,
>   Count Öderland goes around the world!" etc.

Genoa, October 1946

The sea again—at last! We are blissful. We have a room on an upper floor, and there is a moon to light up the sea for us, so that we can still see it at midnight. We even, as I later discover, have a little balcony. When I step out on it to look down on the night-covered alleys of Genoa, chasms filled with the sounds of the city, I become aware for the first time of the yawning gap beside us: the rubble has been cleared away with exemplary thoroughness, one can see right down into the cellars, and I make the mistake of telling Constanze what it looks like on the other side of the wall that, with its picture-laden, flowery wallpaper, stands sentinel over our sleep—

A friend's letter raises once more the question whether it is any part of an artist's job to concern himself with the problems of the day. That it is his duty as a human being and a citizen to do this is of course beyond dispute. But a work of art, he writes, must rise above it. Perhaps he is right; but the emphatically negative answer he gives to his own question is no less dangerous than the affirmative one. The best reply I know to this always worrying question comes from Bert Brecht:

"Ah, what an age it is when to speak of trees is almost a crime for it is a kind of silence about injustice! . . ."

On the following morning we go down to the harbor to take a closer look at the sea. The harbor has also suffered considerable damage. A submerged ship, only funnel and masts showing above the waves, reminds me of that dream I had somewhere near Würzburg. We stay watching for the best part of an hour. They are raising it to the surface—a gigantic task. Later we are told it was an aircraft carrier.

Portofino Mare, October 1946

There is something almost ghostly about it: one passes a hand over one's eyes and when one looks up—there is the sea, foaming and tossing, but it is ten years later, and there is nothing to show it in the surging water, in the wind shaking the silver olive trees—

The little church has been destroyed.

We spend a long time sitting on a German bunker. Gorse is blooming around the rusting guns, a lizard peeps through the dark muzzle, and the sea washes ceaselessly about the steep cliffs. It is our first evening and, out here by the lighthouse where we are sitting, we can see nothing but a horizon of water. A returning fishing cutter comes into view and, chugging and puffing, passes with swaying mast beneath the cliffs. The sea begins to look like dark-blue ink as the sun sinks deeper; the waves with their gliding foam caps roll over their own shadows—

Café Delfino

Basically it all depends, probably, on what we call the spirit. Meant in this letter is certainly not art that evades by looking upward. But my own fear of this kind of art, which apes the highest while tolerating the lowest, is perhaps the reason why I cannot agree with this letter, however often I reread it. It is no idle fear. I think of Heydrich, the Nazi governor of Czechoslovakia, who played Mozart; for me a conclusive example. Art in this sense, art as a kind of moral schizophrenia, if one might put it like that, is certainly the very opposite of what we should be aiming at, and in any case it is doubtful whether artistic aims can be separated from humanitarian ones. The hallmark of the spirit we need is not in the first instance talent, which is an additional bonus, but responsibility. The German nation has never lacked talent or minds that consider themselves above ordinary cares, but it is Germany that has produced the most—or at any rate the first—barbarians in this century. Should we not take a lesson from that?

On the beach

Every morning when we go down to the beach we pass by some workers mixing mortar or carrying bricks; dust has turned the red scarves on their heads into a pale pink. A child whose short arms can scarcely lift the bucket above the ground is bringing them the water they need. What they are concerned with is the mole, which was damaged by two or three bombs; not with work itself as a virtue and an aim in life. They do not think themselves better than the others who stand gossiping beneath the arches. What they are doing is not the whole point of their day's activity; they do it skillfully, but it is always in the way one might tie up a sunflower or patch a garden chair: to create a life congenial and pleasing to the eye, a life worth living. Not for an instant can we presume to feel, just because we are on a vacation, that we are freer than these people, living better. We are not more fortunate than any of those who pass us by, noiseless on their bare feet, ragged, upright, composed: each of them an individual, splendidly alive, the master of his own time—

Something can perhaps be divined from the fruit, the black olives lying on the ground, the last figs, purple and overripe. One gets the feeling that fruit ripens here not as a reward, but as a gift; no wonder that this is where mankind began. Here Man is not living in defiance of a creation he has daily to outwit to prevent its consuming him; it is not courage, the empty pleasure of daily conquest, not virtue that keeps him alive, but a joy in existence; he is more innocent, lighthearted. The gifts that grow in this country on trees: freedom from anxiety, faith in the future, the right to laze in the sun.

The sea is warm but the wind is fresh, and after swimming one seeks the sunshine. Even the sand, when you dig yourself a hole, is reminiscent of the fall; it sticks to the skin, damp and cool. The air, as one lies there with eyes closed, suddenly makes one think of the reds and browns of the woods at home. The brightly painted cabins are now being taken down, the boats pulled up on the sand. Each day could be the last. Apart from us there are only two foreign girls still here. I do not even know what language they are speaking, so loud is the sea as, like rolling thunder, it hurls its waves on the shore. For hours on end I watch them curling and hissing, one after the other, see the wet sand, shining like a mirror, gradually become matte like blotting paper; empty shells, usually different ones each time, remain behind to form little dimples in the sand, until the next wave comes, rears up, and curls over, letting the sunlight through, then breaks with a foaming crest to thud, splash, and gurgle. And out there lies a whole sea, full of such waves dancing beneath the sun. A black freighter is creeping along the horizon, its smoke visible half the morning.

Reading

Books that provoke us to contradiction, or at least to further consideration, are often the most gripping: we think of a hundred things the author has not even mentioned, though they are apposite, and perhaps it is one of the main joys of reading that the reader should above all discover the wealth of his own thoughts. At least he should be permitted to feel that he could have said it all himself. All he lacks is the time—or, as a more modest person might put it: all we lack are the words. And even that is a slight delusion. Those hundred things that the author did not think of—why do they occur to me only when I am reading him? In those passages that incite us to contradiction we are obviously still in the position of receivers. We blossom from our own branches, but on the soil of another. But at any rate we are happy. Whereas a book that turns out to be always cleverer than the reader gives little pleasure and neither convinces nor rewards, even if it is a hundred times richer than ourselves. Maybe it is accomplished, but it still puts us off. It lacks the gift of giving. It does not need us. The other books, those that make us a present of our own thoughts, are at least more courteous; and indeed they are perhaps the only truly effective ones. They lead us into a forest whose paths are laden with bushes and berries, and when our pockets are full we are quite convinced that we have found them ourselves. Well, haven't we? The effectiveness of such books lies, however, in the fact that no thought can convince and so vitally affect us as one that nobody has had to spell out to us, that we take to be our own because it is not there in print—

Naturally there are also other reasons why the books that contain it all, and only require our admiration, are not always our favorite ones. Possibly it depends on what at the given moment we are most in need of, a summing up or a new departure, satisfaction or stimulation. The need surely varies from person to person and also from age group to age group, and certainly (in a way that could do with more investigation) it has something to do with the times in which we live. It is conceivable at least that a late generation, such as we presumably are, has particular need of the sketch, in order not to be strangled to death by inherited conceptions which preclude new births. The tendency toward sketchiness, already long mastered in painting, can now be seen in literature too—and not for the first time; a predilection for fragments, the breaking down of traditional unities, the painful or teasing emphasis on the unfinished—all this was a feature of the romantics, so alien to us in some ways, so close in others. Perfection: not in the sense of mastery over, but as a definition of a certain consummate form. Looked at thus, there could be a consummate sketch and an unskillful "perfection"—for example, a clumsily written sonnet. The sketch has direction, but no ending; the sketch as reflection of a view of life that is no longer conclusive, or is not yet conclusive; it implies mistrust of a formal wholeness which pre-empts the spiritual content and can only be a vehicle for borrowed ideas; mistrust of ready-made formulas which prevent our time from ever achieving a perfection of its own—

Cesario says:
"Every ruin has a fascination which has nothing to do with art and is therefore for the serious artist nonvalid. One does not create ruins on purpose. The sketch, the aphorism, is a ruin pointed toward the future. Take, for instance, the Acropolis: this, like all ruins, exploits the melancholy of having once been a living whole; but the Acropolis cannot help being a ruin. You writers of sketches are quite another matter: you exploit, not melancholy, but its very opposite—hope, the promise of a living whole which will one day come, but which you yourselves cannot in fact deliver."
Is Cesario not right?

The aphorism as a thought process that never produces a genuine or tenable result; it always leaves the question in the air, and its outward ending is just a sign of fatigue, due to the fact that the thinking powers are not up to it, and so, in a mood of sheer melancholy, the writer causes a short circuit. It is a sort of conjuring trick to extricate oneself from the insoluble by creating a moment of bafflement in order that the questioning may stop. By the time we realize that we have experienced nothing but a bang, the conjurer has disappeared. The most that maybe remains is our own feeling of bafflement that the opposite of what he has just been baffling us with seems no less true. Of course, there are also aphorisms that are not true whichever way you look at them.

And another thing:
The aphorism provides no experience. It does of course spring from an experience, which it then attempts to generalize. But the reader, who did not share the original experience, sees only the generalization, which claims to be valid; and although one might expect a generalization to apply to everybody, what the reader in fact does, if he is interested in more than just a passing titillation, is to apply it to specific people and cases he himself knows. In doing this, he is of course helped by the fact that the more generalized the statement, the easier it is to interpret as

one pleases: most aphorisms are tipped in our own favor. "Hollow heads contain the most knowledge," I have read in Karl Kraus, who was of course a master of the aphorism, and at once I have a whip in my hand which I can crack with schoolboyish glee at all the people I know whose greater knowledge has always filled me with shame. Who can stop me? Certainly not the aphorism, which does not say at whom it is directed: and consequently we enjoy it for what is in fact its weakest point, which is that it provides conclusions, but no experiences. Unless we know the details of his life, the writer of aphorisms is like a child who picks only the heads of flowers, without the roots that nourish the blossoms, without the soil. The brightly colored flower heads remain a riddle which soon fades. Thus we turn to narration, which provides roots, whole clumps of earth attached, and fertilizer aplenty.

Narration: but in what form?

It is at any rate open to question whether the current trend toward sketchiness has to do with any individual deficiencies. For anyone who has devoted his life to it, the question of what one can do, in the sense of craftsmanship, resolves itself sooner or later into the question of what it is permissible to do; that is to say, preoccupations with technical skill give way to moral preoccupations, the combination of both being probably what produces art. Thus no one can do what he finds so admirable in the old masters, or even if he can do it, he cannot imbue it with any significance, and whoever takes on more than he can accomplish stands revealed as a mere bungler. There may be times when only bunglers will dare aspire to perfection. We have not yet got that far. A Catholic, for instance, who can believe he is part of an ordered existence, has the right to attempt perfection, since his world is a perfect one. But the attitude of most of my contemporaries is, I believe, one of questioning, and as long as a complete answer is missing, the formal framework can be only temporary. Perhaps the only form they can decently use is indeed the fragmentary one.

Portofino Monte

High above the sea. Its horizon has risen with us, higher and higher, and only the bays have stayed below. The sea, when one looks down into these bays, appears as black as night. A network of silver waves across it. Like gleaming brocade they lie there beneath the sun, noiseless, only the breakers betraying their movement; white foam around the cliffs.

Happiness in the flash of recognition: this is a sight you will never forget. But what do we experience at the moment, while it is still before our eyes? We look forward to a journey, maybe for years, and once we are there the main part of our pleasure consists in knowing that we are a memory the richer. A certain sense of disappointment, not in the landscape, but in the human heart. The vision is there, but not yet the experience. We are like a film at the moment of exposure; it is memory that will develop it. At times one wonders to what extent one experiences the present at all. Could one depict experience with complete objectivity, for example in the form of a curve, it would certainly not conform with the curve of the actual events; it would, rather, resemble a wave, which is related to the other waves that went before and follow afterward like an echo; not the events themselves would be depicted, but the sources of expectation, the sources of memory. The present moment remains somehow unreal, a nothingness between expectation and memory, these being the true dwelling place of experience; the present as a mere passage; the familiar feeling of emptiness, which one does not care to admit to oneself.

"Go hence, that I may be with you!"

In relation to a landscape we come nearest to acknowledging it. One is never quite where one actually is, yet where we are cannot be a matter of indifference, for it provides the vantage point from which we can bring distant objects into our experience. If it were always written on our foreheads where our thoughts were straying, nobody would wish to share the present moment with us. Wrongly so. Only if he has been there can we return to him.

Milan, October 1946

At heart one is always something of a nationalist. When I read that one of my compatriots has been awarded a Nobel prize or has been received by the Emperor of China, I refuse to feel proud, because we know only too well from history where this sort of patriotic pride leads, when it is not confined strictly to the sports field. In this effort I succeed more or less. But when the opposite occurs—as incidentally it more often does—my cosmopolitan pose is scattered to the winds; when I see my compatriots plundering the Italian shops with their Swiss currency, I turn pale with anger—

Why exactly?

My obvious disappointment betrays the secret assumption we all have that the nation to which we belong must be a model nation, simply because we ourselves happen to belong to it—which gives one every reason to feel angry, rather, with oneself!

Die Chinesische Mauer

Today at the final rehearsal. I am seeing my play (*The Chinese Wall*) for the first time. A shock rather like this: you visit China, where you have never been before, come to a public square full of Chinese people, and watch a dancer, whose doings partly astonish or even delight, but also partly disgust you. And everybody says: This dancer is yourself. You and nobody else! At the moment when, though not really taking it in, I believe, accept, and admit it, I am unable to take in anything at all of what is going on, what is being played—neither a sentence nor a scene; it is all a foreign language, impossible to say whether it has any meaning—

Première the day after tomorrow.

The theater, a terrible distorting mirror, is most terrible when it is not that: nothing can be stranger than seeing one's own experience from the outside.

Café Odeon

Discussion with students from both universities. The Waagsaal turns out to be much too small, so we walk through the city to another, larger restaurant for the hearing and judgment. I do not deny that such a large audience both surprises and pleases me: whatever happens, it shows interest. I soon realize that students like anyone else want a play to provide solutions. The need for a guiding hand comes out again and again. And what if one were to provide it? Such as, for example: Go out and give away all your possessions, forget your rights, do as Saint Francis did. What would happen? Nothing. What would have been gained? One would know the author is obviously a Christian. Good for him, maybe, but purely his own concern—as indeed it is. The solution is always our concern, my concern, your concern.

Henrik Ibsen once said:

"I am here to ask questions, not to answer them."

As a playwright I should consider I had done my duty if I succeeded in a play of mine in putting a question in such a way that from then on the members of the audience were unable to live without an answer. But it must be their answer, their own, which they can provide only in the framework of their own lives.

This constant appeal for an answer, a general one, which one so often hears uttered in reproachful and moving tones, is perhaps not as honorable as those who make it tend to think. Every human answer, as we well know, is open to attack the moment it goes beyond the personal and claims to be generally valid, and the satisfaction we get from contradicting the answers of others is due to the fact that it enables us at least to forget the question that is vexing us. In other words: we do not really want an answer, we just want to forget the question.

In order to rid ourselves of the responsibility.

Pfannenstiel, near Zurich

Another series of golden days, the last of the year. The mornings, when I ride to work on my bicycle, are cold and damp; the leaves cling to the road surface, the lake is silver-gray, and all one sees are buoys floating in a shoreless waste, lonely and empty of boats, unreflecting, white seagulls on the railings. Usually the decisive moment comes at about eleven o'clock, when the bells are ringing. There are still no shadows to betray the sun; but one can feel its presence; the clockfaces gleam on the church towers. Mist, when one looks up into the sky, glitters like bronze-colored dust; then suddenly it is gone, leaving only blueness; suddenly a strip of watery sunlight falls across the drawing board—

And now, once more, there it all is: the fermenting wine and the wasps buzzing in bottles, the shadows in the gravel, the golden silence of decay with all its magic, clucking hens in the meadows, a teeming mass of brown pears scattered over the highway, asters hanging over a wire fence, starlike shapes of blood-red fire dissolving in all directions, a bluish light beneath the trees. It is as if everything were now taking leave of itself; the rustling foliage of a poplar, the metallic sheen on the fallen fruit, smoke from the fields, where they are burning shrubs. Below, behind a trellis of vines, the lake glitters. The sun is already rusting in the haze of midafternoon. Then the journey home without an overcoat, hands in pockets, a damp carpet of leaves which no longer rustle, wine presses in the vineyard, the dripping barrels in the twilight, the red lamps on a landing stage shrouded in mist—

Draft of a letter

You write to me as a German, a young corporal who fought at Stalingrad, and you write very scornfully; you are angry that a foreigner, one who stood outside it all, should write about death.

What can I reply?

Because you are right: I have never seen a soldier die, and, as you know from my short preface, I am not without doubts whether we have the right to comment. As a youngster I was made to place a carnation in my grandmother's open coffin, and I found it repulsive; a yet greater impression was made by a horse that once lay dying outside our house. Later, when I was your age, I stood by the zinc coffin of a young woman I loved: incidentally, she was German, and the memory of her, to whom

I owe so much, often seared me in moments of hatred against the Germans. These things and many others were, I admit, just glimpses of death or, as you very scornfully call it, mere theater. I ask myself what would be different if I could watch a soldier die; for me, the survivor, it would again be only a glimpse, and I still, as you have proved to me, should have experienced nothing. Once I stood beside a child's bed, a very small child who had suffocated during the night; outside it was a lovely morning as I stood there holding back the young mother, who again and again was trying to restore life to the tiny blue limbs. Or again, we stood in a quiet railroad station, giving out cups of tea to the skeletons who had just arrived from German concentration camps. They could no longer retain the lukewarm tea, and one could see how it ran out immediately through their anuses. And there are many other things I could tell you that I should describe as experiences. Yet it does not alter the fact that in some sense you are right. There is another side to death, an unusual one that only war reveals: I have never had to fire a gun, and perhaps that is the decisive factor in your experience that makes it different—

Why do you not speak of it?

"The only ones who can advise and help us will in the long run be ourselves. Our experiences have taught us. With these experiences behind us, I believe it is we who can help the foreigners, rather than the other way around, except perhaps in a material way."

Yet all the same you ask me for an answer, and the more often I read your passionate letter, which has been occupying my mind for nearly a week, the more helpless I come to feel; you wrote all that in conditions of bitter cold, hungry, and here I sit in a warm little attic room; for me you are a young German, and for you I am a foreigner, and you reply to reproaches that I have never made:

"It is not true that the German people knew about all these horrible things, as is believed abroad. A few individuals may of course have known of such shootings, or even as soldiers have taken part in them, but none of their comrades, their friends, parents, or acquaintances knew, and all of them were horribly shocked when they were eventually told; very few could even bring themselves to believe it—"

89

When you yourself read such sentences again, do you not get the impression that you are hitting out blindly, that you are always defending yourself without really knowing what it is against which you are defending yourself? Probably if you yourself knew that, it would be enough. What you said earlier about help and advice is what I think too, at least to some extent; my play (*Nun singen sie wieder*) did not stem from the presumptuous aim of offering advice to the German people, but simply from the need to relieve an anguish of my own.

"What your old pope says about love: it is beautiful, because it knows it is vain, yet all the same it does not despair—how do you know that?"

I do not know it.

An explanation that someone attempts to make does not oblige you to accept this explanation. I shall also not accept yours, if you make one, but we should try to make sure that I understand it. That means primarily: that I should be able to hear what you are trying to say. As the next step I have to consider to what extent your differing explanation, which arises from your differing experiences, is valid for me also, to what extent it can widen, reverse, limit, or deepen my own earlier explanation. All this would amount to a discussion, and it would still be difficult for us to talk together about these things, which are of significance to our own continent at least and which of course, having been in different places, we have experienced very differently. Your attitude, which makes a discussion so difficult, stems perhaps from the fact that you have up till now only had either to command or to obey, and thus have no view of your own concerning the things you saw happening around you; at any rate you do not mention any, but write at the end of your letter:

"I must emphasize that everything I have written here has nothing to do with a political opinion."

Would that have been something to be ashamed of?

It is not impossible that we shall meet in Munich sometime in the next few months. At any rate I am keeping your address. Perhaps things will be easier if we discuss these matters in person; without a face before me I increasingly get the feeling that I am not replying to you, but to all the German letters I have so far received, and they would fill quite a sizable box.

Though these should be of value to us, almost all of them show an arrogance which permits no answer, and because of their touchy resentment at having once again lost a war, they teem with willful misunderstandings, more than one can possibly hope to correct, and in the whole box there is scarcely a thought that could be regarded as original. I tell myself: this comes from hunger, cold, misery. But why should I, as so many demand, worship their misery? Misery brings maturity; that may be true in some cases, and certainly in our days there is no lack of misery. But the sort of misery that brings no moral reward, misery that is of no value to the mind and soul, that is the true misery: it is hopeless, bestial, and nothing else, and to worship this would seem to me shameless, a glorification of bombing, a literary show of reverence amounting to an idolization of war, and therefore the very opposite of what we should be doing, which is to fight against misery: with bread, with milk, with wool, with fruit, and not least by refusing to admire misery for itself, by refusing to fall down on our knees in silent prayer before it, even when those who are suffering it demand that we should. Repugnant as it is, one can become proud of one's misery; that in itself is an argument against the moral value of misery. The idea that ordinary people are changed, deepened, and sublimated by having to live among dust and ashes is a hope with which literature has made us familiar. A dangerous hope, which has perhaps influenced you: you are no longer the victor, but the man who took part, and as such superior to all others, who have experienced nothing because they have not experienced war; your poor nation is no longer the supreme one, but the nation that is suffering most on this earth, that is, if we ignore the Jews, the Poles, the Greeks, and all the others; it is the nation that God has tested most sorely, which implies that it is the nation that God most favors. Your best poets find words for it: Nations of the world, we suffer also for you and your sins! As if it had not enough sins of its own, as if no one else suffered in the years when your own comrades and parents and acquaintances were, as you say, refusing to believe what the reports told them. Why is it never one nation among other nations? That is what I meant previously by arrogance, and I ask you to let me withdraw that ugly word. So long as I am sitting in this warm attic I have less right than you to give way to grudges. I keep coming back to your handwritten postscript, urgently asking me to reply to you. But what can I answer as long as you are not content to accept a human equality which we regard as self-evident?

Second draft

You write to me as a corporal who fought at Stalingrad, and I have already attempted a reply; your letter moved me, but in an area, I believe, that has nothing to do with the fact that we belong to different nations. Early this year I spent a month in Germany; and even there, day after day, I found myself making judgments, now in this direction, now in another. One is torn all ways and—what makes things even more difficult—one reproaches oneself for making judgments at all. I mean that quite generally; somehow one always remains a foreigner. How can we judge women when we ourselves will never bear children? How can we judge our own father when we have not yet experienced what it is to be his age? How can we ever judge a human being, when he is and always will be another person? Judgment is always presumptuous, and thus your anger is probably legitimate, even though the Germans, as you know, have always judged other people.

What can be done?

Nobody wants to be a hypocrite, anything rather than that; but perhaps one really is that, if not all the time, certainly in the moments when one is concerned about one's own appearances and not about the misery we see before our eyes and recognizing its causes. Forgiving, which offers the nearest way out, of course presupposes a judgment; there is no real difference in the degree of presumption, it is just that one has the additional fear of seeming presumptuous and is therefore a coward into the bargain: one does not take up the dagger for fear of cutting oneself when one judges. One keeps silent and imagines oneself to be a good Christian, while in fact enjoying one's own compassion, a compassion that alters nothing; mere refusal to venture on a judgment is not justice, and certainly it is not kindness or even love. It is simply noncommittal, nothing else. But it is precisely this failure to commit oneself, this silence in the face of a known crime, that is probably the most widespread form of complicity—

Third draft

You write to me as a corporal who fought at Stalingrad, and since, the more I read your letter, the less I can understand you, all I can do is to describe matters as they look from our point of view, if that is of interest to you. The question you raise about our competence to judge is one that indeed worried and confused us even during the war, when our prospects of remaining untouched by it were by no means certain. Whoever was writing in those years and chose to keep silent about the happenings that came to our knowledge and shattered many fond illusions— he too was of course giving a clear and perfectly definite answer to the question: he was replying not with imprecations, not with judgments, but with peaceful work aimed at showing the existence of another world and indicating its permanence. He reacted to world events not by accepting them, as others demanded, as the only true reality, but, on the contrary, by contrasting them with all the other things that still constituted a part of life. Perhaps indeed, as long as it was not mere escapism, that was the most immediate and necessary task. Of course the danger of taking refuge in mere escapism is one with which all who stand apart are constantly confronted. The writers of a country engaged in war have passed through a fire, a public one, a generally visible one, and what they can still find to say has at any rate gone through some sort of test. In our eyes as well, indeed particularly in our eyes, they wear the halo of a purified soul. Of course there were some false halos, to which, as could be expected, some Helvetians bowed the knee. But let us stick to the genuine ones. What, compared with them, had the creative artists of our country to tell the world?

The question is difficult.

We did not experience war in person, that is true, but on the other hand we did of course experience certain things which have influenced our destiny. Everyone knew that the war concerned us, even if we should once again emerge unscathed. Our happiness was illusory. We were living next door to a torture chamber, we could hear the screams, but it was not we who were screaming; we ourselves were not deepened by suffering, but we were much too close to the suffering to be able to laugh. Fate had placed us in the vacuum between war and peace. Our way out was through helping. Daily life, here in our island, was full of foreign faces: refugees of all sorts, prisoners, and wounded. We had, whether we liked it or not, a view of events that, for a nation outside the war, could not have been more oppressive. We even had something that the warring countries themselves did not have: a twofold view. The combatant sees the scene only when he is present at it; the onlooker sees it all the time. Of course we had our passionate longings, but we did not have the participant's distress, or his urge for revenge. Perhaps that is the true reward that falls to those who remain unscathed and determines their function. They would have the privilege, now rare, of remaining just. And even more: they must be allowed to have it. It is the only possible way in which we can uphold our esteem in the circle of suffering peoples—(Not sent.)

1947

Marionettes

Yesterday at a marionette show, and at the end we were allowed behind the little stage. In a narrow room with stale air we wonderingly eyed the hanging puppets, somehow not quite believing that they were the same that had just been enchanting us. Even the devil himself was now suspended from a rail, shabbier than expected. While on stage they always keep on changing, in line with the scene, the words they themselves neither speak nor hear. One explains it by the effects of lighting, the various positions of the heads, and so on. As the puppet master soaps, rinses, and dries his hands and talks of plans, one has a feeling of disappointment, secretly affected, at any rate, by the way the puppets suddenly seem to be staring into space, mindless, as if they no longer knew us. . . .

What strikes one every time:
How easily marionettes can depict the nonhuman characters as well—gnomes, goblins, monsters, and fairies, dragons, spirits of the air and the heart's desire. Even on large stages such figures are sometimes needed—the *Meerkatzen* in *Faust,* Ariel in *The Tempest.* In these cases there is always a danger of embarrassment: the best an actor can do is to avoid making them ridiculous, but the desired effect of ultimate horror or of unearthly bliss, which should emanate from such nonhuman figures, is hardly possible on the stage when living persons depict them. Marionettes can do it. This is of course largely due to the fact that the puppets depicting human beings and those depicting gnomes are made of the same material. In consequence, the puppet representing the gnome is just as convincing or unconvincing as the other puppet we are being asked to take as a human being. On the live stage, I feel, we cannot believe in the gnome, because it cannot get through to us in relation to the human being. The human

character confronting it is a genuine human being, a creature of flesh and blood, whereas the gnome remains an image, a symbol. Thus the scene, however well it is played, is being presented from the start on two different levels, which cannot convince us to an equal degree. On the marionette stage it can. As also in the masked theater of ancient Greece: when Pallas Athena and Odysseus are both wearing masks, when both remain sketchy and unreal, we can believe in the goddess too.

Another delightful thing about marionettes is their relationship to the spoken word. The dialogue in a puppet play, whether one will or not, is always a heightened form of speech which cannot be mistaken for everyday language. It is unnatural because it is not part of the puppets, it lives and moves above their heads; and in addition it has more volume than their wooden bodies could produce. It is thus more than the accompanying noise that comes daily out of our own mouths. It is the word as it was in the beginning, the absolute, all-creating Word. It is speech itself. The puppet show can never for an instant be mistaken for Nature. It allows of only one possibility—fiction; and fiction remains its only sphere.

A comparison with the ancient Greek theater, which also made use of rigid masks, is possible in other ways as well. Both theaters, the largest and the smallest, make their effect by distorting dimensions. In the former, masks (and later the buskin too) were employed to make the figures larger; in the puppet theater the figures are diminished. In both cases the effect is essentially the same: we can no longer place ourselves beside the figures, shoulder to shoulder, and indeed we should not; on the contrary, the differences of dimension forbid any efforts to get close to them. We are here and they are there, and we see what happens on stage from an unbridgeable distance, whether this is achieved by enlargement or by diminution. And to our astonishment we find that, the longer they play, the more compellingly alive they become to us; at times we forget entirely that they are smaller than ourselves—dwarfs, wooden dwarfs in fact, which we could pick up with one hand and hurl from the stage; thus we discover, and feel for ourselves, the relative nature of all outward dimensions, including our own. And as long as their actions are not disturbed by some trick, by some accident of gesture that is out of place and thereby betrays the nature of the place where it is all happening, the mind is not conscious of size. While acting, these dwarfs virtually take over our lives. They become more real than ourselves, and moments of true magic emerge; we are, quite literally, beside ourselves.

And afterward:
How shabby they look as they hang there on the rail, now that they no longer have possession of our lives, now that we have returned to ourselves.

Christ as a puppet?

Incidentally I remember as a student once seeing a puppet show depicting the Last Supper. It was quite shattering. It was devout to an extent that would not have been possible had a human actor attempted to depict Jesus Christ. This Christ was of linden wood, like Marion's. And, just like a crucifix, it gave no sense of sacrilege; the puppet, unlike the living actor, appears to us from the very start as an embodiment, an image, a creation of the mind, which alone can visualize holiness. The living person, even when he is representing an image, always remains a creature of flesh and blood. The puppet is wood, a good, honest wood which never makes the insidious pretense of portraying the real Christ, and for that we should never take it; it is merely a symbol, a formula, a document which says something, but does not try to be what it is saying. This is play, not pretense; it is a thing of the spirit, as only play can be—

Davos

A delicious day, full of sunshine, clear and certain, and we are standing scarcely a hundred paces from the white cross at the summit, around which black jackdaws are flying. Suddenly a sharp sound from the blue sky or from beneath the glittering snow, a short dry note, almost soft, almost like a vase cracking; for a moment one does not know whether it has come from far away or close at hand. As we look around, we notice that the whole slope, a steep one, has been transformed into a heaving slide. It all happens so quickly, yet at the same time it is as if decades have passed since the vacation, which we have only just begun and which has left no other memory. The summit, its white cross standing out against the cloudless sky, seems farther off than a moment ago. All around us things are exploding, silently to start with, and the snow is already up to our knees. On all sides clumps of snow tumbling over one another, and at last I realize that we too are sliding downward, helplessly and with growing swiftness, in the midst of a rolling, rumbling mass. But all the time one is wide awake. Luckily our skis are on our shoulders; I call out to Constanze, whom I see for fleeting instants, telling her what to do. More and more comes on us from behind. Snow, wind, a sense of suffocating. One's feeling of terror, though great, is at the same time calm—in some way familiar, as if this were not one's first avalanche.

En route

Since Strasbourg, whose cathedral we could only glimpse through the dusk, we have been traveling in a sleeper and, when we wake in the morning, have just reached the bombed railway sidings of Karlsruhe. A cloudless day. At times, for minutes on end, we see the scenery only through a latticework of burnt-out railway coaches, a tangled line of red rust. Later we open the window in the corridor; we are in Pforzheim, where there is hardly a roof to be seen, nothing but jagged walls and ruins full of snow. Smoke is coming from a cellar somewhere, and children are standing on a snow-covered road, watching us. It is Constanze's first journey through Germany; she shakes her head when she sees that:

"Completely wrecked—"

One of the victors, a young officer who is just passing along the corridor on his way to the restaurant car, looks at her:

"Thank goodness, madame—"

To Maja

You are a woman, perhaps a girl, and secretly you sometimes ask yourself what I want of you; a whole afternoon we went walking together, too far for your narrow shoes, and we spoke of nothing in particular. As we walked down the slopes, you

gave me your hand. We kissed, and next morning I awake as
one awakes beside the sea. My hand is still full of yours. But do
not take it too much to heart; no letter will call you back when
you go. You are young, and I am glad that you exist. The earth
you have trodden is again a place for wandering, and everything
within it is you. I can see the blossoming branches which you
break from the tree, see the dogs chasing the stones you throw.
The fruit you place between your lips, it is all there, round and
full, as your brow is full and young and impenetrable; you are
the present moment behind everything. It is as if here, where
you have never been, the fields are growing from you, and the
air is full of the radiance of your eyes. I should like to be able to
tell of all these things I see, the landscape of fir trees and elms
with strange gables between, of rivers and endless woods and
castles, their windows shining in the evening sun, of bridges
and ruins of bridges, domes towering above ruined cities. You
are all that is in these pictures, the colors before nightfall, and
all the light the sun squanders would dissolve into darkness, were
there nothing for us to love—

Prague, March 1947

I did not know that Theresienstadt, which we visited yesterday
on our way here, was a historic place named after Maria
Theresia. Heavy high walls of reddish brick entirely surround
the little town, as well as a broad moat full of weeds and water
seeping away in brown puddles. Outside the little town, which
served as a ghetto, is the fort: the actual death camp. A fine
old alley links the two places; beside it a field of wooden
crosses, placed there afterward. In the first courtyard, where the
German wardens lived, there are still trees; it is a warm day
in early spring, birds twittering, and on the red walls, which
suddenly cut us off from the world and the surrounding landscape, single blades of grass sway in the wind, Nature's final
gesture. Over the inner courtyard, where the prisoners were
kept, there presides a little house with searchlight and machine
gun; the cells, ranged like honeycombs, are of concrete; the
beds inside remind one of bottle racks. At the far end of this
courtyard, in a spot where we can see bullet holes, those special

executions took place that all prisoners had to attend. The whole place looks today like a mixture between a barracks, a chicken farm, a factory, and a slaughterhouse. Adjoining it is a succession of further courtyards. Through a sort of tunnel, known as Death Gate, we come to a mass grave of seven hundred people; later they used the ovens of a nearby brickworks. Here stand the gallows, a simple wooden beam with two hooks, on which the prisoners themselves had to fix the rope, with two wooden trap doors beneath. Here too we can see nothing but the reddish walls, the whipping grass on top. Not far from the gallows, whose primitive construction is almost laughable, is the spot where the shootings took place in rows; in front of it a water-filled ditch, which separated the riflemen from the victims, and at the back an ordinary fascine to stop the earth into which the bullets plunged from slipping down as time went on. There is room for ten or twelve people. A shelter, like that provided at a rifle range for the markers, housed the so-called funeral party, a little group of Jews whose job was to clear away the bodies and where necessary to see to it that all were completely dead. We move on; on the other side of the wall, but still within our camp, we are suddenly confronted with an immaculate swimming pool, and on the slope in front of that wall whose other side we have just seen, there is even a little alpine garden with beautiful stones and plants, though now overgrown and neglected; this is where in summer the German wardens spent their leisure hours together with their wives and children. In the next court-yard, where prisoners had to assemble to hear each of the Führer's speeches, it is for once not red walls that surround us, but old stables. We enter one of them. This was the torture chamber. Fixed in the stone floor are two iron rings, on the ceiling a pulley, and directly beneath it, mounted on the stone flooring, an iron spine the size of an index finger. It is a room of old vaults, and between the pillars hangs a curtain of thin sackcloth, a screen to conceal the onlookers. Leaving the stables through a door on the other side, we find ourselves back in the open air, standing on a bridge looking down into what was known as the Jews' Trench. Between two especially high walls, so high indeed that one can see nothing but bare sky, there is a canal of green water with grass banks on either side. There is also a wooden ladder. Ten Jews were sent down it, each armed with a hayfork, and with the promise that the last two survivors would be given their freedom. From the iron bridge, on which the watchers stood, one looks down as if into a bear pit. The freedom for the two survivors, says a former inmate who is here with us, consisted of a shot through the back of the head. Eventually we come to the final place. We are standing before the urns. It is the first time I have ever seen human ashes; they are gray, but full of little bones, which are yellow. The more recent urns are of plywood, but the German model placed in our hands was simpler and more economical: a bag of strong paper, each inscribed, after being filled, with a handwritten number. The concentration camp of Terezin, as Theresienstadt was called, had twenty thousand such paper bags in stock when it was liberated. Naturally we took off our hats, but it would be a lie to speak of feeling moved; the sight of these urns, which can be opened, arouses no associations; they stand in rows like tins in a drugstore, like pots in a garden nursery. What most made me think in this place were the two portraits hanging above the nameless urns: Beneš and Stalin.

The day continued.

We went on to Leitmeritz, where we had lunch, and in the registrar's office, where the same two portraits looked down on us, we were told why the Sudeten Germans, all three million of them, had been banished from the country, and what was now being done with their houses, with their fields. We were shown plans. But, whatever was said or done, it still remained the registrar's office, which I find oppressive the whole world over. Death or marriage or birth, what does it matter? What business is it of the state, which is not a human being, yet nevertheless works with a hairy human hand? I see the changing portraits on the wall, the emperors and generals and liberators who, to save it from the hairy hand, try to give the state a human countenance, but even then all the human affairs that are dealt with in such offices remain as nonhuman as the yellow ashes we have just seen; even though one has not come here for anything, one still feels uneasy. The plans rolled out before us on the table are full of good sense and the will to make things better. As we wait for the French translation, I think of those refugees I saw in Frankfurt, a year ago; I think of the wagon in Munich which, when opened on arrival, was simply full of death, and I think of the two rings in the stone floor, the pulley, and the iron spine; that too. It is important to see many things in conjunction. Since I say nothing, what is really only concern perhaps looks to them like suspicion; if so, I am sorry; from my very heart I wish for this diligent man that the red marks he is drawing on his map do not signify the blood of his sons—

What most potently remains in my memory of the concentration camp, and always with increasing clarity (though at the time I hardly noticed it—at any rate no more than anything else): the whipping grass on the red walls, and the fact that, wherever we were standing, we could see nothing but sky.

Prague

Yesterday the performance in Czech. Of course I did not understand a single word; the exits and entrances, the changing positions were all a pantomime for me; color, form and gesture, movement, all the means of emotional expression peculiar to the theater, these I saw, and I heard what one might call speech without words, speech purely as sound, as rhythm. All those things that go to make up a play—who confronts whom, who goes off, who comes in, who returns, and so on—everything suddenly becomes quite patent, and one can read it like an X-ray picture.

Tomorrow a public discussion; I shall speak in German, which is causing the promoters some anxiety. How they hate this language! But they fully see that it is as much the language of Switzerland as French or Italian. To admit the right of hating a language, whatever it is, would be to admit that the very people we justly hate in all languages—that is to say, the nationalists— are themselves in the right.

Something else that makes this production so stimulating to me: language not as a means in itself, but as one among others. Napoleon and Brutus speak in Czech, which is just as ludicrous as to make them speak German. But here I am able to realize how natural it is, either way. . . . There is our own particular language, which restricts and isolates us, and there is the language of art, which is language as a means in itself, speaking to all humanity. I see Macbeth, and I feel in German what was written in English and is being spoken in Slav. I understand not a single word of it, and can only note with consternation how closely related all of us really are—or, rather, how often we forget it.

Hradcin

Gulls sitting on the glittering ice of the Vltava; stone saints standing dark on the long bridge, in the blueness of approaching spring; everywhere dripping trees; streets full of melting snow shining in the sun; the moss-covered wall of the Hradcin above, on which one sits with dangling legs, before one the vista of a foreign city full of green domes; thus it had once been. Thirteen years ago, when I sat on that wall with no inkling of what was to come, it was also March; it was the first foreign city I had ever seen. For fun I wonder how it would be if I had to relive everything that these thirteen years brought me—everything exactly in the order it happened, without alteration and without leaving anything out, the ugly, the beautiful, the unimportant, all exactly as it had been, but without the hope of the unknown which always precedes any new step—

Who would want that? Who could stand it?

Prague

Our departure has been put off again, since we stayed up talking all night. We sat in the dressing room with the young actors: there was candlelight and black coffee, and songs in the way people sing them here, songs of melancholy, of passion and joy. We still had a few good cigarettes left; somebody brought along some wine, and there was also an accordion. Sometime after midnight we heard footsteps; it was a sleepy janitor who had seen the light of our candles; he looked at us over his spectacles, nodded, and vanished. The stage, when one occasionally went out, was dark and empty, and in the high corridors there was a clutter of regal candlesticks, of drums which boomed when one knocked into them, or one stumbled past marble staircases and pillars, all of them hollow; the walls, which the probing beam of our torch could just reach, glittered with swords and pieces of armor; elsewhere there were flags, hanging down in the shadowless dark, the flags of our whole Western history.

We all want change—on that we are agreed, and it is always only a question of how this change can be brought about; it is not the first night we have sacrificed to pursuing this question. Some believe the only way is through the discovery of the human soul, the adventure of truthfulness, and they see no other paths of hope. Others are convinced that people cannot be changed in the world as it now is; so we must aim above all to change the world, its exterior circumstances, so that mankind, which they see as the product of this exterior world, can set about renewing itself. For them the solution lies in the discovery of a new economic system; the new spirit, they say, will emerge in the moment it becomes possible for it to do so, and they believe this so implicitly, so undoubtingly, that they are even prepared to use force to bring about this liberating change in exterior circumstances. And so we come back every time to that other basic question. Is there an end that can justify our means? Is it permissible for me to enslave and even kill those who try to prevent what I consider to be our salvation? Do I achieve in this way the salvation I can achieve in no other? I came with the conviction that there was nothing more to be said on that subject, but now I see that I have not given it enough thought, otherwise I could have convinced them, since after all we are entirely agreed on the goal our changes are aimed at. It is respect for the dignity of all mankind. We have to keep reminding ourselves of that in order to keep our discussion to the point. A man's dignity, it seems to me, lies in his freedom of choice. It is that which distinguishes human beings from animals; animals are always just the result of something; they cannot know guilt any more than they can be free; animals invariably do as they must; and they do not know what they do. Human beings can know it, and even God, the Almighty, leaves them free to choose whether to follow their good angel or their bad; because God does not wish us to be animals. It is the freedom to choose that gives rise to responsibility, to guilt or freedom; to human dignity, which we would sometimes willingly exchange for the easier existence of a seagull. My friends say: The goal is freedom. And thereby mean the same thing: freedom as a part of human dignity. Why do we both condemn the economic system, the prevailing one? Because it leaves individuals or groups—indeed the majority of all mankind—no choice; because it sins against human dignity. The animal quality does not lie in need alone, where it reveals itself as poverty, visible because one goes about in bad shoes or even barefooted. That is bitter. But the real bitterness does not lie in the bodily discomfort. No one will seriously assume that these exterior things are not important for the spirit; they are a constraint, an obstacle. A hungry man has no choice. His spirit is the outcome, not of his will, but of his hunger. However, there are other things besides hunger that can be used to condemn the existing system. If a man is a skilled worker and his son is obliged to become a worker simply because there is no money for anything else, the element of indignity is not in the work itself or in the kind of work, but in the fact that the son has absolutely no choice. Where can he learn a sense of responsibility toward society when its economic system abuses him? He is its victim, even though he does not go hungry. He will not become what it is in him to become, and he will never know what his capabilities are; perhaps he really can do nothing else. But how can that be decided without putting him to the test? Others are able to become what they are, sometimes even more: because ability is so rare, because millions of births are squandered. That is why we want a system that robs nobody of choice, and my friends even believe they have a pattern for such a system; much of the pattern is exciting, and when we speak of the final goal, we are always of the same mind. But if this effort to ensure that all may wear good shoes and no one may be restrained by the economic system and thereby be deprived of choice and therefore of his human dignity—if this grand, unremitting effort leads to the erection of a state that immediately deprives me of my freedom to choose what I think, what shall we have achieved? We shall have realized the means, but not the end. Human dignity, as we call this end, means choice; not the bathtub the state gives a man for not doubting the state. How can I believe, when I am given no choice? Indeed, the very power that forbids me to doubt takes away even the belief that I already had—

Question:

"Have we the right to assume that tyranny becomes a blessing when it is we ourselves seeking to impose it?"

Answer:

"It will be only a transitional stage."

Question:

"Can we see anywhere in history a transition of that kind, a tyranny that did not go up in smoke but turned itself by the natural processes of growth into the opposite of tyranny?"

Answer:

"We'll talk about that in a hundred years' time."

Laughter . . .

Nuremberg, March 1947

Children on the railroad embankments, particularly where the trains have to travel more slowly on account of the damage; they are waiting for us to throw them something to eat. The embarrassment of doing so when others are watching. Why? Women too, standing at crossing gates or in open fields; not waving, silent, gray-faced and haggard. Raggedness of a kind I have hitherto seen only in Serbia. Six track workers share the sandwiches our Czech friends had prepared for us. We are glad that we have nothing more, so do not have to go on discriminating. A rumpus on the platform; somebody has thrown out cigarettes. The youth who wins them: tuberculosis, an army cap, the black market, the law of the strongest, syphilis.

Home again

Ursel is delighted with the Czech doll and also the picture book we brought back; the fact that the children in its charming illustrations speak differently and that we too cannot read what is written there gives her no rest; for two days she has been constantly asking. Peter as well, the younger of the two, is entirely dominated by a journey he himself never made; he is now at the age when railroads are everything, and he savors his newly acquired knowledge that one can even sleep on a train and never have to set foot outside it. They already know most of it from the letters that Constanze always draws for them; there is nothing in these picture letters that did not happen, and every time I have to explain them again to the children I am amazed how much in our path was worth experiencing—

Café de la Terrasse

What I notice, when I return from abroad, is the inhibitedness of my Swiss compatriots, the constraint in their manner, in their faces, so industrious yet so disinclined. Unbearable when they talk of their modesty; in fact, once certain inhibitions are overcome, one sees the contrary; there is no lack of pent-up ambition lying in wait for world championships, and in higher circles it is Pestalozzi, Gotthelf, Burckhardt, Keller, and others of the illustrious dead whom one sticks in one's buttonhole; one is often shocked by oneself, over one's almost pathological touchiness when somebody else is not impressed by us. We somehow lack an inborn self-confidence. Particularly noticeable is the way the Swiss treat their artists, how the best they can do is to pat them on the shoulder with a sort of grudging recognition; genuine encouragement, an anticipation not hedged around with misgiving, comes mostly from foreigners. Fortunately, at the time we had to close our gates, emigrants at least were already there among us. The sober reticence of our fellow countrymen toward them would be wholly admirable if it were genuine, but what makes it questionable is this unreflecting obeisance before all things foreign. The afore-mentioned lack of self-confidence, betrayed in this and other ways, does not make our artists modest, which would be a gain; it is, rather, that our fellow citizens, when we are dependent on them alone, simply reduce us to faintheartedness, and the inevitable reverse side of that is arrogance, another form of inhibitedness. On the other hand, it can be a blessing to belong to a nation that never spoils its artists by pampering them. That without irony: the German mistake—typical perhaps of the whole of the West—of imagining that because they have symphonies they also have culture could hardly happen here; the artist not as the upholder of culture, but as just one link among many others; culture as a reflection of the whole people; we recognize it not only in bookcases and at the grand piano, but just as much in the way we treat those dependent on us. So long as one means culture in this sense, which seems to me its future sense, we must not be alarmed if we are occasionally treated as an anachronism, though here I mean less the reality than the image of Switzerland, which I love above all things, and if I could voluntarily choose what birth has already decided, I should not in spite of everything want to be other than Swiss. Beyond the image, where we find our true home, there are of course particular landscapes that one also loves, if only in second place. What I least know is whether I love my fellow countrymen—certainly not more than the corresponding faces among other peoples—and it would not in any case seem to me to be a goal to aim at. On the contrary; love for one's native country, interpreted thus, is a betrayal of the idea of home; our home is mankind; to that above all we owe our loyalty. The real good fortune of belonging to a small country is that in it patriotism is not at odds with humanity.

Pfannenstiel

Already the first buds! The long branches of the willow trees hang down like chains of pearls, reminding one of the tinkling bead curtains in certain guesthouses, and everywhere the birds are twittering, blueness streams through the brittle foliage, the sun shines everywhere, bushes and shrubs are like a sieve. Somehow it is too much, especially the twittering of the birds; but at least there is a smell of manure as one walks through the fields, and a cackling of white hens in the farmyards. Occasionally a cloud passes, and one is glad of one's coat, but the washing hanging outside in the green meadow is fluttering splendidly, cracking like a whip, and the fountain gleams, its wind-blown jet splashing over the trough. The familiar house fronts of our Swiss farms, these seem more noticeable than usual; the rows of low windows are shining, their glass panes full of little shoots, not yet entwined with flowers or shadowed by vines; the espaliers are nothing but a skeleton of slender blue shadows, a floating arabesque above their faded vitriol-stained walls. Planes are practicing in the sky. In the schools, as one passes through the villages, they are already singing at open windows, the sound of their choruses echoing across the empty playground with its horizontal bars and its lopped plane trees. From a wooded valley comes the whine of a sawmill, setting one's teeth on edge, and in the graveyards, where the first flowers are blooming, they are raking the gravel paths. For hours on end I walk over tranquil hills. The paths are soft, and one must walk on the edge; there are puddles like fragments of glass, bicycle tracks and hoof marks reflecting the sky. One trudges through woods with scarcely a shadow; only a very occasional depression filled with soiled snow, gray and granular and sprinkled with pine needles; above a gravel pit I see the first butterfly. One can hardly lose one's way, since everything is so transparent, and when one emerges, one sees a further undulating line of hills and brown hollows, birch trees lining a marsh; on the dark fields steaming horses are pulling plows and harrows, or people are scattering manure; the blue distance seen always through the black branches of an apple tree. The mountains beyond loom over spaces filled with a silver mist, the glitter of melting snow; the air is full of promise, the air is full of Easter, and it seems to me as if it had been spring only yesterday—

If time is really only illusory, a mere aid to our comprehension, separating into a one-thing-after-another what is in fact an omnipresence; if all these ideas about time which are now always in my mind are indeed true (if only for myself): why is one startled by every manifestation of the passage of time?

As if death were a matter of time.

A young man and a girl spent their youth together until they could no longer go on, and that was all a long time ago. The idea that love could simply come to an end was something they could not accept; each felt guilty that love had deserted them, and it was out of the hypocrisy in which they took refuge that the real sins emerged. There was that promise of marriage which could not be kept; one cannot get married just out of good manners. When they finally took leave of each other for

111

the last time, the girl fainted away on the doorstep; he had to take her up in his arms, and when she regained consciousness, there he still was, finally determined that they should get married. He did not wish to be a scoundrel, not toward this one person he had loved above all others, but he was a scoundrel, whatever he professed; he could not stick to his promise. To leave was betrayal, to stay was betrayal. The situation led to much error and bad blood; it was a hateful time, ugly and confused. . . . Once, many years later, he wrote her a letter. He did not really know what he should write. He knew that time did not cancel out his guilt, and there was no point in apologies or regrets. Our guilty acts remain our own affair. It was to be simply a greeting. The urge was such a clear one, and he saw no reason for repressing it. He sent the letter, which contained no questions, expecting nothing in return. But even then he was expecting too much. The reply, when it came, was angry and bitter and full of self-righteousness. There is a male self-righteousness, which is obstinate and stupid and perhaps violent, and there is a female self-righteousness, which is dif-ferent—spiteful and petty. Having read her letter he felt ashamed, as if he had gone through the wrong door and seen a nudity of no concern to him; he put the letter in a fresh envelope and sent it back. He cursed himself for having been an ass; she would have been the first woman able to be magnanimous when no longer in love, and at the age he had now reached this discovery should not have surprised him—

More years passed.

One day, in a different town, he was going down some steps, preoccupied, unconscious of his surroundings; he just had the feeling that someone, coming up the steps, had suddenly stopped and was blocking his way. It was a woman, who was regarding him in obvious dismay, and for a while, looking her straight in the face, he was not sure who she was. He cast around in vain. Of course they knew each other; it was a face that even in silence spoke of a former intimacy between them—a good, mature, warm face whose owner began gradually to smile at his helpless groping, and in this way forgot her own embarrassment. At last he realized, and they shook hands. What should they talk about? He did not want to ask questions, but they could not just talk about the weather; he said:

112

"So you are well. . . ."

"And you?"

"You have children. . . ."

"Yes," she said happily. "You too."

Their conversation was quite light and easy. Only the fact that he still could not recall her name made everything seem as if it were happening behind a veil. He should have foreseen that one day they were bound to come face to face again. Just as little as her name, which he replaced with a nameless "you," could he at the moment remember what had in fact happened about that letter; whether he had really sent it back or had only thought of doing so—

"This is my wife," he said. "And this is Annemarie."

The name had come back to him, and now it was he who did all the talking, while the two women regarded each other without using their eyes. Somehow the fact that there were two of them seemed improbable. As they parted, Annemarie said exactly what he himself had wished to say. All he said was:

"Goodbye."

While she said:

"I am so glad we have seen each other once more."

That sounded almost as if there were a death in the offing; but she was certainly not thinking of death: it was just a sense of something definitive and final. The same feeling accompanied him down the steps. All the idle thoughts that come later—whether our life might have taken a different course—what are these, after all, but waves breaking around the rocks of a finality which we cannot otherwise perceive?

When today, walking or sitting beneath the leafless trees at the edge of the woods, I think of this meeting, what I particularly remember is its happiness and ease; also the special quality arising from the use of that intimate form of address which the German language provides. The women to whom one says "*du*," however different in age, origin, manner, and appearance, seem like sisters who must surely know one another. That is both wonderful and terrible. Somehow, the moment we become intimate with them, they always become like ourselves. To another man they are completely different presumably, unrecognizable to me, more like the other man himself. . . . I sit there for a long time beneath the trees, smoking, seeing the path along which seven weeks ago I walked with Maja, and it is not really surprising that all their faces, different to the eye though they may be, become almost like one, the closer they are to my heart. The *"du"* is always ourselves. It is our own loneliness that shows us the same face— our own face, which is definitive—and beyond this *"du"* we never come. Just now and again another person enters into it, for a shorter or a longer time.

What we call unfaithfulness: our attempt for once to get out from behind our own face, our desperate hope of eluding the definitive.

Never shall I walk on the Pfannenstiel hills without thinking, briefly or at length, about the writer whom, of all my Swiss contemporaries, I love most—Albin Zollinger, who has described this landscape for all time. It was six years ago, in the fall. I had just read his latest book, and Constanze had to listen to a great deal about it as we walked along this path for the first time together. I took her into the little inn, which I knew well from previous wanderings; in a window corner there is a little walnut table, where people can sit together and chat and enjoy a glorious view over the countryside; I was pleased that I knew about this table, and since it was a weekday, I had no doubt that it would be ours. Great was my disappointment when we entered; the table was already occupied by another couple, and naturally I was convinced that they deserved it less than we did. They seemed to be a married couple, middle-aged; they were drinking wine and eating ham, and my vexation provoked me into studying them. The man, who looked rather insignificant but had a remarkable head above his slim body, could be no other than Zollinger himself. We too ordered ham. Since my eyes kept wandering to him, our own conversation proved scrappy. His face was hard and decisive, manly, but at the same time delicate and shy. He spoke in a very soft voice. I could feel my heart beating as I debated whether to speak to him or not. Their plates were empty, and any moment they might get up and go. He was wearing a pullover beneath his jacket; his whole manner of dressing reminded me of a village teacher. As he settled his bill with the landlord's daughter he had the intimate air of a little man from the neighborhood who was not used to being waited on; somehow he did not care for it. He asked for a piece of paper in which to wrap the remains of the ham (this was in the war years). Meanwhile I was wondering what, if I were to speak to him, I would have to say to him. On the other hand, I had just been talking for a whole hour about this man whose work I so much admired; why should I not tell him so? He was already asking how far it was to the station; all very inconspicuously. I had once heard him giving a lecture; somehow, now that I was seeing him close up, he seemed smaller, but also more youthful, like somebody who, behind his shyness, is rejoicing and dancing without letting the world see; he seemed to me like a Rumpelstiltskin, going through the woods and thinking that nobody knew his name, nobody knew of his visions. As he raised his glass to drain it, I suddenly heard myself speaking:

"Pardon me—"

He turned in pained surprise.

"You are surely Albin Zollinger—"

"Yes," he said. "Why?"

His eyes no longer suggested rejoicing and dancing; the diffidence he had shown, at least since our arrival, increased almost to the point of hostility, at any rate to a wary mistrust. I told him I had just read his last book. His expression remained reserved. He did not look encouraging. But now, somehow or other, I had to go on; having once written about him, I told him who I was. I was very much aware of the embarrassing situation that I, the younger man with nothing to show, was bestowing praise on the more mature man, and I could somehow understand his mistake in persisting in addressing me as *"Herr Doktor."* What saved the situation was his touching delight; he looked like a youngster being praised for the first time in his life, at any rate happy at not being vulgarly misconstrued. He talked about Thomas Mann, whom he called a master of precision, about the limitations of verbal expression, about the disturbing realization that all attempts at communication are dependent on the good will of others. He did not complain of the lack of good will; he simply burned with the desire, once in his life, as he said, to write a page that nobody could misconstrue. Unfortunately he broke off the conversation when he noticed that it was confined to the two of us; he did not wish to take me away from the young lady, he said, and asked me for my address, so that we could meet in town. It was also time for them to leave if they were to catch their train. As he took his leave, he thanked me. Since there was nothing I could say in reply, he asked me again whether we might not meet again in the near future. Then suddenly he seemed to feel he was being importunate. His curious, almost ceremonial courtesy, which made us feel all the more awkward, was like a dam which he had to erect against his overflowing heart: that diffidence of his in another form. Alone in the dining room he had just left, I felt as happy as a bridegroom striding toward certain felicity. Through the lattice window we could just see them walking away down the hill. It was already growing dark. I was pleased that I had spoken to him; our walk home was exultant—

The next I heard of him was the news of his death. He died of a heart attack at the age of forty-seven, torn from the midst of a tempestuous creative life whose work arouses in one a feeling of exhilaration; his words, whenever one hears them, give one courage to face the ramifications of one's own life, confidence and delight in all the human heart may encounter.

As evening falls over the lake, where boys crouch on posts to fish between the green beards of weed, I stand waiting for the little steamer; the sun has already vanished behind the clouds, but the lake still glistens like the inside of a shell, a shimmering somewhere between brass, silk, and bluish smoke; so for a while it hovers again above its greening bed of weeds, whose surface is mirroring a day with ivory clouds; in half an hour, when the steamer comes, it will look like dust and ashes—

The lamps are already shining.

In the churches all around the bells are ringing.

Perhaps one should make a distinction between time and transience; time as that which the clock shows, and transience as our experience of it, the consciousness of something else beyond our existence, a nonexistence which we call death. Even an animal is aware of its transience; otherwise it would not feel fear. But an animal has no consciousness, no time, no aid for its thinking; it is not upset by a clock or a calendar, not even the calendar of Nature. It carries death within it as a timeless entity, as an omnipresence, whereas we live and die every second, both at the same time, only with the difference that life is shorter than death, rarer, and since we can only live by at the same time dying, we use up life as a sun uses up its glow; we feel this perpetual decline toward nonexistence, and so we think of death whenever we see a decline, symbol of the unknown; whenever we see some visible manifestation of time's decline, such as clouds passing, leaves falling, trees growing, a gliding bank, a budding avenue, a rising moon. There is no life without fear of the other thing; for the reason that without this fear, which is our depth, there can be no life: it is only the consciousness of a nonexistence which allows us to realize for moments that we are living. One delights in one's muscles, in one's ability to move, one delights in the light that is reflected in our dark eyes, in our skin, and in the nerves which allow us to feel so much. In all this one delights, feeling with every breath that all that exists is a blessing. Without this reflecting state of wakefulness, which fear alone makes possible, we should be lost; we should never have existed. . . .

Letzigraben, August 1947

This municipal plot of land, so named because in earlier times there was a defense trench (*Graben*) here, is situated in a workers' district. The swimming-pool complex, which I, as winner of an open competition, designed, has to cater for forty-five hundred visitors.

Now at last we can start the construction work. The first workers are already on site; their brown backs glisten with sweat, and around the hut where our plans lie waiting there are rows of empty beer bottles; somewhere planks are being noisily piled; the first trucks are there, and today, when I arrive at the building site, I find a whole mountain of brown earth; a bulldozer is eating up the meadow, bushes and all. In two years, and that seems to me a very long time, it will be ready for opening: an open-air swimming pool for the general public. A century ago this was the gallows hill; our excavations will not lack skulls such as Hamlet once held in his hand. Farther on is the old gunpowder factory, which is now being pulled down; with hardly a sound the old walls crumble and disappear in a rising cloud of dust—

If only it were all the gunpowder factories in the world!

Portofino, September 1947

We were already wondering why all the limousines were still standing there beneath the palms; nobody wants to go for a drive. They are all drinking coffee, glancing through Italian newspapers. Today, it is reported, the great strike will start in Genoa and other cities. Some of the guests are playing ping-pong. The atmosphere a curious mixture of apprehension and boredom. Unfortunately the summer heat is still intense, no desire to walk, not even to swim; a sea without waves, sound-less, as smooth as ice, not a sail, not a blade of grass moving.

Yesterday I received the page proofs of my previous diary; it is always a tedious business, this retrospective working—having to read one's own stuff! I need a lot of Cinzano. Which is not to say that writing is not a pleasure! I won't give it up. But now and again, proofs in hand, one does ask oneself what possible interest this can have for others; one takes a cigarette and sneaks a glance at the other tables, watches people strolling across the piazza, sizes them up—there are so many sorts of people in the world; a sportsman and man of the world who makes a habit of snapping up the only available sailboat before my very nose as soon as a puff of wind crinkles the waters—a healthy man, a nice man, but no reader, I should say, any more than the seven anglers who are just crossing the piazza, barefoot in their rolled-up trousers; or the lady of questionable virtue who has copied their style of wearing trousers; or the elderly married couple, the loitering money-changer and black-marketeer with the classical features, the two lovers who always hold each other around the hips . . . A writer, I believe, has to think up his own readers; it is an integral part of our work, this inventing of a reader, sympathetic, not uncritical, not too much above us, but also not beneath us, a partner who is pleased that we are mulling over identical questions and is not annoyed when our views conflict; not condescending when he knows better, not stupid, not unserious and not unhumorous, above all not vindictive. He is a creature of the imagination, no more unreal but also no more real than the characters in a story, a play. The reader as an unwritten role. Unwritten, but not undefined, brought to light by that which is written; whether it be the role of a schoolboy under instruction or the role of a judge who enjoys catching one out in an inconsistency, the role of a disciple whose job is to admire, the role of an idol who has to be cajoled by flattery, or the role simply of a partner, a collaborator, who seeks and asks the same things and complements one, a human companion—the choice is up to me, the writer, though I cannot insist on anyone's assuming the role I have assigned him; I can only be pleased if someone, he or she, does assume it—somewhere out there in the sunlight or beneath a reading lamp, in a train, in a café, in one of the waiting rooms of life—and particularly if he plays it with skill.

Santa Margherita.

A fishing cutter brings in the week's catch. Boxes full of cuttlefish, everything dripping wet, a green and violet glittering, slimy as shining entrails. Little dinghies flit to and fro; there is always at least one on its way between the anchored cutter and the mole, which last year was still in ruins. The fishermen are all equally dirty, oily, cheerful, and tired, also a little proud: both the men who hunted and caught the quarry and the women who take it over and do what is necessary to convert it to domestic use. Market under shady vaults. They tip the wet catch onto stone tables festooned as for a feast with fig leaves and ferns. Selling begins at once, haggling with chanted cries and gestures. Whole hills of silver scales. Of course it stinks. The splendor of the colors: the fleshlike pink, the gray which is like a veil, the greens and blues and all the indescribable opalescent variations between. Lovely the long eels with their white bellies, their green and brown backs, their black fins. Or the fine sweep of a tail hanging over the stone table. Then the knife which slits them, and the wet, thick, red female hands which fling them onto the scales; then search among the paper money for change. *"Signore?"* they cry. *"Niente!"* And already the next is calling: *"Signore?"* A starfish is among the pile: in the air it has lost its shine and is now just a gray piece of dough, repulsive with the slow, blind groping of its many feelers, a headless thing, life without choice or will. We move on. To the crabs, the red ones, where one does not know what is front and what back; a whole slowly crawling mountain; here too: life is damnation. And on how vast a scale! Each time the fishermen bring in just as much as their cutters can carry; numbers beyond imagining, a dip into the incalculable, the inexhaustible. I watch an old woman who is holding a yellow lobster, uncertain whether the thing is worth so many lire. Meanwhile the men are busy spreading out their brown nets on the jetty; others are in the taverns, drinking, chatting about the strike. The yellow lobster is too expensive for the old woman; a young lady in trousers seizes it quickly. What most fascinates me is the simple fact that here for once one is seeing everything together: the hunters, the sellers, the buyers. All quite factual. And behind it the evening tolling of bells from an old church, the sun casting its last rays on the tiled roof of a convent, a priest wearing a flat black hat. Two rather ragged children are dividing up a fish which is not of the freshest; they are slicing it on the curb. Back through all the silver scales, the mother-of-pearl iridescence, the pink silence of open mouths . . . At the piss-stained corner stands the usual beggar, a notice in English tied around his neck:

"Blind, please help."

The entire staff of a grand hotel going on strike, the guests having to share in all the daily housework, make beds, peel potatoes, chop wood, wash dishes, dry glasses, cook soup, soup with bread, as long as the bread lasts, but every day soup:

Background to a comedy?

A walk in the glowing heat. Whole burnt-out slopes, a dead snake among the charred bushes; butterflies dancing . . .

Somewhere along the road a tablet in marble:

"Qui la bellezza del mondo sorrise per l'ultima volta a Francesco Pisani. 8.9.1941."

(Here the world's beauty smiled for the last time for Francesco Pisani.)

At last a gravestone that does not insult life; dignified; no obscene misrepresentation, cowardly glorification of death.

The strike, we are told, has been put off. Remarkable the family feeling among the guests, who previously had scarcely even exchanged nods; one cannot now get into the elevator without becoming involved in a conversation, and one's consent is taken for granted. A class consciousness such as I had not previously believed to exist. We belong together, whether Italian or English, Swiss, Dutch, or Belgian; whether racketeer or physician, officer on leave or lovers or little man with large purse, we share a common inconvenience, and an unjust one; we want to enjoy our vacation and that is all, we are foreigners and we have paid for it. The landlord, dressed in black from head to toe, stands in the foyer and assures us in all languages that there will be no strike now. He can even speak German: his memories of the German army, on which he once waited, give me a claim—since I speak their language after a fashion— to a certain respect that I as an individual could not hope to receive from him. The guests read the newspapers of their own countries, which print no reports of any unrest, nothing at all in fact about Italy; one feels faintly reassured. But it is still annoying, sad, and incomprehensible that there should be people in this country too (one calls them "elements") who want what others already have. I play ping-pong with the young Italian whose girl friend prefers just to watch; she goes in search of our mis-hit balls among the night-covered aloes. . . .

Nothing would be nicer than a comedy, but not an antiquarian one: it would have to be a contemporary one, played in costume if you like, but a comedy about the problems of our own day. Would that be possible? The demand for it would be great, altogether the demand for a cheerful and basically undoubting affirmation, but all the same an affirmation that does not evade the real issues and the contemporary values of today.

That is what counts. A comedy that just evades the problems can be no more than mere entertainment; compared with that, a tragedy that would face up to our awareness of things as they are would, I think, prove on the whole more comforting—

Why is there no such comedy?

One might laugh for three hours at a stretch, tickled by one witticism after another, and still have no comedy. Wit alone is not enough. Laughs are just the trimmings, never the essence, of a comedy. A possible way might be merriment without any wit at all, a sort of cheerful reassurance arising out of some incorrigible optimism which, in view of all the trials and tribulations to which it is subjected, becomes disproportionate and so, to that extent, comic. Comedy, I think, is not a question of plot, but of climate. It cannot work without a basic optimism, a feeling that all is for the best and the world is heading for redemption— and without this gilded background we so fervently desire there can be no real comedy. . . . In Kleist's *Der zerbrochene Krug* there lurks, behind the comedy of people sitting in judgment over other people, the unshattered faith that there is a judgment beyond the human one outside the realm of comedy; here it is Gerichtsrat Walter, as representative of a truly merciful God, who supplies the gilded background. There can be no doubting him. In Lessing's *Minna von Barnhelm* and in other true comedies, of which there are precious few, the optimism is not always metaphysical; it is sometimes enough when we can believe in the social order. One may laugh at its degeneracy and its tiresome excesses, but fundamentally one still approves of it; the social order as depicted in comedies is the best possible order. There are noblemen and servants, and sometimes, as comedy shows us, the servant is a much better person, nobler than the nobleman. By rights the servant should straight away be raised to the aristocracy, and so—in this particular case—the distribution of titles is comic, because it is incongruous. All the same, that there are such things as noblemen and servants, masters and slaves—that is something comedy does not question. Otherwise it would cease to be funny. Society is approved, in theory at least, and unquestioningly; and so one can laugh all the more cheekily about its unsatisfactory appearance in practice, without being heretical. Comedy is devout—in the sense that Aristophanes was devout: he believed in Athens unquestioningly, otherwise he could not have trounced the Athenians so vigorously; and indeed he had every reason to believe in his polis—in spite of Cleon. Aristophanes believed; otherwise he would not have become Aristophanes, but a clown or a tragedian. The least that can be expected is of course that the human being should be approved, Man as a species; the least or the greatest. Man as God's finest creation, his masterpiece. Our emotions may in specific cases perhaps seem foolish; a person continues to believe after he has been betrayed, and his faith becomes incongruous, comic, because he is always squandering it on the wrong person; but in the same play there will be someone else, who—if only he could see it—would certainly make him happy. Or we laugh at hypocrites, knowing that the Tartuffes of this world achieve nothing in the end. In the end; that might mean the fifth act or heaven. Virtue is always triumphant; the gilded background remains unblemished; it is this alone, and not individual jokes, which induces in us the merriment from which comedy (meaning merrymaking) after all takes its name—the gilded background of belief that right will always prevail and everything has its meaning: a hidden one, if you like, but nevertheless a meaning; without this belief, which must be devout and undoubting, the result can only be satire, witty, but not cheerfully reassuring. . . . Don Quixote is comic because everything he does and says is out of proportion; the good man has read too much, and now we see him, primed with archaic modes of speech, riding out into a completely bourgeois world, a victim of Literature, which at all times has consisted of antiquarian modes of speech; everything is different from his lofty illusions, more practical, uglier, less grand, but easy to live with and worth living. The world that ridicules the knight has Cervantes's basic approval. It is after all a real world, a possible world, and our sympathies are not with the landlords and the goose girls for not being princesses, but with the nobleman of La Mancha who always takes the landlords and the goose girls for the wrong thing. How would it be if the world that makes such a touching fool of Don Quixote were equally impossible, an empty specter, outdated, lost, unreal and unlivable, unworthy of approval? What would become of our enjoyment of his mistake—which would then not even be a mistake?

Today, Sunday, in Santa Margherita, they pass by now and again in open trucks, crammed together, but singing. A girl holds the banner with hammer and sickle.

But where to find the faith? Where the gilded background? I can see the portents well enough. Approval of a coming social order that has not yet proved its viability is seldom unclouded; the desire for faith which fills a revolutionary is still not faith. How rare to find a revolutionary who does not regard humor as something monstrous . . .

I am reading Jakob Burckhardt, an antiquarian edition with brown stains on the paper and marbled binding, and enjoying his golden, Indian-summer faith, which betrays that a young man is writing. I read him as if entirely unaware of his later fame, praise him as if he stood in need of it, reproach him as if that were my right. I reproach him, for example, for his utterly constrained, blinkered, prejudiced contempt for his own times—this sort of thing: The spirit is going more and more to the dogs—which means of course us. I spell out for him the names of those who were living and creating at the time he wrote that; a club of quite worthy gentlemen, after all. Most of them—well, no, he could not have known them. You have to be careful in judging your own times . . . ! The Renaissance starts with Brunelleschi, and with the Renaissance Burckhardt starts to be a splendidly informative guide; time and again I take up my pencil to mark delicious passages with one, two, even three strokes. Styles are creative goals; but why they change is something even my great Jakob does not mention. With Brunelleschi the Renaissance begins, that is beyond dispute, but then, a hundred pages on, others come along and simply throw the Renaissance, which my author describes categorically as the only right way, out of the window. The wretches! Suddenly everybody goes baroque, and at once Burckhardt turns from an enthusiast into a professor—that is to say, he suddenly loses his antennae and hears nobody except himself, his own opinions. I permit my pencil its first question marks, which turn gradually into exclamation marks, and finally I put the book down on the table—not exasperated, just reflective: it does really look as if even so penetrating a contemplation of created work

—and who is better than Burckhardt at that?—cannot get beyond the outer defenses; the conditions of creation may perhaps be revealed to the creator, though hardly in so conscious a way that he can describe them—and that is anyway not his concern. The observer, on the other hand, starts from a preconception which he has accepted as right, as generally valid, and the precept the creator is following is probably not this particular sort of rightness; it is, rather, what is possible and necessary for him, a living precept which comes to an end when he finds the proper form for it. All success is of short duration. And unrepeatable. Peaks in ancient Greece; the Renaissance. Only imitations can endure. The best saying I know about the need for changing styles is in Goethe's *Faust* (Part II):

> Forming, transforming
> Eternal sport
> Of the eternal spirit.

But what, if we look at it like that, is this rightness that one style is supposed to have over the others? Jakob Burckhardt and baroque art; his disapproval is so understandable, because he is measuring baroque art not against its own creative precepts, but against those of the Renaissance. I permit myself to note in the margin: *"Et tu, Jakob?"* For in this way even he, one of the worthiest of men, is showing himself no better than the little reviewers who for example reproach Brecht because his plays are not dramatic, when for whole decades his aim has been epic theater. . . . Oh, this business of our judgments! When even so rare a spirit as Burckhardt is hemmed in by inhibitions toward bygone epochs, receptive to one, blind to others, how can the creative artist, the one who is interested and involved, ever hope to achieve an impersonal judgment?

A heavy storm . . . The little sandy beach from which we swam daily is now a mass of debris. Trees, snapped in two, hang over the cliffs. A feeling almost of liberation. We walk along the shore in pouring rain. Pillars of spray. The sky is gray and violet, metallic. Stones on the road. Floods in Santa Margherita, half the public square under water; white-coated waiters standing behind streaming windows. The flapping of torn curtains. The great bunkers, which last year were still standing, have now been demolished. During our walk we flee beneath an arch for shelter; a deluge, with more thunder. In front of us the rolling sea; why should it not rise still farther, three meters, ten meters? The feeling of panic is almost blissful, all barriers become suspect, insecurity prevails, the adventure of living. Later we take a bus, drink a schnapps in Rapallo. The rain has eased off, but not the wind; the quay, still under construction, has been damaged, laborers and fishermen try to save what can be saved; the finished concrete stands firm, but the supports are gone, and the huge flat surface, just ready for concreting, is a mass of twisted steel, the mold smashed; the crashing waves are throwing single planks ashore, church bells are ringing; I don't know why, but they seem superbly fitting. . . .

On architecture

Well worth taking to heart, writes Burckhardt, is the lesson that no material pretends to be something other than what it is, and a hundred other sentences like this which, although referring to the Renaissance, belong to the ABC's of our existence. The congruence of function and form—only with essentially different objectives, which are required to meet other needs, and above all with different materials which have their own different laws; the basic principle, however, remains: a syntax with other materials. And yet we see our intellectuals, faced with a Corbusier for example, often as helpless as before a South Seas mask.

Why?

Our relationship to our own times, precisely that attitude of "the spirit going to the dogs," meaning us . . . On the Acropolis there are the Persian ruins, those sculptures of a previous generation which were used as a lining for the new wall; the men who did it were in no doubt that they were creating a new work of art of their own. It is the same thing in Italy: the bare-faced plunderings of antique buildings, done not by vandals but by architects who needed pillars, marble for their own buildings. Give it here! It's our turn now! A tremendous feeling for the present, as lacking in piety as life itself, an antihistorical attitude that is seen even in the Renaissance, which professed to emulate the ancient world. However, they did not call it re-

construction then, but renascence. Everywhere the active awareness that it is, primarily, not the created work that is important,
but the act of creation itself. I should say: even if the new
thing is of lesser value, it is more important that it should be
created, more important than conservation, though the need
for that is not denied. One of the fascinations of Italy, inducing
a warm feeling of personal happiness, is the way each epoch
takes its existence so seriously, how ruthlessly it sets out to make
use of its time on earth.

And we?

A few years ago a competition was held for a new art gallery
in Zurich; everybody knew that the allotted site permitted no
solution that would be completely successful, free and pleasing
to the eye, but nobody had the courage simply to tear down an
old house of moderate architectural value that stood in the way.
And so the new building, our building, stood condemned before
we even took up our pencils. This is the atmosphere in which
we are now permitted to create: there is no feeling of expectation,
we are tied to the apron strings of an excessive historical piety,
beset by the unquestioning self-surrender of our own generation. . . . Culture as a perverse devotion to the past—

Florence, October 1947

In the street in front of our hotel two children are playing; a
boy of five, rachitic, and a girl with a toy pistol: they are playing
at highwaymen, and the little boy, rather petulant and unwilling,
is told to stand up against the piss-stained wall. He can't understand that he is then supposed to fall down; the girl shows him
how—with all the experience of her seven years.

In Savonarola's chamber: the man has a fascination, his profile,
beside it the little picture of the stake, the black tribunal of
right-thinking men. But for them at least one thing can be said:
they did also look on at the execution, there was a unity of
time and place, a wooden platform leading straight from the
courtroom to the red fire. I can again feel something of what I
recently felt in the fish market: all the connections are straight-
forward, visible in a way one understands, not anonymous. Fish-

ing and trade, tribunal and execution, whatever it is, it does not fade into a mere conception; everything is factual. We, on the other hand, live among conceptions that we can usually not check up on for ourselves; the radio convinces me of a hundred things I shall never see for myself, or if I do happen to see them, I am not seeing them properly, because my mind is already made up; I have a point of view, though I have viewed nothing. The majority of our conceptions we find unbearable when they assume a factual shape; we live beyond our own powers. When I see a pig slaughtered with a gleaming knife before my eyes, I feel sick and have no more appetite for ham; normally I like it very much. Our thinking must become more factual! One should be made to see what one is thinking, then either accept it or change one's thoughts to something one can think. In *Dantons Tod* Georg Büchner makes Danton say, as he is led away to prison: Follow up your phrases to the point where they become reality, then look around—this is what you said! A motto that today hangs over almost the whole of Europe. And in this sense I do not feel that these judges sitting beside the fire and fanning the flame with their claims to know best are the lowest form of humanity; at any rate their words and their deeds are one.

"*Marxismo—Cristianismo?*"

If the latter in its two thousand years of existence had given as serious attention to its precepts concerning life in this world as to those concerning the other, I cannot believe that the former would have ever become a real threat.

Many beggars even here.

I have no time at all for people who station themselves outside the churches whose cloisters we have come to view in the hope of profiting from my Christian impulses. That is not the way! I prefer those others who, when one is eating outside, come up to the table, stand there until the bustling waiter has brought the black coffee and I am lighting a cigarette, then say: "*Mangiato?*"

Michelangelo's *Pietà*. (From the Capella Barberini in Santa Rosalia in Palestrina.) This is where beauty ends; the weight of the corpse with its bent legs and its hanging arms, the horrifying quality of a body that now obeys only the laws of gravity, the fear that its accidental movements will suddenly become grotesque, puppetlike, and ridiculous. And behind it the mother; unfinished, a piece of stone, the remote awakening of a figure, emerging from a primal darkness which has never seen the light, her tenderness hidden behind a heavy veil of stone. Beyond the beauty: the bodies that were loaded on trucks and then thrown into a chalk pit—one can recall them without disgust at one's enjoyment of art; they too are contained in this. They are not mocked and betrayed by fine sculpturing. Only when the element of horror is included can there be any hope of salvation, which is more than just premature harmony.

An Italian newspaper, which Constanze translated for me, reports the following facts: the atom bomb in Bikini developed a radioactivity equal to the yield of seventy thousand tons of radium. The amount of radium used up till now for medicinal purposes is: one hundred and fifteen grams. The afore-mentioned radioactivity will remain active in the atmosphere for twenty-five years. Five hundred bombs, dropped within twenty-five years, should be enough to wipe out all living things on this earth.

Festa dell'uva . . . Sunday evening; we get caught up in a huge throng, streets cheerfully lit, garlands of electric bulbs, a brass band playing Verdi, all around us happy people eating grapes; women lean from open windows, breasts between their folded arms, enjoying the scrimmage from above, children screaming, a full moon over San Lorenzo, everywhere stalls with fairy lights, piled with grapes, stalls with cheap toys, stalls with cakes just baked in rather smelly fat. A man buys a sort of cherry pancake, breaks it up carefully, gives bits first to his ancient mother, then to his wife and child, and stuffs the rest in his own mouth. Everywhere a festive spirit alive with expectation, without visible signs of fulfillment; a harlequin cracking jokes with a guitar, surrounded by happy faces. The people give the impression of infinitely simple and modest children, glad to be alive, eternally hopeful, harmless, playful, guileless; even the men drinking their wine, who suddenly start quarreling in bitter earnest; even the little, uncertain prostitutes, who stand on the shadowy outskirts, listen to Verdi and do not quite know what one means when one looks into their faces or at the crucifix on their bosoms. A cripple in the uniform of the Italian air force sits on the ground fiddling, even the youths stop to give him something. A truck sounds its horn as it tries to nose through the crowd: two fine white bullocks on their final journey. An old man is selling little paper flags, the Stars and Stripes, but also the Hammer and Sickle, in addition to jumping jacks, tin planes, and woolly apes. The sound of singing from a bar. Smell of latrines. Gossiping mothers sit on the curb, babies in their arms—all infinitely modest, eternally hopeful. . . .

I make a lot of sketches, as an aid to seeing, then throw them away. Little remains either of what I write. I have just brought out my little notebook to jot down, for the benefit of all genera-tions that may still be interested in Europe, that the Palazzo Vecchio (do not let yourself be taken in by its size) is a miserably botched piece of work. Further details on request; how falsely the tower sits on the façade! What has the mighty Jakob to say about that?
"Size, memories, stone colors, and fantastic tower construc-tion give this building a value far in excess of its artistic merit."
It's all been seen—and said—before.

Fiesole.
(I think again about those gentlemen from the trust who do not wish to supply cement for our public swimming pool. The industry, with whose management they feel associated in an advisory capacity, has at the moment so many urgent building projects to invest in. The industry, they say, cannot now approve an undertaking of this type. Is it theirs to approve? The people have voted for it. Their shameless proposal: that the city should use imported cement, which is not only more expensive, but also can be had only through this trust. The pits for our pools have already been dug. I wonder what the decision will be.) The remains of a Roman bath . . .

Farewell visit to Michelangelo . . . His slaves, unfinished: the blocks, still recognizable as such, are much smaller than one would judge from the figures he began to carve in them.

Their gestures were designed from the start in the shape of a strict cube. True sculpture: a figure is not kneaded, but carved out, released from the stone. That is the fascinating thing about Michelangelo's many fragments—here, as seldom elsewhere, one sees the creative process at work. Procedure, not result. Birth in all its torment and wonder. Who desires it? Maybe those giving birth; the born themselves—defenseless, victims. This is the moment he took as his theme in the Sistine Chapel—the awakening of Adam—and here as nowhere else I realize the herculean nature of his figures; it is as if they are fighting for their birth or defending themselves against the being who is trying to force them into birth. In Adam too, as God's finger wakes him, there is this conflict; half grateful and wondering, half grieving, he receives the life that he has neither willed nor pleaded for. He is God's creation and God's victim. In his shining eyes there is both defiance and humility. . . .

En route

Two hours in an overcrowded bus. We are the only foreigners in this rocking sardine can. Constant stops; a worker gets in. Another stop: a woman with a baby gets out. What a handsome set of people! On lengthier examination: they are mostly not all that handsome—simply happy and gay. Not high-spirited, not loud, but happy, lively, polite. How cheerfully they accept all the jostling, help one another—and this is not the special atmosphere of some festival or occasion; it is a workday, laborers, priests, women going to the market, baskets of eggs, children, rucksacks stuffed with poverty, a sickle, a lamb to be sold in Siena. A workday: yet rarely has one been so conscious of culture, of living humanity. One should not generalize about a nation— but I shall do it just the same: I love the Italians.

Siena, October 1947

Towers: unadorned brick with no special features, simply a slender body of red material, then the sharp edge between light and shadow, just as sharp as the edge between body and space, tower and air, stone and sky, yet different. We always like to talk of relationships; but they are often, on a closer look, not so happy, they are crippled, spoiled by later extensions, blunted by an added story, as here in the Palazzo Pubblico. But there still remains, deliciously, its sheer corporeal being. All corporeal things in this country have an unusual, almost disconcerting being of their own. What moves us, what pleases, surprises, and fascinates us, is the being that confronts us in such corporeal things, pure being, familiar yet puzzling, ordinary yet mysterious—that such things can be—

The feeling of oneself as a being.

Siena will be our last call this time. Waiting buses marked Arezzo, Orvieto, Roma. Even at such times, when my feelings are painful, I consider the ties of work a blessing. Restriction leads to greater enjoyment.

Sitting in the shade, I read the history of the new cathedral, the tale of a presumptuous act. Siena wanted to possess the largest cathedral of all. The cathedral standing at the time, I read, would just have served to form the transept. The gigantic new nave, which was never completed, got only as far as a side wall, five axes with round arches and a complete front wall. Then came the plague, which ravaged Siena for several years, but did not succeed in diverting its inhabitants from their extravagant undertaking. Their grandchildren continued to build. The imprudence characteristic of paranoia is apparent as soon as one examines the plans more closely; the central dome, already standing, could never have been reconciled with the new nave; and, to add to that, the foundations turned out in the grandchildren's time to be unsound, the vaults, already begun, started to spread: work was abandoned. The result of all this is a wonder! It remains open to the sky, but the interior can be visualized as it was planned. One sees how this enclosed space that never was would have been snatched from infinity, cut off from the sun. Space as a being, like the body of that tower; that is to say, space confined, shaped, and formed, which makes us conscious for the first time of the space that is limitless and intangible.

Form: when the unimaginable quality of being succeeds in making itself apparent?

En route

In the restaurant car. The train has stopped in a small bombed station, opposite an open cattle truck which is also standing still. This is full of people: Italians on their way to work, men and women, youths, girls, all looking at our plates; without expression or reproach, weary and apathetic, as if there would always be two sorts of people: those who sit and those who stand, those who eat and those who do not starve, those who find this quite in order and those who cannot change it, though there is only a pane of glass between, though they are in the majority. . . .

Why can they not change it?

Café Odeon

The word with which one can at the moment make the most mischief is "nihilism"—you have only to look through any of our newspapers and you will soon find it. Sartre is a nihilist, so is Wilder, so is Jünger, so is Brecht. . . . What a very obliging word it is! I can just visualize them, all these second-rate reviewers of ours; they blunder around armed as if with a Flit-gun; the moment they see something moving, they shut their eyes and squirt:

"Nihilism, nihilism—"

In the sense in which our newspapers mean it the doctor who today X-rayed me instead of rouging my cheeks is also a nihilist; what will emerge from his X-ray will not be pretty—

What they call positive:

Fear of the negative.

(Obviously the fact of whether one says yes or no is less important than to what one says it; the belief that finds expression in a no is not always the least significant—most often indeed it is the purer.)

133

Their yes: connivance with a lie.

With regard to Brecht, the subject of this particular essay, I ask myself whether a nihilist, a genuine one, would be capable of desiring change. Brecht, as this critic well knows, certainly does want change, a quite familiar sort of change, completely identifiable. A person who does not desire change because the present situation is to his advantage, or another who favors change of a different kind, may call him an opponent, but never a nihilist. By rejecting bourgeois values you are not rejecting all mankind, just as by photographing the body you are not denying the spirit—rather, you are making use of it.

Another thing: our attitude toward ugliness, why the artist who shows us ugly things is usually denounced as inartistic—
The bourgeois says:
"Art should concern itself with the beautiful."
(So that it should not concern itself with him?)
Goethe says:
"Art concerns itself with the difficult and the good." (*Maxims and Reflections*)

Only a person capable of beauty, it seems, can bear the sight of ugliness—and succeed too in depicting it.
What is the mark of a dilettante?
The objects he depicts are always beautiful.

Letzigraben

My building site still has very little to do with architecture. Pits full of muddy water, pipes, mounds of excavated soil, already with a green shimmer of sprouting weeds, and scattered between them huts, latrines, sheds full of bits of apparatus or cement in paper sacks, piles of planks, a vista of log roads and puddles, props and pulleys where they are laying the heavy pipes. Of the future buildings one sees so far only the first foundations, a pile dwelling of ferroconcrete. I am pleasantly surprised by its growing size. For all the many pits (some of them seven meters deep), nothing has yet been found, not even a human skeleton, only horses' bones. On this spot the Russians once fought against the French; there are bricks from a Roman villa scattered all over the gallows hill, the burial grounds, and the allotments. . . . At the moment it is I who am imposing my will on this little patch of earth, monarch of an area more than thirty-five thousand meters square.

En route

That there are very many different degrees of nonfreedom, yet no real freedom (though everyone out to subjugate us proclaims it)—this is something it is vitally necessary to recognize if one is not to make a fool of oneself when, disappointed and disillusioned with one persuader, we yield in a similar mood of childish hope to another.

The difference in degree: whether people revile and misrepresent you and you cannot defend yourself, or whether they arrest and ill-treat you and you cannot defend yourself.

A member of the bourgeois class, an academician, well read, much traveled, anxious to impress as a man of good will and an upright intellectual—can we say he is lying when he maintains that our social order is the only one that represents true freedom? He is quite convinced that here in Switzerland every person of talent can develop and use his gifts; and his only reaction is dismay, surprise, and embarrassment when he finds I am not equally convinced. I quote cases in point, which arouse in him genuine regret, but do not basically upset his beliefs. He has two kinds of answers. Firstly: All the instances I have mentioned are exceptions, special cases, misunderstandings. Secondly: Do I think Communism means freedom? He is unshakable in his belief that there can be freedom, freedom for all, that it does in fact exist—and precisely in this country of ours. . . . The reason, of course, is that he himself feels completely free: as everybody does in a society that he approves because it protects his interests.

Perhaps most things we condemn as lies are in this sense not lies at all, but the honest expression of an opinion that fails to recognize its relative nature. Lying is a conscious process. People lie much less than we think. Lying requires strength, in contrast to untruthfulness; lying is a deliberate act, and an evil one. Lying is the deliberate suppression of a different knowledge, it requires an act of will and is always hazardous, whereas untruthfulness, even when the words are the same, is always ingenuous, moral, complacent. And that is why the untruthful person cannot be converted, but only made indignant, as he would be by the desecration of a temple; his temple is the confident belief that everything that most benefits him must be the truth—not just his truth, but pure truth, eternal, unassailable, sacred—and absolute.

The prerequisite for tolerance (as far as there can be such a thing) is the awareness, hardly bearable, that our thinking is always relative.

Tolerance is always the sign that a governing system considers itself to be secure; the moment it feels endangered, it claims the right to act unconditionally—hence mendacity, the divine right of personal prejudice, the Inquisition.

Zurich, November 9, 1947

"The writers whose names appear below, having met together in Zurich, are of the opinion that the existence of two differing economic systems in Europe is being used to make propaganda for a new war. Concerned for the future not only of their own nations, but of the whole world, they request the writers of all nations to add their signatures to the enclosed appeal and to act in its spirit."

The preliminary group, the result of a chance meeting in Zurich, consists of seven people: despite one American passport, one stateless, and one Swiss, the voice being raised is for the moment a very German one, but it is intended to become worldwide. Each person will try by means of personal letters to get further signatures, in order to widen the basis of this preliminary group; I myself have undertaken to seek support among my Swiss compatriots. The main thing must of course be to unite the writers of both West and East. If only half of them sign, the whole appeal will be pointless, its possible effect nil. Do not both sides assure us that they want peace? But not, of course, peace with the enemy, and so the word has become a mere lying battle-slogan, for what does peace mean but peace with the enemy? Gradually we are beginning to see where the drawback lies; the tone of our discussions is becoming drier; a good impulse, the human earnestness that prompted us to take up our pens, the spirit of intoxication which on such occasions can take possession of even the most inveterate cynic—it has all ebbed away before the last signature is quite dry—

The appeal would read:

"Anticipation of a new war is bringing the rebuilding of our world to a standstill. Today we face the choice, not just between peace and war, but between peace and total annihilation. To the politicians who are not yet aware of it we declare categorically that the peoples of this earth desire peace."

In the train

The absence of men, most of whom either have been killed or are still in captivity, strikes one as soon as one touches German soil; one is aware of it less on the streets than in private circles; aware most of all in the presence of women aged between thirty and forty—

Frankfurt, November 1947

On the whole, if I am not mistaken, things have become rather better than they were a year ago. Though not much. Or has one simply grown used to the rubble? There are newspapers now on the stands. The people themselves look rather worse. Need has lost its novelty, it is daily routine, and there is no way of knowing what is in store. A certain kind of hope that arose with Germany's collapse is now looking shabby, like the last clothes. I read the public placards: appeals for the rebuilding of Goethe's birthplace, a lecture on Buddhism, an English language course, a cabaret, surrounded by a desert of small advertisements: Wanted, a room within reach of the city. And again and again: Who can supply information about my son? Coupled with a photograph: the smiling face of a healthy soldier, the unshadowed confidence of a young face, to be seen nowadays only on advertising pillars; it is moving, yet at the same time depressing: we should never have understood one another.

Evening in the library of an old friend, with view over the river Main. We unwrap our food, and everything is uncomplicated, we can sleep here, a lively and cheerful conversation till three in the morning.

On writers

Even if this writers' appeal were to come to anything, would it have any real significance? The peoples of this earth desire peace; would writers, even those with famous names, count as the voice of the people? I imagine myself as a newspaper reader catching sight of this appeal; my reaction: Just look at that— the writers of the world! And after skimming through to see which names I know and which are missing, I turn to other pages to find out something factual—for instance, where uranium has been discovered—or something amusing—for instance, Adamson's newest escapade. Oh, the writers mean well, no doubt. Some of them enjoy our deepest respect, no less than Eisenhower, but in a different way; and I don't find anything wrong with their making yet another such appeal, in fact I find it praiseworthy, it does them credit and it is nice, like Churchill painting. . . . And, abandoning the paper to my companion, I might perhaps say as I sip my coffee:

"Pity that writers and poets have so little real influence these days."

"Why?"

"Peace or total annihilation," I say. "That's exactly how I feel. It's utter madness—"

"Sure it is."

He too takes up his cup.

"If writers and poets really had any influence," I say, "perhaps many things in the world would be different."

He turns to another page.

"Do you think so?" he merely replies.

(He is perhaps a doctor or something like that.)

"When I was still a student," he goes on, "that was sixteen or seventeen years ago, we were sitting in my room in front of the radio—just before a Hitler election—and we heard the voices of two people who were using their fame to tip the scales: Gerhart Hauptmann and Max Schmeling."

"What of it?"

"What of it!"

"What are you trying to say?"

"If our writers have no real influence," he says, his eyes again on the newspaper, "maybe it's a pity, yes, but maybe not. Anyway, it's not our fault. Even fame can only be sold once—and as for influence, real influence—well, I think you can only influence things you know something about, when you've already proved to the world that you know something about it. . . ."

In the train

How pleasant that you can journey for days on end, knowing the field you are just passing is still called *Feld,* not *champ,* not *campo*—how odd that landscapes I am seeing for the first time seem familiar, though completely different from our own landscapes, just because they belong to the same language as myself . . .

And the people?

From the start one feels a tie with people who call things by the same name. One enjoys the delightful extension of one's inner home, and when the foreignness begins to show as it inevitably will, one feels it more painfully than elsewhere; one also hates much more easily, more swiftly, more wildly than in places where a different language is spoken.

Berlin, November 1947

Arrival at dawn. Lakes, the sun rising behind pine trees, clouds, bridges kneeling in water in which the sun is reflected like brass.

The roofs are wet. Between the tree trunks a tangled mass of bombed searchlights. Then the first red flags, gaudy against the leaden sky, like fresh blood. Red as the color of warning; one is reminded of rifle ranges, etc.

Lichterfelde.

The American officer whom I met for the first time in the train invites us to breakfast, which ends with our becoming his guests from now on; so the accommodation problem is already solved.

Morning on the Alexanderplatz. The youthful gangsters and prostitutes. A lot of bartering going on: *Dreigroschenoper* without the songs. Behind it all one senses a secret language. Unsettling not in the sense that one fears being molested—at any rate not during the day—but, rather, because of the sure knowledge that people of one's own sort, if suddenly faced with living this kind of life, would go under within three days. One feels very keenly that even a life like this has its own laws, and it would take years to learn them. A truck full of policemen; at once they scatter, some stand still and grin, while I look on and have no idea what is happening. Four boys and three girls are loaded into the truck, where they squat down among others who have already been picked up elsewhere. Indifferent, impenetrable. The police have helmets and automatics, therefore authority, but no knowledge of what they are doing, one feels. Not even they! Life in the lower depths develops along quite different lines; I am reminded of those captive crabs in Portofino. . . .

Later to the Brandenburg Gate.

Now and again one trips over the tracks of a light railway; I wipe my trousers, listening in the dusk. A silence as in the mountains, only the trickling of a glacier stream missing. The newspapers carry a daily column of street attacks; sometimes naked corpses are discovered, and the murderers come as a rule from the other side. Whole districts without a single light. The amount of rubble is immense, but one gets out of the habit of asking what ever will be done with it. A chain of brick hills, beneath them buried people, above them twinkling stars; nothing stirs there but rats.

Evening at the theater: *Iphigenia.*

"What do you think of Berlin?"

A word of praise from a foreigner is highly coveted; the need for recognition colossal; avow that Berlin's spirit is unbroken and you will be treated as a very important person. . . .

The weather is again lovely, a November sky, its blueness spacious and almost silvery; it is true that the air in this city is unrivaled. One feels more awake here than anywhere else, even after nights with hardly any sleep. The soles of my feet burn, for I have been walking all day, but my head is like a torch in the wind. Midday rest in the Tiergarten. A treeless waste, the familiar statues of the Brandenburg princes surrounded by vegetable-garden patches. Some of the statues have lost their arms, on others the face has been shattered. One statue has apparently been turned around by bomb blast and is now striding masterfully in the wrong direction. Somewhere else one sees just a pedestal with two stone feet and an inscription; the remainder lies among the proliferating weeds. Except for a dog attracted by the smell of my sandwiches I am alone. Behind it all the towering Red Army Memorial, which at night is illuminated.

A lot of faces.

A lot of personal destinies.

I get hardly a chance to write anything down, though almost everything seems worthy of note; not a single sentence for days on end; a forest of destinies, a flood of impressions, all jumbled up, conflicting, there is no overall sense in it, just stories, views, isolated happenings—

An exhibition of Soviet culture. It is indeed not irrelevant to be shown pictures of Smolensk or Sebastopol, devastations preceding those now daily on view. But, for the rest, one already knows what to expect from exhibitions of this sort. Whichever great power is engaged in glorifying itself, one feels discomfited. I cannot see what need it has for such retouchings: Russia conquers Japan. At the door a small letterbox: What is your impression of this exhibition? Give your views frankly and freely. The little box is empty. For the best part of an hour I am the only visitor. It is raining outside; the rooms, I believe, are heated. In order to get beyond merely emotional reactions I inquire about the Russian housing program, taking care to identify myself as a Swiss citizen and an architect. A friendly army captain in civilian clothes conducts me to the library. Picture of a classical palace with pillars three stories high.

"What I particularly want to see is houses," I say, "workers' developments and so on."

"Workers live here."

"Behind these magnificent pillars?"

"Oh, yes."

My expression, my somewhat speechless surprise—since by architecture we mean something so completely different—is obviously taken to betray doubt and mistrust and is answered accordingly:

"Oh, yes, workers live here."

"Then why such—such pillars?"

"This is the main street in Moscow."

In time, and because I am seriously interested, we come, after leafing through many books, nearer to the matter at hand. What interests me: whether the designs, evidence of an attitude to life, are very different from our own designs for middle-class housing developments, and in what way. Picture of a small house: with two little columns.

"This is in the country?" I ask.

"Oh, yes."

"But not part of a development, surely? Rather a house on its own," I suggest, in view of the two columns. "Or am I wrong?"

"Oh, yes, workers live here."

We are not quite on the same wavelength; my questions, I feel, are being made to look, in the way they are taken, like police inquiries. Searching for a design that will give me the information I want without further words, I take the liberty of turning the pages for myself; the obstinate way in which I linger over little wooden houses without columns makes the atmosphere even more oppressive. A design for living room, bedroom, kitchen. Neat, simple, familiar. I do not dare say anything more. I climbed the stairs to find out something about a subject on which I have expert knowledge; and now I stand there like a spy, turning pages, feeling myself being watched sideways.

(Suspicion as a feeling of physical discomfort.)

Every evening in the theater. A lot of good actors, but no directors, no new ones. And no new German playwrights either. Or they are not being played—also possible. As if you can have living theater without living writers of your own! Afterward another party: actors, critics, occupation officials, doctors, civil servants, economists, all talking about the theater, sensible, lively, and curious. It is somehow intoxicating; at least for someone like myself; theater as a matter of public concern. In time perhaps a bit disconcerting, since it feels like escapism. But later one understands; what else can they talk about?

"Have you seen Gründgens?"*

"Not yet."

"Oh, you must!"

"I know."

"Things are happening here, you know, like nowhere else in the world maybe—"

(What?)

Grunewald, Krumme Lanke, Schlachtensee, Wannsee, a lakeland scenery which today, almost before we have ordered the tickets, is sure to fill me with nostalgia. What is there about it? The pine trees growing in sand, the sky between the pines, the air, the crisp spaciousness—at any rate I feel tremendously well, hardly know myself, even come at times to believe I have become a completely different person, a much happier, more sparkling person; I feel like a fish of advancing age that one day, God knows how, suddenly finds itself no longer in an aquarium with its scanty ration of bubbles, but in flowing water: Aha! it says. . . .

Frank, our host, tells me of a case during the Russian occupation, a period that tested the nerves of many women and also a number of men, even more than the bombing.

His account:

* Noted German actor, theater manager, and director.

May 1945, West Berlin, the cellar of a large house, scarcely damaged. Upstairs the Russians—noise, dancing, laughter, victory celebrations; down in the cellar, in hiding, a woman and her husband, an army officer who has escaped from a prisoner-of-war camp, has no other clothing, and must on no account be seen. One day somebody comes down looking for wine, forces the scullery door. The woman has to open up. The husband hides. It is an orderly, rather drunk. He tells her to go upstairs. Does his commandant speak German? Yes, says the orderly. Her hope of saving herself by speaking. His stammerings about the many fine books. She asks for half an hour to prepare herself. Her husband does not want her to go; but what if the Russians come down and find him? She puts on her best dress, an evening gown; they vow to take their own lives together if her plan does not succeed. Upstairs she meets a group of rather drunk officers. She as the grand lady. After a lot of jostling, from which she extricates herself with a few slaps, she manages to speak with the colonel alone. Her pleas, her request for humane treatment, etc. He is silent. Goaded by his silence, which she can only take as evidence of deep suspicion, she even goes so far as to tell him about her husband: in order to win his confidence. When she at last realizes that the colonel understands no German, she collapses. She feels trapped. The colonel fetches the orderly to interpret; in this moment she gains possession of a weapon, which she hides under her dress, hoping it is loaded. Then her last desperate proposal: if he will send everybody else out of the house, permanently, she will be at his disposal, she says somewhat obscurely, every day at an appointed hour. With that she at least gains a little time; at all events she is resolved to shoot, the moment he makes a false step. (Herself or him?) But nothing like that happens. Every evening for a whole week she goes upstairs to keep the colonel company, so to speak—always in her evening gown. Down in the cellar she pretends the commandant can speak German, invents conversations she has had with him about Russia and so on. Her husband is to some extent reassured, feels, however, that she is not unwilling to go upstairs, that she seldom looks him straight in the eye, that she really is combing her hair with the intention of looking her best, and so on. As time goes on (the account is full of holes), it is evident that a genuine love has arisen between them and is being actively pursued. Without words. In the end the colonel has suddenly to leave, having been posted away from Berlin; both hope to meet again, but he does not return. The husband, now rescued, always speaks of the Russian in tones of friendly respect; the Russian way of life, as described to him down in the cellar by his wife, seems to have made a considerable impression on him. Where did she get her knowledge, since the colonel could speak only Russian, she only German? From the Russian broadcasts in German, to which she used to listen when her husband was a prisoner of war in the East . . .

Small party at the Kulturbund, which is banned in the West. Some familiar faces—people who had emigrated to Switzerland. Publishers making offers: genuine and with astonishingly large editions, well produced. Supper in the so-called *Möwe,* where artists can eat without ration cards: two potatoes, meat, even some greens, beer.

In the morning at the American radio station.

Both sides busy recruiting mercenaries . . .

Then in the subway: practically everybody with a bundle, a rucksack, a paper bag tied with string. Beside faces of mud and ashes there are also healthy, taut, and full ones, but equally withdrawn, often masklike. What are they trying to conceal? Only when they are squashed together in close proximity does one see the poverty—in the collars, the elbows. Berlin wearing its last suits. The women, even when dressed in trousers, heavy shoes, and head scarves, are mostly well turned out.

Evening with friends.

Everywhere you meet people with whom a close understanding exists from the very start, everywhere a few at least; the differences, when one does not try to ignore them, bring their own rewards. Why are most friendships made abroad successful?

Today with the Russians. Courteously received by the two men, who speak faultless German. We put forward our petition, which is accepted with impassive faces. Then to a communal lunch, *chambre séparée,* a simple but ample meal on plain china, with vodka in large glasses. Their knowledge of German literature, German philosophy; a discussion lasting over three hours. The Russians take matters of the spirit very seriously; it is evident that they send their best people, who find themselves confronted on the other side, apart from a few exceptions, with amiable nonentities. In Frankfurt we met an American, a paragon of helpfulness, who heard of T. S. Eliot for the first time from us—a Theater Officer! But of course the Russians who listened to us so politely for three whole hours do not have the option of leaving their posts if some other field of activity tempts them. Colonel Tulpanov appeared for a few minutes. A very strange, impenetrable, strong head, round and bald. Quick exchange of greetings, all standing. Our conversation, always carefully confined to theatrical matters, produced not a single name with which they were not familiar, in both a literary and a political sense. All rather like a card index. Afterward I am so tired that I fall asleep in a chair without removing my coat—in a dressing room in the Deutsches Theater, which as a young man I looked on as Mount Olympus. When I eventually awake, I find myself alone; the performance has already begun. . . .

Tartuffe.

Our petition will be translated and telegraphed to Moscow. An answer could come the day after next. It will be a polite no. Nevertheless, there are things one must attempt before one can decently give up.

Kurfürstendamm.

Kurt buys a little sketch by Liebermann. Also available: three small cups of Meissen porcelain, an old etching of the garrison church in Potsdam, a brass ashtray, letter openers, earrings, and other things of which one does not stand in need. All beyond one's means if reckoned in terms of wages, but cheap if reckoned in cigarettes. A little Buddha, a fine piece, for five hundred cigarettes. A hundred yards farther on women with buckets and spades are clearing rubble, wasting their energies on the immeasurable. It is more like a penal colony than work. Forty marks a week, which is four cigarettes. Naturally they are not the people responsible for all these ruins. Those people are living in heated prisons, well fed, healthier than all the rest, or in their country mansions. . . .

"Things are happening here."

It is undeniable that there are moments of tingling excitement. Many people assert they would want to live nowhere else, particularly artists, and they mean it. Who does not love the place where he has a role to play? Many are playing a bigger role than they could ever have dared dream of, managing offices that one still enters respectfully, whoever is in charge. And indeed this is a good thing; fame is a bridge that can extend for miles even without supporting piers. For miles. Many consider themselves to be piers, simply because there are no others around. And the work that comes from such encouragement is astonishing, superhuman in its effort. Added to that is the natural, often feverish desire to make up for the lost years. It is important these days to talk with older people; the present day has no standards to measure things by. One could do with a companion like Wölfflin, the Swiss art-historian. Already most people's standards date only from the Hitler era. The lack of people is discernible everywhere, and, obvious as it may be that every historical change starts with a step backward—since the new men were for whole decades denied the chance of gaining practical experience—nevertheless there is something melancholy about that condition, something even dangerous; we are constantly in jeopardy of calling good what is in fact only the best we can find in our own days. . . .

The no has arrived.

Yesterday at a cabaret, but I find the Berliners I can hear in the street or the subway infinitely wittier. Cabaret cannot be based on self-pity. There is no point in just swimming with the stream, and what is the use of a cabaret that does not attack its audience? The boxes, however, are filled with occupation uniforms; I ask myself what else our own cabarets could have done, for instance under German occupation, except just this: to abandon self-criticism. . . .

Our final evening.

Visit to a bar with music and watery beer, waiters playing their parts in stained vests. I feel hungry. A hot drink with rum flavor. The place reminds me of waiting rooms; and not just because of the rucksacks. Everybody looking like the work of some bad artist who cannot draw people sitting down. Even when they are leaning back they are not really there. A resting place for ghosts. From the ceiling, supported on marble pillars, hang naked electric bulbs. Crumbling white stucco, beneath it the usual rush lining. Here too it smells of latrines. And in addition the rather grotesque dress suit of a pianist with consumption already showing in his wrists—

Departure from Lichterfelde.

An American major refuses to sleep in the same compartment with a Negro who is also wearing an American uniform. The German guard, a Swabian, is ordered to find a bunk somewhere else for the black victor. The guard nods, implying: Okay, you don't need to put it into words; then goes hunting through the corridors, not without a gloating grin, which he does not conceal from us. Still, it is not directed against the Negro himself—just against the way things are; the racial problem, re-education. The Negro, a young sergeant, meanwhile lights a cigarette, to provide some reason why he should be standing outside in the corridor. He stares out through the rain-covered window, although it is dark outside, completely dark. When the guard comes back and indicates to him in dialect where he may sleep, he nods without looking at the guard, who repeats the number. He remains standing there, still smoking and staring at the black windowpane. . . .

(World history has not yet reached its end.)

Lengthy stop during the night, a station without a roof, no name signs, but a lot of people lying on bundles and paper parcels. The rain is pouring down. Zonal border post? In a newspaper I read that Wolfgang Borchert, the great hope among young German writers, has died in Basel.

Letzigraben

There are so few people who do not sooner or later take advantage of you if you admit to having made a mistake: they try to turn you into a mule and load their own mistakes on you. . . . And then, when the mule suddenly kicks out, they are genuinely astonished. But only for a moment; once they get their breath back they remind you, completely unabashed, of the mistakes you yourself once admitted to—as proof that it is you, not they, who make mistakes.

Postscript

The story of the Russian colonel and the German woman: the whole thing lasted three weeks. The woman was in no doubt that his love was genuine; for her it was the love of a lifetime—
    What fascinates me about this affair:
    That it represents an exception, a special case, a living contradiction of rules and prejudices. Everything that is human looks like a special case. Overcoming prejudice: the only possible way through love, which creates no graven images. And in this particular case: helped through the absence of spoken words. It would hardly have been possible if they had been able and obliged to express themselves in speech. Speech as the instrument of prejudice! What could unite us has become the opposite, fatally dividing us through prejudice. Speech and falsehood. The monstrous paradox that people come closer to one another without words. It seems to me significant too that it was a woman who won this victory over prejudice; women experience things in a more factual way, they are better able to accept an individual for himself and not bury him beneath a stereotype. She goes to a Russian, an enemy, she has a weapon concealed beneath her dress, but, since they cannot understand each other, they are forced to look at each other, and she is able really to see him, to see the individual, really to be herself, to behave as a human being in a world bewitched by fixed patterns, in an age in which language has become unholy; no longer a language between human beings but a language of radio, a language of newspapers, a language inferior to the dumbness of animals. A tower of Babel; at a time when this sort of language should be torn from us. I find in this woman something I have seen in so many others with whom I have spoken or whom I have seen in thousands in the subway: women are sounder than men, more real, less confused in their basic outlook.

149

Lyric poetry

People complain that our poets, above all our lyric poets, are no longer taken seriously. Their complaint contains an unspoken reproach against the world, unspoken because they have to admit the sad truth that the fate that has overtaken our lyric poetry is after all the fate of the intellect generally. They complain, instead of finding it right.

The fate of the intellect?

A man who makes use of his intellect to build bridges or fight cancer or research into atoms is still taken seriously enough. He is doing what he knows; working in full awareness of our world and our time. Just imagine an engineer who knows quite well that there are such things as communicating tubes; but when he comes to build something, what does he do but push aside all his knowledge and build aqueducts like those of the ancient Romans? What would happen to him? He would be clapped into jail, or at least dismissed from his post. . . . Poets, when they write poetry that lags behind their and our knowledge, are not clapped into jail—but only for the reason that the damage they do is restricted to themselves; they have, so to speak, disqualified themselves, for none of their contemporaries —at any rate those who are up-to-date—can take them seriously.

Unlike the English and the French, who possess a modern lyric poetry, Germany demonstrably has very few poems to offer that are not second-hand—second-hand even in their imagery; they often sound splendid, but mostly have no real language: no penetrating verbal reflection of the world in which we live. Scythes, millstreams, lances, spinning wheels, lions—these are not the things among which we live. The banality of the modern world (or of any world) is not impaled, only avoided and timidly circumvented. Their poetry is set invariably *before* the banalities, not *behind* them. There is no victory, only flight— and into a world already sufficiently sung. What has happened since, what now makes this world our world, all that is simply ignored in their imagery. . . . The fear of appearing banal: flowers are placed on the table before poems are read, beside them a candelabrum, curtains are pulled—to shut out awareness. The poet has perhaps arrived in an airplane, at least in an automobile, but the poems he is to read cannot stand up against the sound of a distant motor: not because this makes his words harder to hear, but because it makes us only too conscious that the world he is talking about is not the world in which both we and he live. How can a man like that hope to transport me? Or we turn on the radio; after only half a sentence we know where we are: Poetry!—for no one with anything serious to say ever speaks like that. What does his singsong arouse in me? Only the feeling that he is putting it on—maybe out of respect, just because he sees a few rhymed lines in front of him. And he cannot even admit that it means nothing to him—though obviously he realizes something is not quite right, or he would not relapse into singsong in the hope of lulling my consciousness to sleep. And the annoying thing is that he expects me to join in the pretense, just so as to convince myself that I am "artistic"! None of this is necessary when the poem is a genuine one: such a poem *can* stand up against the world in which it is spoken. And why? Because it does not avoid this world, but reflects it penetratingly.

> The city of my fathers, how can I find it?
> Following the swarms of bombers
> I come home.
> Where does it lie? Yonder where huge
> Mountains of smoke arise.
> There in the flames
> It stands.
>
> The city of my fathers, how shall it receive me?
> The bombers arrive before me. Deadly swarms
> Announce my approach. Conflagrations
> Precede the son's return.

One of the few whose poems stand up in this sense is Brecht. For this poem to get through to me I do not need to be in a drugged state or tired, which is what so many people mean by meditative. It remains a poem even when I speak it in a kitchen, without a background of candles, string quartets, and oleander. It does have something to say to me. And above all: I do not have to forget anything in order to be able to take it seriously. It demands no particular mood; but equally there is no mood it needs to fear. Most of what goes by the name of poetry looks like irony of the crassest sort when I compare it for even only a single day with my own life. Romantic irony is the trick of anticipating this sort of irony, and agreeing to regard poetry as something set apart from real life. Heine cannot ever trust himself, though the feelings of which he writes may be to a high degree genuinely felt; but they do not stand up against all the other things he knows. Behind the rose, to put it crudely, lurks syphilis. The things of which he is aware—and which are not contained in his poetry—oblige him to make fun of his poetry before anyone else can, in order to show that he himself does not take it seriously. And why not? Because it falls short of his own awareness, does not stand up against his awareness. He sees himself as two-faced (a feeling that would not come amiss to many other poets). Heine is honest, and to that extent he is significant. But the next step, surely, is to become even more honest and not to write down things of which our forefathers have already, according to their awareness of things, made poetry, but to write about real things, about our own world. Then the poet will no longer need to fear this awareness and will need irony as little as he needs curtains, candles, and oleander; because there is no longer any pretense, any two-facedness. . . . It can all be said:

> Indeed I live in the dark ages!
> A guileless word is an absurdity. A smooth
>   forehead betokens
> A hard heart. He who laughs
> Has not yet heard
> The terrible tidings.
>
> Ah, what an age it is
> When to speak of trees is almost a crime
> For it is a kind of silence about injustice! . . .

And later:

> I would gladly be wise.
> The old books tell us what wisdom is:
> Avoid the strife of the world, live out your
>   little time
> Fearing no one,

Using no violence,
Returning good for evil—
Not fulfillment of desire but forgetfulness
Passes for wisdom.
I can do none of this:
Indeed I live in the dark ages!

I came to the cities in a time of disorder
When hunger ruled.
I came among men in a time of uprising
And I revolted with them.
So the time passed away
Which on earth was given me.

I ate my food between massacres.
The shadow of murder lay upon my sleep.
And when I loved, I loved with indifference.
I looked upon nature with impatience.
So the time passed away
Which on earth was given me.

In my time streets led to the quicksand.
Speech betrayed me to the slaughterer.
There was little I could do. But without me
The rulers would have been more secure. This was
    my hope.
So the time passed away
Which on earth was given me.

Man's strength was little. The goal
Lay far in the distance,
Easy to see if for me
Scarcely attainable.
So the time passed away
Which on earth was given me. . . .

Brecht himself once read this poem to us: shyly, but not
inhibitedly; he was the same afterward as before. His voice was
soft, still bearing traces of its usual dialect, almost whispering,
but clear and precise, particularly in the rhythm, with no apparent emphases, factual, demonstrating words in the way one
demonstrates stones, fabrics, or other things that have to make

their own impression; the bearing of a man who, cigar in mouth, has to read out a text simply because not everybody has a copy of it in his hand; more or less as one reads out a letter—simply to pass on the news. And it was not disturbing when the bell rang, a new visitor arrived, or the daughter of the house walked through the room because there was no other passage. "I am just reading a poem," he told the new arrival. "It is called 'To Posterity.'" Meaning that the other would have to wait a little while before speaking. Then he read on, informing us what else he had to say to those born later:

> You, who shall emerge from the flood
> In which we are sinking,
> Think—
> When you speak of our weaknesses,
> Also of the dark time
> That brought them forth.

> For we went, changing our country more often than
>   our shoes,
> In the class war, despairing
> When there was only injustice and no resistance.

> For we knew only too well:
> Even the hatred of squalor
> Makes the brow grow stern.
> Even anger against injustice
> Makes the voice grow harsh. Alas, we
> Who wished to lay the foundations of kindness
> Could not ourselves be kind.

> But you, when at last it comes to pass
> That man can help his fellow man,
> Do not judge us
> Too harshly.

The usual pause that comes after the reading of a poem—since we are, so to speak, leaving the church and have suddenly, slightly dazed and without the help of an organ, to return to a world that is after all very different from poetry—this pause is not necessary; a poem, a genuine one, does not need to fear the world; it stands up to it, even when a bell rings and an unexpected guest arrives to tell us, while the same coffee is still in our cups, of his fourteen years in captivity. . . .

"Indeed I live in the dark ages!"

Not all his poems have this ability to stand up, to be spoken at any time. The weakness of the others, I find, is not that they are too aesthetic, but too ideological, which is another way of being unreal.

"To be real."

Goethe, I would say, is real. For his maxims and reflections he often needs to use only four lines. At the outset there is a statement, followed by the birth of a thought so compelling and unequivocal that one goes down on one's knees to offer it service. But then, when lesser people could not resist drawing conclusions overruling all doubts, conclusions with the force of a crusade, the unexpected happens, the opposite of an epigram: without taking back the thought, he contrasts it with an experience that contradicts or at least modifies the thought. To this experience, coming from the same mind that has just given birth to the thought, he gives equal validity, simply because it *is* an experience, something living, something real. That is why his reflections are apparently so conciliatory: because almost always they possess both light and shade. Apparently; for in fact they do not reconcile the contradictions at all. They simply hold them in the balance, in a state of mutual fertilization, the balance between thinking and observing. There is no fight to the death, because the contradictory experience is not overruled or arrogantly suppressed. The thought has the strength to accept it—the strength to remain real or, more precisely, constantly to renew its reality.

Letzigraben

Now they have found one after all—the skeleton of an executed man seemingly, for the skull is missing; probably, as the custom then was, it had been placed between his feet. Only half the skeleton lay within the bounds of the pit, and since we live in an economical era, they did not widen the pit even a single centimeter on his account. A spade, and snip-snap, they cut him off below the knees—two bones vanish in the mud. . . . They think me comical for having expected to be called, as instructed, for a find of this sort, and assure me rather tartly that there were no gold coins or chains with it. Close by I find a few ribs, a shoulder blade. But at least we shall leave him his skull, though I should like to have possessed it.

En route

Every thought, at the moment we first have it, is completely true, valid, right for the conditions that gave rise to it; but then, when we express only the conclusion, without being able at the same time to define the extent of its relevance, it is suddenly hanging in the air, meaningless; and this is where falsehood begins, when we look around and start searching for analogues. . . . (For words, even those left unsaid, are never able, at the time the thought arose, to capture in a moment all we know, let alone what we do not know. . . .) So there we stand with nothing but a conclusion, remind ourselves that this conclusion was once completely valid, apply it to matters that themselves would never have given rise to this particular thought, overstep or at any rate shift the bounds of its validity—since we no longer know the extent of its relevance—and at once we have let in error, distortion, prejudice.

Or, put more shortly:

It is easy to utter a truth, a so-called *aperçu*, of an unrelated kind; it is difficult, virtually impossible, to apply this truth, to recognize how far its validity extends.

(To be real!)

1948

Vienna, January 1948

Is it the city, or is it something in myself that makes me feel, after a week here, that I have still not woken up? To see a play of one's own is seldom a pleasure, even when the theater is the enchanting Theater in der Josephstadt, graceful as the summer pavilion of an archduke, private, sociable as a Menzel painting of drawing-room music, with a chandelier that floats slowly up to the ceiling, lights dimming, as the curtain goes up. . . . The man who originally built this theater was a simple innkeeper in love with the muses, an honest citizen whom one can picture to oneself in his gray top hat and short green jacket. Beethoven wrote the music for the opening, and since then what has not been seen on these boards? Here Raimund's sweet "Hobellied" was sung for the first time. A gay, opulent, brilliant century hangs over us like the chandelier, slowly floating upward, slowly dimming. . . .

Everybody is charming. A stranger was the first to greet me. "Master," begins the little blue note, written in a childish maidservant's hand straight from a guileless heart; to her regret she has not yet seen my splendid play, whose twenty-fifth performance we are deigning to honor with our personal presence, but she will not miss it. She bids me welcome in the name of Vienna: May, dear sir, our city please you! Everybody is charming. As I go out, I am stopped by a lady who has just seen the play for the fourth time; she must see me, she must, and we discuss how she can go on living as long as the printed text is nowhere to be had in Austria. The best solution will be for me to give her a copy; she seizes my hand; I know she will never forget me as long as she lives; unfortunately, she is already very old. But others who are less impressed by me are no less

159

charming: nobody utters a critical word, not straight out; each of them lives in a shell of impenetrable charm, in which he feels at home, and when one feels at home one is tolerant. *Aber geh!* That is the magic formula that wards off all evil. "Come on, now!" Here the deluge itself will stop in its tracks and subside, evaporating in the warmth of so much good feeling. Vienna is always Vienna. Why should they worry how things look elsewhere? Don't talk of other cities: be glad that you are in Vienna. What has happened, after all? Even the Germans, who alone were to blame that Austria was on the wrong side, they dismiss with a shrug. Stop worrying, and try to be charming too. Have you been to the opera? The opera is wonderful. Particularly Mozart: only in Vienna do you get performances like that. You must always hold tight to the best things in life, you see, to the pleasant and nice things. Have you been to the exhibition of Old Vienna? Grillparzer's room, Nestroy's writing desk, Metternich's bed, I have seen them all; a city councilor, left-wing, showed us around personally on his free Sunday morning; people are really charming; tomorrow we shall be given an official car, we simply must visit Schönbrunn—

We have already been to the Prater.

The giant wheel, of which my mother had often told me, is working again. We did not miss the opportunity of going on it and letting ourselves slowly be borne aloft in an evening full of rainy twilight. The view over the gray city, the black towers, the distant Danube, which always reminds us of the Balkans—and of course beneath us the Prater itself: here and there a bomb crater, a puddle of brown water which refuses to drain away—though perhaps, I think later, they were just holes where trees had been, pits full of charred trees—then a ruin minus a roof, so that one can look inside from above, weeds and grass on the paths and squares, a signboard advertising fresh *Würstl*, elsewhere the remains of a merry-go-round, a wrecked slide down which one can slip into oblivion. I thought of the treeless Tiergarten in Berlin; there it is history, the elector princes, which has been turned into a desert, here the pleasure gardens. Apart from a jolly, plumpish woman who unlocked the cabin for us, there was nobody in sight, though somewhere a loudspeaker was booming loudly and brassily into the night as it slowly began to rain; a waltz, a very familiar one. . . .

Three whole days of traveling around in taxicabs and street-cars, accompanied and advised by a respected Viennese lady, who uses all she has—her name, her time, her elbows, her femininity—to procure for us the rubber stamp we need to continue our journey, a stamp that the office of the allies in Bern forgot to provide us with; waiting rooms, barriers, corridors, lines, forms in septuplicate; the Austrian officials are friendly, even long after our cigarettes have run out, and help as much as they can; our embassy helps with testimonials and phone calls, which give us hope, but that is all; I don't recall how often, hat in hand, we had to explain the whole silly affair, always to people who were not competent to deal with it, the competent authority being Russia, France, America, and Britain: not singly, but together—only all together. Without this stamp I may be in Vienna, but I can no longer leave Vienna. It was all very interesting, exasperatingly boring, but revealing, ending with a captain whose nose, now that I have got the stamp, I should like to punch.

(Uniforms ruin every character.)

The time of day that best suits Vienna is the evening twilight, the violet grayness of fine façades standing behind old trees, a sprinkling of snow on the roofs, the unradiating brightness of early street lamps, baroque outlines, a fountain with silenced jets, its bowl lined with dead leaves, three stone cherubs with flutes, stillness, twilight, people crossing a park, hands in coat pockets, a gate of elegant wrought iron, steps, broad and ceremonial, everything in some way monumental, a Sleeping Beauty undisturbed by the streetcars or even by a bumping truck with a trailer, everything as if seen through a violet veil . . .

Coffeehouse.
American soldiers meeting their girls. Every day between seven and eight. They come in and leave the girls standing there while they chat together, hands in pockets, caps pushed back off their foreheads. The girls are uncertain whether they should sit down or what; they do not dare order anything. Anything but worldly cocottes. Poor little strays who are prob-

161

ably seamstresses or waitresses, unable to make out on what they earn. (Like most of the others: the rail workers, I have just read, cannot pay for what is on their ration cards.) Most of these girls are fat, pale, and rather puffy, their attention to their outward appearance only very superficial; as one watches them and the young men sprawling astride the chairs, chewing, utterly lacking in any sort of courtesy, one truly does not know whom to pity most. Against the marble background, its tall mirrors reflecting the dreary scene, there stands an old waiter who might once have served Schnitzler, or at any rate Karl Kraus, a much-folded serviette in his hands. Among the soldiers there is of course the joker, while the others laugh and the strays remain standing there like mules left outside the inn while the farmer goes in for a pint. Their open secret seems in some way to isolate them; they scarcely speak to one another, each trying not to see the others. It all looks so wretched. Later they get something to eat; the waiter, white-haired, preserves the conventions, behaves as if he were on a stage, pretending. The boys, leaning back with outstretched legs against the red upholstery, now somewhat tattered, have already eaten in the mess; so they just smoke, wordlessly, as the little girls fortify themselves. I can see only one soldier who is flirting, not particularly nicely, not very inventively, but all the same giving some hint of being a man in love; he looks like a god among a herd of cattle. . . . Horrible but compulsive vision of the couples when later they are alone together; otherwise relieved not to have to see how our soldiers would behave in similar circumstances: in uniform and abroad, where the individual is unknown.

Afterward to Mozart.

Uniforms here too, Frenchmen in steep caps, a Briton towering above the crowd, ladies in long dresses and furs, Americans, Viennese, foreigners, black-marketeers, broad-faced Russians in boots—

Die Zauberflöte.

Once again in Wotruba's studio; he lived for a long time in Switzerland as an emigrant, but it is here we first really get to know each other. Not the only, but certainly one of the few contemporary sculptors who really carve instead of just kneading; he does not put things into the stone, but works out of the stone itself. It is something really quite miraculous, rather like looking at the act of creation itself. His more recent works preserve the quality of the original stone to such a degree that, looking at the figure, one has the impression of a continuing process of birth. A raw block, the beginnings of a figure which, wiping off the stone dust, one feels with one's fingers, two or three figures standing out in the yard—this is quite enough to outweigh the museumlike effect of a whole city. The artist, however subjectively he expresses himself, has in some mysterious way a universal quality; his creative need, the mere fact of his existence, his failures, his successes, his individually conditioned striving seem like symbols of the way things are in the invisible universe about us. One feels: the whole cannot be a museum—there is a living person chiseling, searching for new things—

I think often here about Berlin. The historic similarity; both cities with four occupying powers. I notice that nobody here wants to hear about Berlin, not even about professional matters such as the theater; their faces take on an uncurious expression, as if one were talking about some obscure village activity. Amusing how each city considers itself to be the center of the world, or at least the German-speaking world, and hence the center of human culture; the background to such illusions is, however, not at all amusing. . . . Morning chat with a waiter: I ask him which of the occupying powers gets most on his nerves. The British are the best. Between the others he sees nothing to choose. Vividly he adds to my stock of reported misdeeds. Since I keep silent, attending to my scanty breakfast, he adds:
"Of course, the others did something for us too. But all the same it's hard for us—"
"What others?"
"The Germans."
That is the usual line of talk here. . . .
In Berlin I feel more at ease.

Charm, adopted as a mode of behavior, has something frightful about it. A truce with one's own falsehood. Hence the lack of struggle, the weariness, the museumlike quality.

The storm (apparently all over Europe) has snapped off numerous trees, everywhere shop signs rattling, bricks falling from the ruins (two people have been killed that way), in the ruin next door an iron shutter that nobody can reach: it clatters, bangs, rattles, and flaps like a flag of brown rust.

On the way home everyone walking arm in arm.

A young woman, whose auburn hair I am not the first to compare with Botticelli, assures us that she was never raped—

Prague, January 1948

Reunion with friends, re-encounter with the Czech production of my play. The situation very much tenser. They are still arguing together on the last bridgeheads of personal friendship. Public discussion such as on the previous visit would now hardly be possible. Open speaking in a cabaret: Voscovic and Werich, who had once gone into emigration, as Communists. Unfortunately I understand only the visual side, the jokes are translated for me afterward. Beside us an officer who is roaring heartily with laughter; but since I am not laughing (on account of not understanding the language), he suddenly becomes silent and wriggles on his seat, eying me surreptitiously from the side. . . .

Next day on to Brno—and only later do I understand the reason for this enforced journey, which did not fit into our plans at all. Splendid journey through Bohemian villages, exemplary in the unity of their style, then Moravian villages, now and again little towns with decorative market places, then deepest country again, as far as the eye can see, snow in the furrows, winter sunshine, horizons of black woods, pine trees. The performance in Brno, where we arrive just in time, is crazy provincialism, amateurish, but very interesting: the characters speak dialogue I never wrote, and where I know there is dialogue they cut it down or simply stay silent to keep the play with its new dialogue from becoming too long. At vital points, as I later find out, they say practically the opposite. It is one of the weekly performances given for the garrison, and the audience behaves as if attending a lesson in school. The newspapers, which are content with the lesson as it has been given them, report that the author was present in person—meaning me.

Reading

Carlo Levi, an Italian painter, exiled for many years by the Fascists, has written a book about his exile. He describes a desertlike district, an almost heathen backwater which nobody really knows, not even the Italians; the book, well enough written but not extraordinary, is having an extraordinary success in Italy and beyond—

Why?

Presumably for the very reason that Europe, the Europe of today, no longer has any epic poetry such as the Americans have, such as the Russians could have.

Regions of unknown life, unexplored regions, a world never yet described, remarkable purely as fact—this is the realm of epic writing. In all its territorial, in all its historical aspects, even in most of its sociological aspects, Europe has depicted itself frequently and skillfully enough—in fact more than enough; epic conquests such as dominate the literature of young nations might still be possible in the same sense that there may still be a few minor peaks (in Switzerland for example) that have never been climbed; but a whole world, a significantly different one, a terra incognita which might fundamentally change our outlook —there is nothing like that left for our epic writers to work on.

The epic is concerned with description, with information, not with argument. Argument with a world that is depicted only to the extent necessary for the purposes of the argument, this is most fittingly done by drama; the argumentative novel is something of a late crop in the epic field: Thomas Mann's essays in fancy dress.

Description—but it need not be description of an existing world: it can also be an invented one. Initially it is always that; the saga. And at the further end, providing so to speak the last epic opportunity, lies fantasy.

(Homer, Balzac, Kafka.)

Behind the Homeric urge to describe lies the creative need to provide a world for oneself. The Homeric epic as the mother of our worlds: only when it is described does a world exist. And only when it exists can it be conquered, as is still happening today in the American epic. And only when it is conquered can the argument with it begin—

(What I find particularly stimulating in the American epic: its mood of acceptance, its unprejudiced curiosity, the stimulating absence of reflection.)

Terra incognita—if this is truly where the epic has its place, it might be thought that what is new in our present world, for instance the previously unexperienced phenomenon of destroyed cities, would provide an epic opportunity. Why is this not so? Basically because the world that could be brought to light by epic discovery is not a new one: it is just the ruined face of the old world we already know, interesting only because of its different appearance. In other words, ruins require us to know or to be able to surmise what they looked like when they were intact; without the wrappings of their yesterday they are of little account, interesting only for purposes of comparison, reflection—

Café Odeon

Revolution in Czechoslovakia. It all happened very quickly. As always when a house of cards collapses. Concern for our friends. The self-satisfied grins of people to whom I had always held up Czechoslovakia as a model of social democracy; the general complacent opinion that this could not have happened to us. Now I keep remembering what I saw in Theresienstadt a year ago, but did not note down at the time:

"*Ici,*" the young man explained in a tiny cell, "*ici les Allemands ont arrêté plus que vingt hommes—sans aucune installation sanitaire!*"

It was not until we stood on the threshold, after inspecting a sign laboriously scratched on the wall, a cross and the German words "*Gott mit uns!*"—it was not until we were on the threshold, looking back on the empty cell, that we noticed a spick-and-span toilet, newly installed.

"*Pourquoi ça?*"

No answer; the Czech officer who had been our guide was

already outside, and the young man was only there to interpret.

"I don't know," he said, and went on: *"Ici vous voyez la cour des exécutions—"*

(Why did I not note this down at the time?)

Burlesque

One morning a man comes to your house, a stranger, and you cannot help yourself, you give him a plate of soup and some bread. For the injustice he has suffered, according to his own account, cannot be denied, and you don't wish him to take it out on you. And there is no doubt, the man says, that he will one day have his revenge. Anyway, you can't get rid of him, so you give him some soup and bread, as I said, and indeed even more: your sympathy. At first through your silence, but eventually with nods and finally with words. You agree with him, for if you did not, you would have to admit, more or less, that you are being unjust yourself, and then you would perhaps be afraid of him. But you do not wish to be afraid. You also do not wish to modify your injustice, for that would have too many consequences. You wish for peace and quiet, and that's all. You wish to have the feeling of being a good and upright person, and so you can't avoid offering him a bed as well, since, as you have just heard, he has lost his own through an act of injustice. He doesn't want a bed, he says, or a room, just a roof over his head; he would be quite happy, he says, with your loft. You laugh. He likes lofts, he says. You feel, while still laughing, that there is something rather uncanny about him, at any rate odd, disturbing; there has been so much in the papers recently about arson; but you want your peace, as I said, and so there is nothing for it but to stifle the suspicions now forming in your breast. Why shouldn't he sleep in the loft if he wants? You show him the way, the lock and bolt, the workings of the ladder, and the switch for the light. Alone in your nice house, smoking a cigarette, you find your thoughts returning several times to the same point, and it's no use reading the papers, between the lines you always read the same thing: one must be trustful, you shouldn't always believe the worst of a person you don't know, and why should he be an arsonist?

All the same, you resolve next morning to send him on his way
—in a friendly manner, so as not to offend him by letting him
think you suspect something. You do not resolve not to be
unjust: that, as I said, would lead too far. All you mean to do
is to be friendly and, in a friendly manner, to send him away.
That night you have some sleepless moments; the air is close,
and the stories of real arsonists which so obstinately keep
coming into your mind are really too absurd; a sleeping pill
gives you the rest you deserve. . . . And there you are, you
see: next morning your house is still standing! Your trust, your
faith in this person, even though he is living in your loft, has
been vindicated. You feel a not inconsiderable urge to be noble,
helpful, and good; for instance, by providing breakfast. Face to
face with him, drinking coffee and eating eggs together, you
feel ashamed of your suspicions, shabby: at any rate you cannot
possibly send him away now. Why should you? A week later,
when he is still living in your loft, you have overcome all
your fears, and even when he one day brings along a friend who
also wants to sleep in your loft, you may perhaps hesitate,
but you don't refuse. You hesitate because this other man
has been in prison, God knows what for, and has only just been
released. You would never, obviously, have allowed him into
your loft by himself. He is also much cheekier than the first,
though that is perhaps because he was in prison, and he makes
you feel a little uneasy, the way he admits so frankly to having
been locked up for arson. But in fact it is this very frankness,
quite without shame, that gives you the reassurance you so
much desire in order to enjoy your peace and quiet; in the
evening, when for all your yawning you can't get to sleep,
you reread Max Mell's *Apostelspiel,* the legend that illustrates
the power of true faith, a fine piece of poetic writing; you fall
asleep with a feeling of contentment which makes the sleeping
pill almost unnecessary. . . . And there you are, you see: next
morning your house is still standing! Your friends shake their
heads, can't understand you, ask every time what those two boys
are doing up there in your loft, and get on your nerves so
much that you now seldom go to the bar; all they are trying
to do is get you rattled. And, between ourselves, they are
succeeding to some extent; at any rate you do begin to keep
a bit of an eye on the boys, and not without some result; the

mere fact of their carrying small cans into your loft does not of course disturb your faith in human nature, for after all they are doing it quite openly, and when you rather jokingly ask what they want with all these cans, they reply quite naturally that they are thirsty. And, after all, it is summertime: in the loft, you tell yourself, it must be very hot. Once, when you were standing in their path, they did let a can fall from the ladder, and there was a sudden smell of gasoline. For a short moment, admit it, you were startled. Is that gasoline? you asked. The two men, without interrupting their work, made no attempt to deny it, and when you rather jokingly asked whether they were drinking gasoline, they replied with such a ridiculous story that all you could do, in order not to look a fool, was laugh. But later, alone in your house, listening to those lively little cans that smelled of gasoline rolling about above, you seriously did not know quite what to think. Were they really abusing your noble trust? For a while, lighter in hand, an unlit cigarette between your dry lips, you had your mind made up to throw the two boys out, simply throw them out. And this very day too. Or tomorrow at the latest. That is, if they didn't depart of their own accord. For it isn't so easy—quite the contrary in fact: if they are not arsonists, you are being very unjust to them, and injustice will make them mean. Mean toward you. You don't want that. Not on any account. Anything rather than a guilty conscience. And then it is always so difficult to foretell the future; someone who always draws conclusions from the known facts or takes care to understand what he knows to be going on, maybe someone like that can foretell certain things, but he won't enjoy a single moment of peace; not with all those suspicions of his. The fact that they are carrying gasoline up to your loft—what of it? One of them, the friend, just laughed and said they were intending to set fire to the whole town. That could just have been a joke or big talk. If they meant it seriously they would never have said it. This thought, the more often you repeat it, convinces you utterly; or, rather, it sets your mind at rest. The other one even said: We're just waiting for a favorable wind! It is stupid to be intimidated by such remarks; too contemptible. For a moment you think of going to the police. But when, so as not to make yourself look ridiculous by spreading false alarms, you apply your ear to the ceiling—

not exactly, you discover, a simple operation—all is completely still. You can even hear one of them snoring. And anyway the police are out of the question; you would only be in trouble yourself for having allowed such people to live in your house for weeks without reporting it. But of course it is above all humane reasons that prevent your taking such a step. Why don't you simply tell the boys quite frankly that you don't want gasoline in your loft? It is always best to be frank. Then suddenly it occurs to you, and you have to laugh for not having realized it before: they won't set fire to your house while they themselves are in the loft! All the same, now in your pajamas, you climb once more onto the chair, the bureau, and the closet. He really is snoring. Half an hour later you are asleep yourself. . . . And next morning, there you are, you see: your house is still standing! The sun is shining, the wind has turned, clouds sail over the roofs of the town. If they really are bad lads, then, just for that very reason, it won't be easy simply to turn them out; not advisable; for as long as you're their friend they will at least leave you alone. It is always best to be friendly. And by going upstairs this morning and inviting them to breakfast, you are not just being cunning or pursuing an ulterior motive, you are obeying one of those sudden cordial impulses which, as you rightly say, should not always be repressed. The ladder to the loft is already in place, the door open, you do not even have to knock. The loft, which out of politeness you have not visited for a long time, is full of those little cans, and one of the men, the friend from the prison, is standing at the skylight, holding out a wet finger to test the direction of the wind; the other has unfortunately already gone out, but will be back. So your breakfast idea comes to nothing. But he'll be back for sure sometime during the day, as soon, says the friend in his usual rather bantering way, as he has collected all the wood shavings they need. Wood shavings? All you need now is for someone to mention a fuse. For a moment you are again somewhat bewildered, somewhat dismayed, though you try hard not to show it. At base, you well know, nobody can be as cheeky as this boy is making himself out to be just because he imagines you are afraid of him. Once and for all resolved not to be afraid, resolved to preserve your peace and quiet, you pretend not to have heard; as far as the breakfast is concerned—well, some other time will do. And your friendly gesture as such may prove to have been worth making. Then supper perhaps? you say. With pleasure, says this queer fish, if they have the time and do not have to go to work; that will depend on the wind. He really is a queer fish. And of course you are now not a little curious whether they will in fact come to supper, whether they do value your friendship. Perhaps you ought to have shown your friendliness even sooner. But better late, you tell yourself, than never. You rightly avoid providing an all-too-special and lavish supper, but even so you do fetch up a bottle of wine from the cellar, to have it cooled just in case. Unfortunately, when they at last arrive around nine o'clock, it is not possible to sit on the terrace; too much wind. Did he find the wood shavings? you ask in an effort to make the conversation more personal. Wood shavings? he says and looks at his friend as one would look at a traitor. Then, God knows why, you have to laugh, and eventually they start laughing too. Wood shavings, no, he hadn't found those, but something else: cleaning rags from a garage. Found; you cannot doubt this can only mean stolen. Altogether they have very individual ideas about right and wrong. After the first bottle—not for nothing did you cool the wine—you tell them that you too in your time have done wrong. Since they do not answer, you tell them more and more as you uncork the second bottle (their friendship is worth that). Clearly they are now feeling at home; the friend, the cheekier of the two, switches on your radio to hear the weather report. There is only one thing they still need: matches. Nothing would be worse than if you were now to look startled: friendship can never be built up on suspicion. Why matches? You succeed in concealing your offensive trembling and proffer cigarettes as if you had nothing on your mind, and then—not a bad idea—you offer them a light with your own lighter, which you afterward put back in your pocket. The conversation continues, that is to say, they are listening, regarding you, and drinking wine. Your honest confession of all the wrong you have done moves them no more than politeness requires; altogether they seem very preoccupied. The third bottle is already between your knees, but they decline. Since you nevertheless open it, you will now have to drink it all yourself. Only as they are leaving, while you are expressing your hopes that people might one day come closer together and help one another, do they again ask you for some matches. Without cigarettes. You tell yourself with some reason that an arsonist, if he were genuine, would come better equipped, and you give them those too, a little book of yellow matches; and next morning, there you are, you see: you are burnt to ashes and can't even feel surprised at your own story. . . .

Café Odeon

C. F. Ramuz, the foremost writer of French-speaking Switzerland, who recently died, has already, I see, been set in our national buttonhole: Gotthelf, Keller, Meyer, Spitteler, Ramuz. . . . *Eh bien!* All one can say against this is: a few months ago Ramuz, facing his last operation, was obliged to ask the writers' association whether it could give him two thousand francs to pay for it—

The position of the writer in Switzerland, even one as unique as Ramuz, altogether the position of artists and even intellectuals insofar as their intellectual achievements are not geared to industry, is a pitiable one—pitiable at least in comparison with the average prosperity of our country. All the same, it would be foolish to make this a reason for bitterness. It is true that the press, which is linked with the economy, could be more generous, could pay fees such as one has to pay an engineer or a physician. They are a long way from doing that; and the general contempt for work that brings in so little reward would be an amusing chapter in itself. As far as our newspapers are concerned, I see them as reaping the benefits of a situation that is no concern of theirs: namely, the situation that our publishers are genuinely not able to pay writers well. So long as Switzerland stands alone, its publishers cannot make a living if the writers are to do so as well; the writer, however, has an interest in keeping his publisher alive, and so, if he wants to write, he must perforce practice another profession as well. Not always to his detriment: there is in fact much to be said for it. All the same, a man like Ramuz should not have to beg before he can go to the hospital to die with dignity. But any bitterness directed against our fellow countrymen, against their lack of interest in reading and so on, would seem to me out of place. We have two and a half million people speaking German, of whom many are countryfolk, only a few townspeople. Compare that with Germany, with its sixty million. With the same proportion of readers —well known to be particularly high in Germany—this would mean that five hundred books of poetry sold in Switzerland are the equivalent of twelve thousand in Germany. How often is such a sale achieved? A play of which two thousand copies are sold here would need an edition of forty-eight thousand if the demand were the same. How often does that happen? Our proportion of readers is not bad, even in comparison with literary France, where a dramatist who is all the rage cannot achieve sales of more than five thousand. A Swiss writer, I feel, could easily work out on a cigarette pack that he cannot possibly hope to earn a living—and yet he has no real reason to feel bitter about it.

Pfannenstiel

A rest in the sun, butterflies, the stillness of an abandoned gravel pit—I find myself imagining the following scene: an escort of six soldiers with loaded rifles has led me to this gravel pit, and now, as I stand there with bound hands, I am asked once again whether I will or will not publicly swear that no injury or injustice has been done to my friends.

What should I do?

I do not know whether the friends whom, in order to save my life and my family, my wife and our two children, I should betray with this oath—I do not know whether these friends are even still alive; it is more probable that they have already been rounded up and killed. In any case, as I well know, the salvo that would put an end to me would not save them from their fate. . . .

What should I do?

Assume now I have just heard that my wife has also been arrested; so far she has not been tortured; at any time they could do that, in order to force me—

What should I do?

And further, I know we have committed no crime, not even what they would consider one, have taken part in no conspiracy;

all we do know is that there are torture chambers in our city, and this we know because we can daily hear the screams and see them loading the rough, unplaned, and unpainted coffins into trucks, and so we refuse to stand up in front of our own people and swear there is not a single torture chamber in our city—

The sergeant:

"Think it over," he says. "You have, according to official orders, ten minutes to make up your mind."

A priest is also there.

"I am instructed," he says tonelessly, "to take your oath, if you can bring yourself to make it."

He addresses me familiarly, because we were at school together; he sat in the row in front of me, and I can only remember his forenames.

"Squad, attention!"

After this command, carried out by all as one with mechanical precision, only a single thud coming from the five rifle butts, the sergeant steps aside—after a quick glance at his watch— to piss against a stone; otherwise I hear nothing; the five rifles at the ready, sunshine as now, butterflies, the stillness of an abandoned gravel pit . . .

What should I do?

Café Odeon

The impossibility of living and at the same time retaining our morals—or one simply does both by halves. . . . Morality as it is taught us always includes worldly defeat; we do not rescue the world from the devil, but abandon the world to the devil so that we ourselves shall not fall prey to him. We simply clear the field: in order to retain our morals. Or we do not clear it; we do not allow ourselves to be shot without lifting a finger, without shooting back, and the result is carnage, the opposite of what we wish for. . . .

One can be resolved to promote good, or one can be resolved to be a good person—two separate things that are mutually exclusive.

Most people wish to be good persons.

If we become good persons, nobody is more delighted than the wicked. As long as people who want goodness do not themselves get wicked, the wicked have a wonderful time!

(As long as the poor do not "steal.")

In people of strong mind amorality is probably nothing more than the longing for a different and practical form of morality.

Daily experience on a small scale: your virtuous living is your enemy's best and cheapest weapon. You have, for instance, resolved never to tell lies, and that is nice of you, splendid in fact, if you can keep it up; but it would be foolish for you to assume that in this way you are always serving truth. You are serving your own virtue.

Some moral stipulations would, I believe, have long been forgotten if those immoral people who had abandoned them did not have a natural interest in ensuring that all others felt bound by them—this is true of all Christian stipulations concerning property. . . .

The teaching imparted not only by our churches, but in our schools as well, is directed basically at making virtuous people of us—for example, we should not steal. It is not directed at encouraging us to object whenever we see others stealing, or to fight for the good it teaches us. Goodness, as we all know, can be achieved at most only within one's own heart. A good thought, certainly—good for those in power.

The impossibility of living and at the same time retaining our morals—a dilemma exacerbated in times of terrorism. What instruments does terrorism use? It uses our will to live and thus our fear of dying, certainly, but it also uses our consciences. The stronger the conscience, the more certain our downfall. The greater the loyalty, the more certain our torture. And the invariable outcome of terrorism: the villains slip through its net. For terrorism, it seems, is particularly adept at destroying people with morals. It reckons on a certain amount of morality; its inevitable failure, sooner or later, is perhaps connected with the fact that it uses up morality to the point where nobody remains who can be caught with it. Above all, terrorism reduces the value of life, the will to live, to a point where one no longer needs superhuman courage to pit one's valueless life against it—which one then does: not when it is too late, as a sacrificial victim in a gravel pit, a moral martyr; but before it is too late: as an immoral activist, an assassin.

Frankfurt, April 1948

In front of the Römer, the old town hall; wire stretched high above the ruins, steel masts, straight and free of rust, each with a sheaf of cables anchoring it on all sides; if it were not for the gay bunting one would think of cranes rather than of trapeze artists, or of the rigging of a sunken ship, sunk not beneath the waves of a sea, but beneath waves of rubble, weed-covered brick. . . . Spring as it comes to German cities is each year greener, more rural, richer in blossom. . . . At evening, however, when the ruins are spotlighted, everything looks even more like a fairyland; a milky light spreading out into greenish darkness, in it an occasional gleaming moth, and behind the glittering trapeze one sees the cathedral, a flat outline, a silhouette, a weightless pallor of red sandstone standing disembodied behind a cagework of crossing searchlight beams. Above it all the moon, full, lying at this moment in the net for the trapeze artistes; the moon, a lantern for lovers, a street lamp for vagabonds, the dilettante's jewel, a solace in strange lands, memory's gong, but above all a guarantee that the universe does not lack poetry— the universe, night, death, not lacking in poetry, not lacking a heart . . . The tights of the acrobats, now swaying thirty meters above our earth, look in its beams like real silk.

"Ladies and gentlemen," says the rather brassy and echoing loudspeaker, "even an acrobat wants the same thing as you do, he wants to live! The next number you will see—"

Handstand on a swaying flagpole—extraordinary what people will do in order to live. Now there are three, five, seven people, all hanging from the jaws of one young man, hanging on the presence of mind of a child who only yesterday, the loudspeaker informs us, celebrated his tenth birthday. . . . A cold, cloudless night, springtime, my third evening in a city that is not my main objective, a time when now and again one asks oneself: Why am I sitting here and not somewhere else in the world, here among night-covered ruins and Gothic architecture transformed into a variety show, half bar, half fairground—?

"What you are about to see in the sixth number," says the echoing loudspeaker, "no living person has ever set eyes on before! We are filled with pride that young German acrobats—"

Two youths, each on a gleaming bicycle, supporting on their shoulders a white pole; on this pole appears another bicycle, just as gleaming. Not enough that they ride in this pyramid formation along the high wire: to take away the remainder of our breath the upper one now lets go of the handlebars to hoist himself in a handstand on the saddle, while the other two keep on pedaling—thirty meters above our earth, that is to say, above bricks and twisted iron bars, the remains of a Romanesque doorway, weeds in a rusty bathtub. . . .

"Ladies and gentlemen," says the loudspeaker, "the artistes thank you for your hearty applause. Now please follow the spotlights, transfer your gaze across to the Nikolaikirche."

We transfer our gaze to the church. The sudden roar of a motorcycle, not yet visible, then suddenly it begins to climb a rope which in the darkness cannot be seen, up toward the illuminated church tower, clattering and roaring until it can go no farther and slowly rolls back into the ruins of the nave. The turn has not come off, the loudspeaker asks our pardon, the motor gave out. But another turn is ready to begin: up there on the cathedral, right at the top among the Gothic ornaments, one discerns two little human figures; a wire, five hundred meters long, is suspended from the cathedral right down to the river Main. Unfortunately at this moment a woman asks me for a light, and by the time my lighter at last functions the headlong flight has already begun: attached to a roller, which as it moves along emits a thin, hissing sound like the tearing of silk, is yet another trapeze, and on this the three artistes hang head downward, arms held sideways, three white human crosses hurtling above the missing roofs, followed constantly by spotlights; at times they vanish behind black zigzags, come back into sight, the audience rising to watch them till the last possible moment. It is over. The loudspeaker begs us kindly to withhold our applause until the three artistes, who have meanwhile landed near the river, return to the old town hall. . . . Meanwhile, a swing number, preparing us for the last turn:

"Camilla Mayer, the unforgettable, much-loved founder of our troupe, was the first to achieve this uniquely daring feat. One evening she plunged before our eyes to her death, but at her graveside we vowed that again and again we would perform this acrobatic masterpiece to which she sacrificed her life. Forever shall it bear her name, the name of the much-loved, unforgettable Camilla Mayer!"

All the spotlights focus on a steep wire, so far unnoticed, which, fixed to the spire of the Nikolaikirche and lightly swinging, vanishes from sight somewhere among the ruins; it is eighty meters long; the grade I reckon to be about twenty degrees—

The music stops.

"Camilla Mayer's Death Walk!"

It is a very young girl who—not just once, but evening after evening—observes the great vow made to the departed spirit. Slowly she climbs up from the red ruins, a white pole in her hands, slowly, step by step, she climbs up into the night. There is no net beneath the wire: that is the unique feature. If she falters and falls: soundless, a dull thud in the rubble, hardly heard, a sharp crack as the pole snaps, then nothing more, a thin, unbelieving cry from a thousand onlookers, some of whom rise, some remain seated, a friendly report in the press complete with picture, a curious, lifelong memory for various individual people, a good death, an individual death, a death of one's own, better than death in a concentration camp, better than being shot without witnesses, better than slow, festering starvation in a guarded mine, a personal death, a gambler's death, a human death . . . But she does not fall, she is still there on the soft and noiseless whipping of the wire, one sees her bare thighs, which are full and powerful, her little skirt like a parachute. A Degas seen from below. An occasional word of command to the spotlights, to keep them from dazzling the artiste. Eighty meters is a long way. The girl has just about reached halfway; as difficult now to return as to go on. A deathly hush. During it a heavy American plane bears its three bright lights through the starry sky. Toward the top the wire of course becomes ever steeper, the vow more difficult to keep. Still ten meters to go!

A spotlight has already caught the tower; again that wonderful color of its sandstone, the terra cotta looking brittle in the green night. On the molding another acrobat is already waiting, to take the white pole from the girl when she gets that far. Six meters, five meters . . . Beside me sits a young Negro in uniform, four stripes on his sleeve, which means two years' service in Europe; in front of us people are already rising to their feet so as not to get caught in the crush. Two meters, one meter . . . At last she is standing on the molding, where usually none but birds go, she is holding on to an ornament, her sequins glittering in the spotlights, she waves to the crowds, who applaud, the loudspeaker plays a march. It is cold. The young Negro is still sitting on his seat. He is not clapping. He gropes in his top pocket, takes out a cigarette, which he places in his mouth. . . .

In a few weeks' time it will be a hundred years since the first attempt, in Frankfurt, to establish a democracy in Germany; the celebrations, designed to be worthy of the occasion, are getting nearer and nearer, builders working day and night so that at any rate the Paulskirche will be ready in time. At eleven o'clock one can still hear the scrape of shovels, the whirring of a pulley carrying fresh plaster up to the floodlighted scaffolds.

Theater

Among the expressions that I tend to use without knowing exactly what they mean—not what they must mean, but what they might be made to mean—is the word "theatrical."

What does this stand for?

On the stage stands a human being, I see his physical form, his costume, his facial expression, his gestures, and also the objects around him—all of these being things that I do not have around, for instance, when I am reading, not as perceptions of my senses. And on the stage I have something else as well: speech. I am not just hearing noises, which would remain simply a perception of my senses, but speech. I hear what this person is saying, and that means a second image has been added, one of a different kind. He says: This night is like a cathedral.

Besides the visual picture I am now receiving a verbal picture, and one that I acquire, not through my senses, but through my imagination, conjured up by the words. And both I have simultaneously: sensory perception and imagination. Their interplay, their relationship to each other, the tension created between them—that, it seems to me, is what one could describe by the word "theatrical."

Hamlet with the skull of Yorick:

When this scene is told as an anecdote, one has to imagine two things: the skull in the living hand and the jokes of the departed Yorick which Hamlet is remembering. The anecdote, unlike theater, is confined entirely to speech, and everything the teller has to impart reaches me on a single plane, that is to say, the plane of the imagination. Theater works in an essentially different way: the skull, which is just an object, the grave, the spade—all these things I am constantly aware of through my senses, involuntarily, keenly, inescapably, while my imagination, wholly reserved for Hamlet's words, has only the task of evoking that vanished life, which it can do all the more distinctly since I need it for nothing else. What is vanished and what is present, the once and the now: divided between imagination and perception . . . The dramatist is therefore working on me through two antennae, and it is obvious that the two things separately— on the one hand a skull, on the other the tricks of a jester— have no particular meaning in themselves; the whole message of this scene, everything in it that moves us, comes from the relevance of these two elements to each other, and from that alone.

Many an unsuccessful dramatist could claim to have a more individual, more powerful, more pointed language than Gerhart Hauptmann; yet it founders on the stage, whereas Hauptmann, whose magic can scarcely be sought in his language, is kept afloat by this very stage to an extent that amazes one. So it seems that for a dramatist language is only a part of the whole. The other part, the appeal to the senses peculiar to theater, has an intrinsic immediacy which operates even when the dramatist forgets it, an intrinsic power, even when the dramatist makes no use of it—but it can also work against him, and that to such an extent that no language can save him.

The best example that language is not enough by itself is of course Part II of Goethe's *Faust*, the greatest feast of language German has to offer, but unplayable except in parts: not because its themes are too lofty—Shakespeare is also lofty—but because they are not theatrical.

Theatrical diagnosis: Do the things I see and the things I hear bear any relation to one another? If not, if the point being expressed lies exclusively in the words, enabling me (if I wished) to close my eyes, then the stage itself is lying fallow, and what I perceive on it at this point (since naturally I do not close my eyes) is not a theatrical situation, but an irrelevant spectacle, a seemingly haphazard gathering of speakers, epic, lyric, or dramatic—

(Drama, dialectical conflict, in which one is now and again tempted to discern the only possible form of theater, or at any rate the quintessential element of theater, is dependent on the stage only to the extent that this does in fact always have something of the ring about it—a circus ring, an arena, a public courtroom.)

ABC's of the clown: the fact that, at the moment he imagines himself to be heroic and dignified, he stumbles over his own feet. An essential element of comedy, I once read, lies in the disproportionate, the inconsistent, the irreconcilable. In the case of the clown: the irreconcilable is not contained in his words, but in the discrepancy between them and our perceptions of him. Self-confidence is not in itself comic, stumbling is not comic; only the two together. The irreconcilable, the disproportionate (an essential part of all comedy) divided up between the words and the image; this applies particularly to theatrical comedy, from the broadest to the subtlest, from the clown up to Shakespeare: we hear from Titania about her tender and blissful illusions, we hear her magnificent words, which are anything but funny, and we smile sympathetically, for at the same time we see that she is lavishing these sweet words, which charm us as well as him, on nothing but a man with an ass's head—this we *see*.

What makes Shakespeare so overwhelming is the way in which the situation (who is confronting whom) is usually itself part of the composition, meaningful already as a situation, so that all the words have to do is to provide beauty: to reap, to pluck, to display the meanings which are already there.

Who is confronting whom.

The very way in which classical plays are written shows how all-important this factor is; in the script itself every entrance is marked, though hardly anything else. Scene Ten: Enter the King and two murderers. That is what we perceive when the curtain rises, and when the two murderers have received their instructions and gone off, leaving the King alone, our area of perception changes; each scene constitutes a caesura. The King alone. When he now says something to betray the burden of his increasing loneliness, he has the whole stage to himself, the empty stage— a state of congruence between the inner situation and the outer one. Counterpoint is another means of theatrical fulfillment: Macbeth feels the burden of his guilty loneliness during a feast, he alone sees the ghost of the murdered man, his solitariness becoming so apparent that all his words, which are meant to be sociable, are powerless to conceal it; the guests depart, leaving behind only Macbeth and his wife-accomplice, the guilty pair. Again the whole inner import of a scene has been given a visual outline; the ghost of the murdered man has not uttered a word— so it is as well I kept my eyes on the stage.

In the second play by Friedrich Dürrenmatt (a name that will one day be as well known in Germany as it already is here) the following scene occurs: a blind man, unaware of the destruction of his dukedom, believes that he is still living in his castle. He imagines and believes that he is still ruling over a healthy, unharmed country. In fact he is sitting amid its ruins, which he (being blind) cannot of course see, surrounded by all sorts of rabble thrown up by the war: mercenaries, prostitutes, thieves, pimps, who now, mocking his beliefs, try to make a fool of the blind duke by getting him to receive them as if they were dukes and generals, the whore a persecuted abbess. The blind man addresses them as he imagines they deserve to be addressed, but what we see is the dissolute wench whose abbess's blessing he trustingly begs for—on his knees. . . . Prime example of a theatrical situation: the expression lying wholly in the contrast between perception and imagination. Theater is here portraying itself.

In the museum in Basel there hangs a painting by Arnold Böcklin: *Odysseus and Calypso,* the relationship between man and woman. He in blue, she in red. She in a concealed grotto, he on a jutting rock, his back toward her, his eyes fixed on the empty horizon of the sea . . . On my journey here I saw this picture again while looking for something else, and I was amazed to perceive that the sea, the object of Odysseus's longing, is hardly shown. Just one tiny blue wedge. In my memory the picture had been full of sea—precisely because in it the sea is *not* shown. No theater could convey, any more than a painting can, the vastness of the sea. It has to be left to the imagination. In Sartre there is a scene in which Zeus boasts of his firmament in order to induce Orestes, the human being, to believe in the gods. Sartre does the only possible thing: he depicts this firmament in words. If a stage director (as I have seen happen) suddenly switches on a heaven of electric bulbs in an attempt to make the stars perceptible to the senses, all theatrical magic is naturally dispelled; the firmament this Zeus is showing now looks so childish that Orestes's scornful refusal to believe in it loses all its point. In spite of good acting the backbone of a scene has been broken by a production effect that fails to recognize the theater's limitations.

The true stage is always within the human soul, and everything is subject to the soul's laws. One of these laws: compensation. When with my eyes I perceive a dungeon, I am particularly vulnerable to words that describe a free, unclouded landscape: the sight of a house- (or grotto-) bound Calypso trying to hold me back makes me particularly sensitive to the slightest word that tells of open seas and foreign coasts; the imagination it requires of me corresponds of course with the measure of my longing. And when I see a merry, riotous feast I am particularly vulnerable to a voice speaking of death; the imagination it requires of me corresponds with the measure of my fear. Theatrical relevance—the interplay between perception and imagination—will always be at its most compelling, its most rewarding, its most reliable, when it observes the needs of the human soul—when, for example, it makes use of the factor of compensation.

The fascination of theater even for a nondramatic writer such as a lyric poet: the stage provides him, if he can control it, with a foil for his words.

No play is ever theatrical all the time. Its theatrical potency does not even depend on the frequency of its theatrical moments. Theatrical effectiveness, I believe, lies in its rarity, its uniqueness: like an eye in a face. A decisive factor would no doubt be whether it is the central or only the subsidiary themes that are theatrical. In the latter case, when the theatrical element remains random, subsidiary, eccentric, every performance, however perfect, will inevitably lead to distortion, to a falsifying shifting of accents. So the theater, the author will then say, is simply a ghastly vulgarization. Of course it is that, but it is not the theater's fault if vulgarization of this sort (which has never ruined a Shakespeare) goes beyond vulgarization and becomes distortion, disfigurement, misrepresentation, destroying all the poetry. It is not the theater's fault if the poet cannot control it. Whoever appears on the stage and does not make proper use of the stage will find it working against him. Making use of the stage means: not being just *on* it, but *with* it—

Berlin, April 1948

The Russians, it is said, have closed the zonal border. A German who has just come from Helmstedt tells a different story: cars are being thoroughly searched, he says, but are being allowed to proceed. However, it is true that since yesterday no trains have been running. A Russian demand for the right to inspect American trains as well has been rejected. For the time being, by a withdrawal of the trains altogether. So all access is now cut off. Berlin is a besieged city. One tunes to all available radio stations to collect news, some of which corresponds to the rumors; in the form of news, however, it always sounds so much more solid.

Telephone call from friends; though they live in the foreign-press building, they know no more than others: a blockade to drive out the Western powers—by starving the Berliners.

Evening at a party.

People in our country love to scoff at the Berliners, but I like them very much—above all their unsentimentality, their wit, which mostly consists of calling things by their real name; their dispassionateness, a particularly welcome quality in view of the prevailing German character. Here in Berlin emotion is not laid on with a trowel; wit is seen as a more modest way of expressing feelings; they are irreverent without being spiteful. I like their soberness—in times like these, where every pose is suspect, they are admirable, because unchanged: unsentimental, down to earth, active.

Together with some fellow Swiss and a British journalist who owns a Volkswagen to the Wannsee. Sunset over the woods beside the lake. Dinner in a hotel that belongs to the press. If people compare the Berlin of today with Shanghai, I suppose they mean this curiously detached manner of living side by side: social life divided up into colonies; they are aware of being in Berlin, but the Berliners themselves seem rather like natives. One sits with legs crossed, drinking whisky, while down below "the German driver" waits. Of course there are contacts in daily life, conversations about unrest among the natives or their lively behavior; no hate, though grumbles now and again about the way the natives seem to think everything revolves about them, but no arrogance, no desire to exploit the natives any more than any other of their fellow men. London, Prague, Chicago, Paris—they all seem much closer than Berlin: people live here as if they were in an outpost, thinking of home, visiting one another and standing around, glass in hand, each maintaining his own tribal customs as he sniffs the air. For that is why they are there: for the air, the invisible things in the air . . . the world.

On writing

Plots—it seems there are thousands of them, all one's acquaintances know some, strangers make a present of them in letters,
each the basis for a play, a novel, a film, according to the hand
that chances to grasp it. Which of its numerous aspects are
eventually crystallized is simply a matter of how and at what
corner it is grasped. . . . *Hamlet:* if it were possible to set out
its plot without any sort of shaping, not even the astutest critic
would say it cries out for theatrical treatment. So much of it
can only be told; to discover what is actable in it needs the
divining rod of a theatrical mind—in this case of a theatrical
genius. Somewhat topsy-turvily expressed, since the way things
happen is not that a creative mind, theatrical or otherwise, ap-
proaches a story and considers whether it is more suitable for a
play or for a novel; the mind itself constitutes the decision: the
painter sees the subject with a painter's eye, the sculptor with
a sculptor's eye. . . . Attempts, mostly unsuccessful, to turn a
play into a short story or vice versa provide the most obvious
proof of what one basically already knows: that a plot has no
real life of its own; it exists only in its precipitates. It cannot be
distilled but only crystallized—in which form it is then immutable,
whether successful or unsuccessful: once and for all.

Berlin, May 1948

Air terminal building at Tempelhof. The plane is waiting.
Berlin–New York; but most of us are flying only as far as
Frankfurt. Customs control was embarrassing, as if we were
deserters or spies against whom nothing could be proved; to
the man who examined my documents in silence it must have
seemed beyond all doubt that I was working for Wall Street.
What else could I be doing? I telephone my friends to say
goodbye again. Splendid weather. The Tempelhof airfield teeming with shining transporter planes—
   "Airlift."

Letzigraben

Snack in the canteen, spareribs and wine, with it a particularly delicious bread—conversation with an embittered ironworker, who earns more than any of the others; though he does grumble about his piecework rates, basically it is not that; his work, as I have often enough observed, really does make one feel embarrassed, so reminiscent is it of galley slaves; one is glad not to be condemned to it oneself, glad of the assurance that ironworkers get good rates and should therefore be satisfied. The gardeners, in contrast, remind one of children at play, even when they are carrying heavy stone slabs, their hands blue with cold. What striking differences one notices, according to the nature of the work! I must admit I have never yet been in conversation with an excavation worker, though they have been around for the best part of a year; a tangible gap: they wading through pits with muddy boots, I standing above with my leather briefcase, I sketching and they getting all the dirt. Not even that skeleton of a hanged man, which came to light one day, got us talking together. The masons are different; their work demands not only brawn, but also skill; there is clumsy masonry and neat masonry, there are experts and there are bunglers; if you can spot the difference, they consider you worth talking to. In all cases where the work gives scope for individuality, one sees a blossoming of self-respect; most noticeably among the gardeners, who are always full of suggestions of what they themselves would find still better; but even the man engaged on preparatory work for the riveting of the ten-meter diving board is the soul of diligence. Work as drudgery versus work as self-expression. In our era, I can clearly see, building provides one of the most congenial places of work it is possible to find; factories cannot compare with it. The craftsman, as distinct from the worker, is always to my mind epitomized by the joiner; wood, a natural raw material which does not come from factories, above all the fact that the joiner does not fabricate parts to be passed on, but produces something finished and complete, a piece of work he can justifiably call his own. Quite different the men who work with metal; their work—assembly—also has the positive advantage of being the outcome of a protracted working process; it calls for ingenuity and provides variety, since every job is always slightly different; it is attractive in that it offers scope for ideas. And yet the nature of all people who work with metal is more ashlike. The objects they handle are always fabricated products. And the result: the flush system works. Their work is important, otherwise it would not be paid for, but it lacks the halo of an individual creation. The worker says: I was working on the swimming pool. The craftsman says: I made the railings for the swimming pool. There is a difference too in their attitude toward the architect: the craftsman considers himself a colleague, and our discussions usually bring rewards; the worker obeys—willingly or unwillingly—but as a rule has no idea of what the architect is doing. Designing plans, yes, but even those he gets others to draw for him! When I explain to a worker that plans do not come out of thin air and show him on a piece of paper the many various ways in which one can design things, how many mistakes there are to be avoided, how many conditions to be filled before he can start to lay down his parquet flooring, he is genuinely astounded:

"Yes, that's true," he says. "I never really thought about it before—"

And yet he has gray hair.

"You know," he says, "I too wanted once to be something quite different—"

"What?"

"An artist."

Café Odeon

The partition of Germany, existing in fact since the end of the war, has now been legally promulgated and put into effect—it reads like the exposition to a drama.

En route

Yesterday morning in the Odeon I heard someone at a neighboring table mention my name. I heard little of what he was saying, but was aware that the man, who does not know me, spoke my name in a tone of real hatred—not just contempt, but hatred.

Should I have introduced myself? I did not do that, but paid my bill, took up my coat, and left. Often enough one hates oneself. All the same, I have to admit that I am upset when I see this hatred in someone else, a stranger. Yet it is easily explained: if one hates certain people oneself and makes no secret of it, there are bound to be echoes. Despite this explanation I am quite unable to go back to my work, though fully aware of the vanity behind my astonishment. In the afternoon to the cinema. Impossible to write down a single sentence, or even to formulate a thought without recognizing how it might be misconstrued; worse still, the thought is hateful even when it is not misconstrued. Without having heard his exact words, I know the man is right. There is no argument against hatred. I realize, almost for the first time, that when one writes one always reckons on sympathy. Perhaps without this imagined response one could not even start, but all the same it is good to know that such a thing exists, and one ought to be grateful for such a shock, such a salutary warning—

Paris, July 1948

The Fourteenth of July . . . No nicer reception could possibly be wished for. Hardly had I arrived, in the morning, when there was a parade, but all I saw were the squadrons with their familiar droning, flying over their own city. Later I saw a military band forming into line in a park, everyone smart in his white leggings and white belt; bugles shining, each decorated with a pennant, the drum major with a decorated rod which he twirled with much bravura in the summer air, like a circus act. I waited until it began: *Le jour de gloire est arrivé!* I can't help it, but the Marseillaise always sends shivers down my spine. I walk along with them for a few paces. *Le jour de gloire est arrivé!* On the Place de la Bastille I find a huge surging crowd, a loud, glittering, hooting, buzzing, and booming fairground. Everywhere an abundance of tricolors. At one street corner a fresh wreath has been laid; three names in stone. *Fusillé par les Allemands.* To please a girl, who has a boy friend with her, I ride three times in the bumper cars; in reality to please myself, for her face, as we ram each other, is delicious. Soon others join in, and such a riot of rammings ensues that the stall-owner simply cuts off the current. Later, when I thought I had lost her, I find her again on the swings, rocking until the chair touches the tent, rocking to and fro with fluttering skirt, magnificent. A hot day, the light glaring above the roofs; it keeps reminding one of painters, as if Paris were trying to emulate the colors of famous palettes. Afterward the girl and her boy friend go down to the *métro*. I too. Stroll in the Bois de Boulogne, where I hire a boat, very contented, very happy, alone, not a soul knows where I am. More and more do I love big cities. A balloon, silver, hangs in the sky. In the evening a fireworks display, dancing on the Place de la Concorde, people of all conceivable kinds: petit bourgeois, city dwellers, families, outsiders, mothers with children, cocottes, little girls with their officer escorts, foreigners, sailors, everybody dancing. Vagabonds with bright tricolors crouch on bicycles, supporting themselves with one foot on the curb. Can one say these people are really happy? All the same, they are dancing beneath the shining street lamps, around which myriads of moths and midges are fluttering, and jazz pours from loudspeakers fixed in the night-covered trees. There are also stars. People are licking ice creams: the nimble vendor has his work cut out to cope. *Le jour de gloire est arrivé.* The Champs Elysées hangs down from the night like a glittering bridge of pearls, very narrow in the far distance, where it ends at the Arc de Triomphe. Very beautiful. Somewhere or other I descend into the earth, take the *métro,* simply because I enjoy it, and ride off nowhere in particular. Back in the fresh air, I don't know exactly where, more music and dancing meets me, for here too it is Quatorze Juillet, dancing in the open street, tables on the curb, waiters in shirt sleeves with white aprons, a band beneath Chinese lanterns, all a bit threadbare, more poverty-stricken. But behind my chair, a wonderful sight, inexpressibly wonderful, a young Chinese girl is dancing. Her black padded trousers, the moon of her tranquil face, which is in love; very beautiful. Then the people from the *quartier,* shopkeepers, cobblers, curio dealers, butchers, officials, all sorts. On the corner hangs another wreath: *Tombé pour la libération de Paris.* Here I stop. Beside the band sit three mulatto girls, all in glaring green silk; I see they will remain unforgettable. They are smoking through long white cigarette holders. A soldier, tall as a giant, can no longer stay on his feet unless somebody takes pity and dances with him; the people move aside as if he were Death itself, and he trips over the curb. At last a man dances with him. The three mulattoes sit and smoke, little animals wearing earrings, silent and beautiful, terrible, mysterious creatures. All this the Germans once conquered, and it was not so very long ago. Did they really conquer it? I stay till long past midnight. Perhaps there are cities that cannot ever be conquered; they can only sink down into ruins. At one stage the mulattoes were dancing too, not wildly, but with decorum, their long cigarette holders still in their mouths; only their arms are serpents. A group of students, arm in arm, have a rather disrupting effect: they are interlopers, childish rather than young. The Chinese girl is young; wonderful how she loves her lean Chinese boy . . .

Autobiography

(*I am sitting in the garden of Versailles, where princes once held their summer serenades. A stillness of fountains. The urge to sketch Paris always dies in the remembrance of all the other humans who have done so, and in masterly fashion. One hardly dares describe it even in letters: everyone knows it, everyone loves it, the air is full of the conversation of distinguished ghosts who need no talking companion. In the morning I was on the Seine bank, leafing through books, as millions have done before me. There is nothing in this city that millions have not already done, seen, painted, written about, lived. And so, thrown back on myself, I will today write about myself.*)

I was born in 1911 in Zurich. Our name is not of Swiss origin. A grandfather, emigrating as a young saddler, brought it from neighboring Austria; in Zurich, which he apparently liked, he married a local girl, the daughter of a simple family named Naegeli. On my mother's side the pedigree is also mixed; there it was my great-grandfather, Wildermuth by name, who came from Württemberg. And so it all began with his son, my grandfather: he called himself an artist and wore a sizable cravat, much bolder than his drawings and paintings; he married a girl named Schulthess from Basel who could never quite forget that her family had once possessed its own carriage, and he became head of the school of arts and crafts in our city. Much more about my heredity I do not know. My mother, desirous of seeing something at least of the world, once worked as a nursemaid in tsarist Russia, about which she often told us, and my father was an architect. Since, as the son of a worker, he could not afford professional schooling for himself, it was naturally his ambition to make scholars of his sons. In which direction we could please ourselves. My brother, older than I, chose chemistry, filling both his childhood and our kitchen with stinking conjurations. A book on the window sill, retorts full of yellow vapors, Bunsen burners, test tubes like glass entrails, now and again an explosion, intended or unintended—those were our Sunday afternoons, the rainy ones when there was no chance of playing soccer.

I do not know why I alone of all my comrades never read Karl May or indeed any other book—with the exception of *Don Quixote* and *Uncle Tom's Cabin*, both of which pleased me immensely and sufficed for my needs. My appetite for soccer, and later for the theater, was more insatiable. A performance of Schiller's *Die Räuber* (a very poor one, I suspect) made such an impression on me that I could not understand how people, grownups with sufficient pocket money and no school homework, could resist spending every one of their evenings in the theater. That, surely, was real life. Considerable confusion was caused in me by the first play I saw in which people appeared on stage in everyday clothing; this meant, neither more nor less, that one could still write plays, even in our own days.

Two months later Max Reinhardt, Deutsches Theater, Berlin, received written notice of my first work, which bore the title *Stahl* (Steel). All I now remember is that it was set on the roof of a high building during the night, and at the conclusion smoke was pouring out of all the windows of the city, yellow smoke such as comes from retorts, and the hero, noble to the end, had no way out but to plunge down into the depths. The postcard with a foreign stamp, briefly but politely inviting me to submit my work, was the first communication I had ever received that addressed me as "mister." I was sixteen. Unfortunately my father who regarded the whole thing as a boyish prank, fetched this postcard from the mailbox and laid it on the lunch table, whereupon I left the room; perhaps—I was not yet quite sure—forever. After seven long weeks, filled with plenty of rash hopes (for, after all, Schiller was only eighteen when he wrote *Die Räuber*), I received back the neat script, which I had typed up in the attic on a borrowed machine; a detailed report, which I could not understand, was enclosed. An invitation to submit my subsequent work was all I had to show my indulgently smiling family. In a store I in time discovered the collected works of Henrik Ibsen, containing plays well worth the money I paid for them. By the time of my final school examinations, which I of course looked upon as unnecessary, a matter of form, ridiculous and philistine, and took only for my father's sake, I had written three or four more plays, among them a comedy about marriage (I had never even kissed a girl) and a farce about a landing on the moon. Of all this work the only part the world recognized was my final examinations. The university was now unavoidable. . . .

I recall two curious years that I spent in lecture rooms, though almost as eagerly in the corridors outside: always expectant, solitary, hasty in judgment, uncertain, usually involved in a secret love affair of which the loved one knew nothing. No poems came off. Pure philosophy, pursued with geninue fervor, revealed to me nothing but my own lack of thinking power. My main subject was Germanics. But there were other lectures that seemed to me more real, closer to life's mysteries. Professor Cleric, who later committed suicide, showed us human existence as it were through the distorting mirror of its criminal aspects. As splendid as he was strange, transcending our perplexities, was old Wölfflin as he stood there, a bamboo lance in his hand, elucidating his basic concepts, all spoken as if cut in marble. I also listened to our well-known theologians, and roved hither and thither; certainly the dissatisfied boy owed more to that unsatisfactory period than he was aware of. But my growing feeling that everything I heard lacked a common center, and the university habit of laying things down side by side in rows as in a store, all this might have been a truly genuine feeling, even perhaps a conviction; but at the same time it served as a welcome excuse for my own ineptitude as a scholar. When I was twenty-two, my father died. I had now to think of earning my own living. As a journalist I described whatever I was asked: processions, lectures about Buddha, fireworks, seventh-rate cabarets, fires, swimming competitions, springtime in the zoo;

I refused nothing—except crematoriums. And as a schooling this was by no means useless. World ice-hockey championships were being held in Prague, I got myself registered as a reporter and set off, after acquiring my first traveling case, with capital of one hundred francs in my pocket. The journey, my first in foreign lands, led me farther afield with every article published at home or in Germany; through Hungary, Siberia, Bosnia, Dalmatia, where, having soon made friends with some German immigrants, I spent a whole summer, sailing all day long around the coast, with no obligations, free, enjoying the present; and that is really my main memory of youth. Later I went on to the Black Sea, of which my mother had so often spoken, and to Istanbul, where I became acquainted with mosques and with hunger, finally to the Acropolis and on foot through central Greece, where I spent my nights in open fields, once even in a little temple. That was for me, though marred by the sudden death of a young woman, a full and happy time. The result was my first, all-too-youthful novel. Back home, I spent a further two years trying my hand at literary journalism, to see what it was like writing to earn a living, even when one has nothing to say. At the age of twenty-five I had once more to return to the school bench. My fiancée was of the opinion that I should make up my mind what I wanted to be before we married. She said only what I myself thought; all the same, it was a shock, the first serious indication that life could go awry. At that time I read Gottfried Keller's novel *Der grüne Heinrich;* this book, in which certain pages were as disconcerting to me as an act of clair-voyance, was of course the very best father one could hope to have. To my resolve, which alone could have achieved little, was then added a stroke of good fortune: a friend offered to support me financially for four years, so that I could return to my studies, this time at the Swiss technical university. Delighted though I was at the beginning to be able to sit down on a working day and devote myself to higher mathematics without a thought for the necessity of earning money for my mother and myself, I did later experience some silent moments of suffering: the feeling of having dissipated my youth, the fear of never achieving a goal. Then, in quick succession, I suffered reverses in all my human relationships. Whether the profession of an architect, to the extent that I was any good at it, would restore these contacts with the world could not be decided while it was all still only on paper. What had attracted me to architecture was, after all, the nonpaper aspects, the practical craftsmanship, the shaping of materials: only a real building job, putting above all my own designs into effect, would show whether this second attempt was also doomed to failure. One day I tied up all my writings, including my diaries, and consigned them to the flames. There were so many bundles that I had to make two journeys into the woods. It was, I remember, a wet day on which the dampness continually put out the fire, and I used up a whole box of matches before I could return home with a feeling of relief, but also of emptiness. A secret oath to write no more was not seriously breached in the next two years; only on the day of mobilization, when I was called up as a gunner, convinced that the war would not spare us and there was little chance of returning alive, did I again begin to keep a diary. There was an army captain who could not bear the sight of me (which of course was his good right), and on September 3 he told me to my face that he would send me to a suitable place when the fighting started. I see no reason to let patriotic considerations draw a veil over this memory; years later I did in fact realize how indebted I was to this officer for a decisive experience in my life. True, his opportunity to decide over life or death never came about: on the border all remained quiet. The diary, broken off during my furloughs, was later published: *Blätter aus dem Brotsack*, 1940. After the downfall of France, which made virtual prisoners of us all, I was given personal leave of absence to sit for my architect's diploma; from now on, as far as my military service permitted, I was in a position to earn my living as an employee. In all, during those years, I put in more than five hundred days of military service, mostly in Ticino, later in the Engadine. A young female architect who helped me at the drawing board and prepared my midday meal became my wife; we were married after we had together built a house, our first assignment. Next came a novel: *J'adore ce qui me brûle oder Die Schwierigen*, 1943. Among the few letters it brought me was one of a few lines from the dramatic adviser of the Zurich Schauspielhaus, Kurt Hirschfeld, who encouraged me to try my hand at a play. Altogether it was a time of slowly mounting confidence. Even if we could not be quite certain of remaining unscathed, the outcome of the war as a whole was already decided; the meticulously planned invasion of Switzerland, the threat of which had hung over us all these years, again became a possibility, as documents have since proved—in April 1943 a minor victory might at least have helped to divert the attention of German newspaper-readers from Stalingrad. Ten days before the planned deadline, which espionage had brought to light, the invasion was called off. With that we were out of the woods. Shortly afterward our first child arrived. Victory in an architectural competition brought me a large and very attractive commission from the city of Zurich, enabling me at last to set up my own office and thus make freer use of my time. After a prose reverie, *Bin oder Die Reise nach Peking*, 1944, came my first work for the stage, *Santa Cruz*, a romance which provided me with two months of great joy during the fall. Six months later—also written in the space of a few weeks—came an attempt at a requiem, *Nun singen sie wieder*. This was my first play to reach the stage: Easter 1945, when the war was coming to an end and peace should have begun. The period of rehearsals, directed by Kurt Horwitz with professional dedication, was for me perhaps the most blissful the theater can ever offer a writer: one's first encounter with one's own words spoken by real people. Then, at last, came the final days of the war, which I spent on sentry duty on the Austrian and partly on the Italian border. After my first visit to shattered Germany there came another play, my third, *Die Chinesische Mauer*, a farce already showing some signs of despair; it too made its first appearance at the Zurich Schauspielhaus, in the fall of 1946. There followed, as far as professional duties would allow, further journeys in all neighboring countries; the desire to get to know one's contemporaries in other lands was particularly strong after our five years in captivity, and in a world bewitched by prejudice it seemed to me of vital importance to see things with my own eyes. Meanwhile the point had been reached at which we could at last start with our building work. Practicing two separate professions simultaneously, as writer and as architect, is of course not always easy, however great its occasional blessings. It is a question not so much of time as of strength. Among my blessings I count the daily work with men who had nothing to do with literature; some knew that I "wrote," but they did not hold it against me, so long as my other work was in order. My last piece of writing to date deals with an incident in Berlin. This play, *Als der Krieg zu Ende war,* is at the moment being read by friends.

Paris, July 1948

To most people it must have been apparent, even before the Second World War made it obvious, that the time when European nations could quarrel among themselves for world dominion is dead and gone. Europe has nothing more to look for in this direction, and any European who still hankers after world power must fall victim either to despair or to ridicule, like the many Napoleons in lunatic asylums. America, once discovered and now busy discovering itself, and a reawakened Russia (not to speak at the moment of China) are now giants to which, quite simply, Europe no longer measures up. Napoleon had at least some hopes of adding Russia to his bag—the Russia of his time. Even that effort did not succeed. He exhausted himself. But what Hitler tried to do was senseless from the very start. It is not only the question of relative size, which ought surely to have made him pause and consider whether it is not a peculiarly German failing to confuse courage with excess; there was also another factor involved: the giants had meanwhile been to school. Just now I am sitting somewhere in Saint-Michel, not far from the Sorbonne, surrounded by a large assortment of students, male and female, among them many colored people, black, brown, and yellow. Many of these are splendid to look at, they dress as naturally as the Parisians and speak French as if it were their native language. But one day, when they have learned what they need to know, they will leave Paris, albeit with a heavy heart, and return to their own world, back to their black or brown or yellow brothers and sisters. It is the natural outcome of any long-lasting dominion, including that of the West: gradually the ruler must lay down his weapons. Through discoveries of many kinds, European in origin, the world, hitherto dominated by Europeans, has—thanks to the export of these discoveries—changed in a way that now puts aging Europe itself completely out of the running. And not only because of its size, which even a cursory glance at the globe will instantly reveal. The deciding factor is that the price that Europe had to pay for the things that mattered does not encumber those discovered and reawakened giants—a price measured in history, in blood, in living strength. And this is the way it has always been. It costs strength to explore the world, to experience, to awaken. To invent or to apply an invention, to build it up and develop it and find new uses for it; to provide a lesson or absorb it, to profit from it, these are separate processes, each of them valuable, but twofold in their demands on creative power. A plane can be flown even by those who did not invent it: one just learns the controls, which are already there: one does not have to spend centuries looking for them. The whole process of flying, the outcome basically of a single invention, now costs nothing except gas and oil, work and intelligence; it calls for no history, no vital substance; and the inheritor is soon flying even better than the original inventor: for he is flying with younger nerves. With Russian or American nerves, for example. In Thornton Wilder's *The Skin of Our Teeth* there is a passage that illustrates this process incomparably; the father, Mr. Antrobus, has just invented the wheel, and hardly has his son spent a minute playing with it when he makes a suggestion to his father: Papa, you could put a chair on this. The father invents, but the son will "take possession of" the invention. Yes, cries Mr. Antrobus, any booby can fool with it now, but I thought of it first. It is less, I believe, a question of priorities than of processes, developments. Younger nerves, the absence of historical experience, of skepticism, those are of course the essentials if one wishes to take over the father's wheel and dominate the world with it. And it is these features —the lack of skepticism, of irony—that we do indeed primarily find disquieting about the inheritors. In Paris I have often noticed that the Germans, yesterday's oppressors, are less hated than the Americans, the liberators. That says nothing at all about oppression or liberation as such. It is, I believe, an expression simply of this disquiet: the Germans, in spite of everything, were Europeans. There was probably the same sort of feeling between the Athenians and Alexander the Great when he ruled the world, but it never occurred to the Athenians to fight to the last drop of blood against this world dominion (which Pericles

himself had never desired). Why should they? It was enough
for them to know that all the good things the young Alexander
was spreading across the world were the fruits of the Greek
spirit—the greatest and most vital qualities of Hellenism, which
have outlasted the dominion not only of Alexander but of a
great many other world conquerors as well—

What Europe has to look forward to:

To be what Greece was under Alexander, what Italy is for
Europe, and to become that for the world of tomorrow.

What has Europe to fear?

That one of its great nations that, in the time of European
world dominion, never reached the top might still be dreaming
of world power: Germany, which almost succeeded in destroying
the resources, human and material, of Europe—the very Europe
that could attain a significance greater than world dominion
through its achievement, its maturity, its example—

Letzigraben

Now is the turn of the woodwork. The rafters have been laid
and look magnificent: that cagework of raw wood, above it the
blue sky, all day long the echoing blows as they nail down the
boarding, wood shavings, sawdust, trucks bringing new planks;
it is unlikely that I shall ever again have so much carpentry
to handle, and I enjoy it thoroughly, walking about more than
necessary. Of all building work I like it best, the bare structure
before the roofs go on. Brick and wood, a series of rooms full of
sky, which one can see through all stories; the cube shape is
visible for the first time, though still transparent, and the space
in which I am now standing has seen the sun for the last time,
at least the last time for decades. Above my head they are
already at work on the covering, pushing one board up against
the next. . . .

Brecht

My association with Brecht, taxing like any association with a
person of superior intelligence, has lasted only six months so far,

and there have been not a few moments when I have been tempted simply to run away. It is Brecht himself who then rings up again or, meeting in the street, asks me in his dry and somewhat reserved, yet always friendly, way whether I have an evening free. Brecht looks for discussion everywhere. I myself get least from our conversations when Brecht checkmates me with his arguments: one feels beaten, but not convinced. Going home through the night, reflecting on his comments, I find myself not infrequently immersed in a reluctant monologue: But none of that is true! Yet when I then hear equally rash and often ugly sweeping judgments from other people, I again feel the urge to cycle out to Herrliberg. The mere curiosity one feels in relation to a famous man would not by itself be sufficient in the long run to reconcile one to these strenuous evenings, which always bring one face to face with one's own limitations. The fascination that Brecht constantly exerts I ascribe above all to the fact that here one sees a life that is genuinely ruled by thought (whereas our thinking is usually only a retrospective self-justification: it does not steer, but is dragged behind). Confronting an outstanding talent—which Brecht incidentally is, the greatest indeed in the German language at this moment—one can of course take refuge in admiration; one bows the knee like an acolyte before the altar, and the thing is done: one can go on. But confronting an attitude, a way of life, that is not enough: the demands are quite different, and because Brecht has less personal vanity than almost any other person I know, these demands cannot be satisfied by attempts to ingratiate oneself. Brecht, perhaps like all other people who live independently, is not at all interested in approval; on the contrary, he is waiting for challenge, is merciless when the challenge is unworthy and bored when it does not come at all. By the expression that appears on his severe, alert face, rustically impassive and often somewhat slyly veiled, one sees that he is indeed listening, forcing himself to listen, even though he finds it all just chatter; but behind those small, withdrawn eyes there are flashes of contradiction; his gaze flickers, impatience makes him for a while embarrassed, then aggressive, thundery. His strokes of lightning, his comments, intended as a challenge to get real discussion going, with blows and counterblows, annihilate at times through the sharpness of their formulation; his companion, especially if new and inexperienced, lapses with a disconcerted smile into silence, and all Brecht can then do is to take a grip on himself and catechize, earnestly but somewhat mechanically, basically rather annoyed, for this is the very opposite of the conversation he had been hoping for, irritated too that so few people are really versed in Marxist doctrines, Hegelian dialectics, the historical background of materialism. Brecht has no desire to lecture, but finds himself in the position of a man who, wanting to talk about poetry, ends, in order to avoid mere chat, in having to give a lesson in elementary grammar. If he considers his time too precious for that, he does it nevertheless, for mere chat would irritate him even more, and instruction is after all instruction, of use at any rate to the other person, potentially. But basically, I believe, Brecht is happy when he does not have to catechize. Our conversations always bear fruit when I leave the reflections to him, confining myself to supplying the facts, which of course in themselves leave room enough for contradiction. His attitude—and with Brecht it really is an attitude covering all aspects of life—consists in the daily application of those philosophical conclusions that reveal our social system as outmoded and its perpetuation by force as despicable, so that this system can only be seen as an obstacle, not as a standard to measure things by. Brecht's concern is with the future; an outlook that inevitably contains an element of restriction, the intermittent danger of a rigidity which admits no modifications. It is no accident that, even in his dealings with actors, Brecht strives so tirelessly to achieve something loose and relaxed; these qualities are indeed always present to a high degree in his poetical work. Loose and relaxed: a staggering requirement in the context of a life such as Brecht leads, a life devoted to a world that as yet nowhere exists, that is visible only in his own behavior, that is a living contradiction, unrelenting and never, throughout his long years of toil as an outsider, crushed. Christians act in relation to the life beyond, Brecht to the life here below. That is one of the differences between him and the priests, whom, because of his differing goal, he loves to mock; yet he is not so very unlike them: the doctrine of ends justifying the means has identical features even when the ends are opposed. There can also be Jesuits of the life here below, and sometimes it is by no means their wish, their paramount duty, to be understood—not, I mean, at all costs. A little piece entitled *Fünf Schwierigkeiten beim Schreiben der Wahrheit* (Five Difficulties in Writing the Truth), written in 1934 for secret distribution under the Nazi regime, heads its fourth paragraph: "Prudence in selecting those in whose hands the truth will be effective"; and its fifth: "Cunning in spreading the truth to many." That must always be kept well in mind, especially in addressing a large and random community. For to plan a peaceful, more just new world and then to sacrifice oneself to it in front of the cannons—that is behavior in relation to the world beyond, heroism, and not in relation to life here below, which is practical, necessitating.

Yesterday we went swimming together, the first time I have seen Brecht in a natural setting, that is to say, in surroundings that cannot be changed and therefore interest him little. ("I looked upon nature with impatience. So the time passed away which on earth was given me.") There is so much in need of change that no time is left for praising what is natural. Like so much else in Brecht, this too is a thoroughly conscious attitude, a second nature: naturally he has no word to say about nature. All the same, he is concerned whether we shall be caught in the approaching storm or not. The lake is green, ruffled by the wind, the sky purple and sulphur-yellow. Brecht, equipped as ever with his gray peaked cap, leans on the somewhat rotten railing, smoking a cigar; it is the rottenness he takes note of: he makes a joke about capitalism. I am already in the water before he goes into the changing shed. Summer lightning flickers over the city, slanting funnels of rain veil the distant mountains, birds are whirring about, the great beeches rustling, dust whirling on the road. Later I see Brecht climbing down into the water to join us; he swims a few strokes, but soon disappears again into the changing shed. His wife and I continue to swim for a while in the choppy, scurrying waves. By the time I return to land Brecht is already back in his gray sports jacket and gray cap, telling us, as he lights his next cigar, how refreshed he feels.

"You know," he says, as if our previous conversation had not been perceptibly interrupted, "that seems to me absolutely right. The actor playing Puntila must on no account give the impression—"

The apartment Brecht has found in Herrliberg is in the top story of an old gardener's lodge. We eat either in the kitchen, where his wife demonstrates talents for which she is less renowned, or in the living room, which has the atmosphere of an attic, as indeed has the whole apartment, something stimulatingly temporary. Afterward we walk around on a gravel-covered roof garden, where one has to stoop beneath clotheslines, and finally we sit down in his workroom to drink black coffee. This has a lovely window facing the lake and the mountains, which are, however, of no interest to Brecht; he likes the window too, but only because it provides a good light. The room looks something like a workshop: typewriter, piles of paper, scissors, cases of books; on a chair lie newspapers, Swiss, English, German, American, and here and there something has been cut out and placed in a folder; on the large table I see a jar of paste and a brush, photographs, stage pictures of a production in New York, and Brecht talks about Charles Laughton; then books connected with his current work, the correspondence between Goethe and Schiller, Brecht reads out some passages concerning dramatic and epic writing. Further items are a radio, a box of cigars, chairs on which one can sit only upright, an ashtray, which I place on the pine floor. On the wall opposite there hangs a Chinese painting which can be rolled up, but at present is unrolled. Everything is such that one could move out within forty-eight hours; unhomely. It would not have looked very different, I think to myself, in 1941, in Finland:

> Over the radio
> I hear the victory bulletins of the scum of the earth.
>   Curiously
> I examine a map of the continent. High up in Lapland
> Towards the Arctic Ocean
> I can still see a small door.

Remembering that, it occurs to me that Brecht has never spoken of his experiences, or indeed ever about himself, except in a very indirect way. We talk about architecture, housing. Brecht paces up and down, at times we are both on our feet in order to speak more easily, moving about as on a stage, where Brecht, for all his reserve, makes much use of gesture. A tiny dismissive movement of the hand indicates contempt, coming to a standstill at the decisive point of a developing sentence implies a question mark, expressed with an abrupt lift of the left shoulder. Irony is indicated with a movement of the lower lip, aping the smug earnestness of all right-thinking people. Then his sudden laughter as some paradox is nailed down, rather croaking, harsh but not cold; his bewildered and dismayed astonishment, his defenseless expression when one tells him something that really affects, worries, or delights him. Brecht is a warmhearted, kind man, but circumstances are not such that this is enough in itself.

> On my wall hangs a Japanese carving,
> The mask of an evil demon, decorated with gold
>   lacquer.
> Sympathetically I observe
> The swollen veins of the forehead, indicating
> What a strain it is to be evil.

We get on best together when our conversation, which Brecht always leaves to the inspiration and inclination of his companion, centers around theatrical matters, production, acting, the technical problems of writing which, when treated objectively, lead inevitably to the core of things. Brecht is an inexhaustible arguer. Side by side with an artistic mentality that loves the methodical ways of science, he has the child's talent for asking questions. An actor, what does that mean? What does he do? What particular qualities does he need? A creative readiness to start again patiently from the beginning, to forget previously held opinions, to collect experiences and inquire into them without dictating the answer. The answers are at first often of disconcerting paltriness. "An actor," he says hesitantly, "that is probably a person who does something with a special emphasis, for instance, the way he drinks and so on." His almost peasantlike patience, the courage with which he will stand helpless on a bare field, eschewing borrowed ideas, his ability to be very modest and possibly with nothing to show, but then again his quick intelligence in seizing on indications of a usable piece of knowledge and developing it by argument, and finally his manly way of taking conclusions seriously and acting on them, unaffected by opinions—these alone are wonderful lessons and exercises which in an hour easily outweigh a whole semester. The conclusions, however, belong to him. Our profit lies in seeing how he arrives at them. And then it is time to go home; Brecht takes up his cap and the milk jug, which has to be put outside the front door. Brecht possesses a rare kind of unaffected courtesy that, if somewhat stereotyped, is nevertheless warm. When I do not have my bicycle with me he accompanies me to the rail depot, waits till I have got on board, then gives a quick, almost furtive wave with his hand; he does not take off his gray cap, which would be lacking in style. Avoiding the other people, he leaves the platform with quick, light steps, rather than long strides; his arms swinging hardly at all, his head held as always slightly to one side, peaked cap pulled well down as if to hide his face, half conspiratorial, half bashful. He looks, when one sees him like that, as inconspicuous as a workingman, a metalworker, yet for a workingman too unrobust, too slender, for a farmworker too alert, altogether too mobile for a Swiss; a refugee, slinking, watchful, who has already left countless rail depots, too shy for a man of the world, too hardened for a man of learning, knowing too much not to be apprehensive, a stateless person, a man of limited sojourns, a passer-by in our time, a man called Brecht, a physicist, a poet without incense. . . .

The manuscript he has given me to read is called *Kleines Organon für das Theater*. Brecht wants to know what others make of it. Even our failure to understand he finds useful; it helps to warn him. I have never met a man who, quite without affectation, is so unconcerned with prestige. An actor, by no means well known, ventures to suggest a textual alteration: he wants to say something where the text calls for silence. Brecht listens, considers, and approves, not just for the sake of giving in, but because what the man says is right. His rehearsals never have the air of a boudoir, but, rather, of a workshop. In all other ways too Brecht has this solemnly obliging manner, which is not flattery, and also tolerates none: it is the impersonal modesty of a wise man who learns something from everyone who crosses his path—from him, not only about him.

———

Prague, August 23, 1948

Wonderful flight through boiling clouds, blue shadows, sheaves of sunshine, mountain ranges of silver foam; scraps of mist race by, now and again an opening through which one sees a pattern of summer fields— Lengthy passport control . . . Prague, it seems to me, is changed: listless, poverty-stricken. I sit in a park. My friends are not at home; on vacation. So I seek out a distant acquaintance; he has emigrated, I am told. My inquiry seems to embarrass them a bit; they answer through lips tight and hardly moving. The sun is shining. There is something ghostly about it all; but I could not say why.

On writing

What Brecht in his *Organon* calls the "alienation effect": according to this, theatrical alienation should be used to divest social practices vulnerable to change of the stamp of familiarity which now protects them from attack. Further, the audience must not identify itself with the action, it must be prevented from going into a trance, should derive its pleasure, rather, from seeing certain familiar processes at a distance, so that it is not carried away by them but really sees them, recognizing what can be changed in them, recognizing the particular relativity of an action. It (the audience) enjoys the higher pleasure of knowing that we can intervene, be productive in the easiest way, for (Brecht says) the easiest way of living lies in art. . . . It would be tempting to apply all these ideas to the novelist; alienation effect by linguistic means, conscious playacting in the narration, the openly artistic approach which most German readers consider "alienating" and reject out of hand, because it is too "artistic," because it prevents self-identification, does not carry one away, destroys illusions—meaning the illusion that the story being told "really" happened, and so on.

Breslau (Wroclaw), August 24, 1948

Arrival at midnight. Large and extensive meal with other arrivals, Yugoslavians, Mexicans, Belgians, and others. A very unhappy feeling, which gripped me as I stepped out of the train, has not vanished overnight. The town hall is labeled "Razhus," not "Rathaus." I do not know where I am. Silesia was Gerhart Hauptmann's home.

The Jahrhunderthalle: its interior of raw concrete makes a strong impression, more than bewildering—I spend nearly an hour sitting in it. Conversation with a young Polish woman who has been translating for me the inscriptions in the exhibition. An exhibition of the new territories that have been given to Poland; both architecturally and graphically the exhibition is a real delight. Proving that Silesia is a Polish land: in the same way Austria could demand the return of Switzerland after seven centuries apart. The charming Pole, who has been three months in Breslau, finds my arguments hostile. Wrongly so. More weighty than these nationalistic arguments, which are incorrect and always at least two-edged, is the detailed description of what the Germans did to Poland; destruction and exploitation on all sides have reached such a pitch that the continued existence of this unhappy nation is endangered unless reparations are made. That seems to me the only possible way of looking at things when one comes to speak of Silesia: it is a question of reparations. In one gallery after another we see what has already been done in this new territory; it is of course always comforting, particularly in lands reduced to ruins, to see actual products, gleaming tractors, plows, bridge girders, new railroad cars, building materials made out of rubble, machines, tools, crockery, implements of all descriptions. The viewing is pleasurable, only one's thoughts are frightening. It works like an act of incantation, all these things that are being presented for our inspection: the new face of Poland all around us, large and small, in paintings and in models, frescoes, reliefs, maquettes, written in electric light bulbs surrounded by flags. Poland without the eastern territories, which Russia has taken; in their place Silesia, this enormous gift. What should they do? The tragedy of the Poles is their geography. . . .
Evening beside the river Oder.
Now, for the first time, I feel more at ease, if only on account of the scenery, which has something heavy as well as spacious about it. Fairground noises in the distance; before me the river,

the evening reflections, the busy tooting of ships, smoke, a sky-line of ruins, gasometers, trees, bushes. Later two policemen come up—sitting down is not allowed here. They see my badge: Congrès Mondial des Intellectuels pour la Paix. They raise their hands to their caps in salute. One asks in flawless French how I like Poland.

"*En Pologne—?*"

"*A Wroclaw,*" says the other.

I answer with cigarettes.

"*Vous êtes suisse?*"

"*Oui.*"

"*Je connais bien la Suisse,*" he says. "*La Suisse m'a sauvé—*"

They pocket the cigarettes, so I have only my own to light as they salute me in an unintimidating way:

"*Beau séjour, monsieur—et bon travail.*"

August 25, 1948

Fadeyev, the leader of the Russian writers, opened the congress by calling us all to task, first in general terms, then with names. If he knows all the writers he reprimands and dubs hyenas or mystics or pornographers, then he is enviably well read. Assembled here are four hundred intellectuals from America, India, Russia, Madagascar, East Berlin, Argentina, England, Indonesia, Uruguay, Belgium, Italy, Czechoslovakia, Mexico, Sweden, Rumania, France, Bulgaria, exile Spain, Denmark, Switzerland, Yugoslavia, Holland, Poland, Brazil, and so on. . . . The hall is decorated with a cluster of national flags; each seat has earphones; simultaneous translation in Polish, Russian, English, French . . . In the evening inaugural reception in the Gothic town hall. The tables, at which one serves oneself, could be by Rubens. A German emigrant whom I know from Switzerland, a man of letters whose brilliant lectures on Thomas Mann are still bright in my memory, has turned out bravely: eating tarts, which are excellent, he explains to me the difference between good terrorism and evil terrorism.

"There is no point," he says, "in talking about culture to people like André Gide."

An Indian couple is wonderful to look at.

"Tell me," he urges, "what cultural values have been created during the last three decades—except in the Soviet Union."

I open the Gothic window to throw away my cigarette; on the midnight street stand large numbers of people looking up at the lighted chambers— *Beau séjour, messieurs, et bon travail.*

August 26, 1948

It is being said that after Fadeyev's speech the British considered leaving at once, then decided to stay. In the discussion each speaker is allowed ten minutes. Ehrenburg speaks for twenty minutes before Julian Huxley, the chairman of the day, ventures to remind him of the time limit. Frantic applause; Ehrenburg should be allowed to go on speaking. After thirty-five minutes an American gets up, wanting to know why Ehrenburg has different rights from others. Frantic applause; Ehrenburg should be allowed to go on speaking. He finishes in the fortieth minute. A clever speaker, a Danton, lively and aggressive, ironic. But he was not being ironic when he spiritedly asked: Can one visualize European music without the Russians? I can; but what has that to do with peace? An Englishman, a scholar from Oxford, replies to the reproaches of yesterday, repudiating them with the remark that his country never made a pact with Hitler and was the only one to take up the fight before Hitler attacked it. The applause, which usually goes on for minutes, is brief and as sparse as if the speaker had been German. Next comes an American, who also takes issue with Fadeyev; Fadeyev sits there without headphones. As I had already discovered, he does not understand English; eschewing the help of the interpreters, he descends from his desk to converse with one of his compatriots, lively and smiling, before slowly returning to his seat, demonstratively slow, demonstratively unconcerned; the American continues to speak; even now Fadeyev does not put on his earphones, but thumbs through a brochure—

Not present at the afternoon session.

Food is plentiful, even for ordinary people; in all the districts I wander through there are potatoes, eggs, fish of all kinds, sausages, beer, bread, plenty of fruit; the clothing on the other hand is very poor quality.

209

August 27, 1948

My fellow countryman, a journalist whose name is easily confused with that of a famous Frenchman, has today suddenly been given a car with a Polish driver, who opens the door with the words: *A votre disposition!* . . . We drive out into the country, visit Silesian farms. A Silesian woman who looks after Silesian refugees in Berlin has already told me much. Now I am here, and I feel once more that it is my duty to see what is here and to remember what is there, always both together; as it is my duty wherever I am. . . . The first farm is a large estate, landed-gentry style, now occupied by thirty families, smallholders from eastern Poland. They work communally, dividing up the yield according to the number of workers. The living quarters, inspected without previous notice, are very clean. In a large yard there are horses standing under autumnal trees, a bullet-ridden tractor which is being restored to working condition. A serious lack of implements, and consequently in the first years the harvest was very poor. No freehold; only the cattle and the household goods belong to them. Every family can leave whenever it wants. They look after the management themselves, with an agronomist as adviser. They sell in the open market. The old manor house: empty, during the day a school for the children, in the evening used occasionally for singing and dancing. In a garage stands a burnt-out limousine, which they are converting in their spare time into a vehicle to take them into town. All in all a mixture between a monastery and *Robinson Crusoe—*

A second farm is very different, occupied by a single family: a youngish farmer, strong and robust. We come on him milking; he speaks German flawlessly—he once worked on a farm in Prussia. You can learn things there, he says. In ten years he earned and saved so much that back home, in eastern Poland, he was able to buy a little farm of his own. Then came war, plunder, fire; hardly had he begun with the rebuilding when they had to move out. Now he is working again on a German farm that at first, since it had also been destroyed, nobody wanted to take on. His answers are frank and free. This is the first year in which no land has been left uncultivated, because now he has a tractor. He shows us his accounts, which he keeps meticulously. For whom? One day, he thinks, someone will come; these books will enable people to see how he has done. Yields, outlays, purchases, takings from each harvest. His ambition is to produce from each hectare as much as previously in Prussia; he is still three percent short of it. In answer to our question as to who will one day come, he shrugs his heavy shoulders and laughs, fetches beer and with it bread and raw ham, later some fruit, apples and plums, and finally schnapps. His wife, who speaks only Polish, silently serves us as he tells us of various kinds of manure that can still be got. A wonderful hour—Sodom and Gomorrah, *one* we have found . . .

At evening back with the intellectuals.

Picasso: one knows his face from pictures; close up he looks more advanced in years, an old man with stabbing bright eyes, mischievous and wise at the same time, the face of a harlequin endowed with genius.

"On est contre les formalistes!" he laughs with raised eyebrows. *"Moi, je suis aussi contre les formalistes—mais ils ne sont pas les mêmes."*

Warsaw, August 28, 1948

One can fly here very cheaply. Thirty francs to Warsaw. The plane is an old transporter, a Dakota, which had once been supplied to the Russians. Inside there are only two benches, placed lengthwise as in a streetcar; no seat belts—flying is an everyday affair. We land at ten in the morning in streaming rain. In the car that takes us into the city I find myself sitting directly behind the magnificent-looking Negro who during that congress on human rights had been the only one to point out:

"The Germans are also men."

As expected, curious faces were made over my decision to leave the congress early and not to participate in the manifesto which is being drawn up today in Breslau; but the hospitality we have hitherto received continues unabated. It is not only the bath that makes me immediately feel happier in Warsaw. Besides that, I also enjoy being alone—

August 29, 1948

Morning on the banks of the Weichsel, work in progress on both bridges, though it is Sunday; far away one can hear the echo of riveting hammers, the dull thud of pile drivers. A splendid sight: the greenish river, broad and placid between banks of raw earth, red paint on the new girders, above and behind them the blue of an autumn sky—the city, seen now from the other bank, is a silhouette of insane destruction, worse than anything I have so far seen; only a third of it dates from the first air attack, unleashed here almost exactly nine years ago, and from the military conquest; complete destruction—systematic, street by street—came only after the collapse of the Polish uprising, a tragedy full of disaster as well as courage. One can understand why the Poles were doubtful whether to reoccupy the city at all; they did so, however—not the least of their reasons being the very fact that a deliberate attempt had been made to wipe out Warsaw forever.

Arrival of the intellectuals. Why is there always something unquestionably comic about intellectuals en masse?

The mix-up with the car has been discovered: now, while the famous Frenchman is being driven around, we go on foot. But the driver is a great fellow and reports to us for duty as soon as his famous Frenchman has gone off to a banquet or for a little nap. François, my journalist companion, visits ministers and priests; the driver and I wait in a restaurant, drinking schnapps and eating smoked eel; he talks little, but all the same we learn a lot. Above all, it is the feeling of unreality which always lurks like a shadow behind collective sightseeings that drives me into little saloons like this, where I can be among ordinary people. I stuff my badge in my pocket. Not a word against Wiska, our official guide! Wiska is a physician, speaks Polish, Russian, Spanish, English, French, and in my case, where ignorance of foreign languages is credible, a flawless German, which she cordially hates. She is different from most other Polish women and girls, who are blond, often as flaxen-haired as Finnish or Swedish women, and have a remarkably healthy, transparent complexion. Wiska is black as a raven; her eyes are

212

not round as in most of the others, but slitted, and her gaze is sharp and narrow above her strong cheekbones. Tartar blood. Her father was a lawyer; at home every child had a room to itself which nobody could enter without the child's permission, a true sanctum. Within this sanctum she cultivated her own thoughts, which later compelled her to go to Spain; her brother fought in the International Brigade, while she was an army doctor. After the defeat she fled to Paris, where she worked for several years as a gynaecologist, an activity that offers little scope in Poland, where children come into the world without much fuss. Eventually she landed up in Gurs, two years in a concentration camp. Her brother escaped to England, had himself dropped by parachute in his own country, and fought with the Polish partisans. He was not caught, but the Germans knew his name and shot both his parents, aged between sixty and seventy, as a reprisal. Her brother died in battle. Her own husband, who fought with the Allies, was also killed. Wiska returned to Warsaw, the sole survivor of her family and mother of two children, a confirmed Communist. At present she is working on the rehabilitation of the wounded, so that they will come to feel like human beings and not waste away in hospitals; after work she translates scientific books that have not hitherto been available in Polish. On top of all this, Wiska is passionately fond of dancing, and her mazurka, danced with a Mexican in a saloon we go to in the evening, is unforgettable. Her present task: to show us there is no such thing as an Iron Curtain. Her first question each morning: What do you want to see? In the once so beautiful old market place, of whose historic façades only one in ten now remains, I raise a basic question: Warsaw has lost almost all its old historic appearance, and that is more than a mere material loss; on the other hand, one wonders whether there is any sense in building exact historical replicas (like Goethe's house in Frankfurt). The mere mention of this question, which I have not been able to answer even to my own satisfaction, was enough to upset our Wiska. Only an enemy of the state can persist in questioning decisions already made; comments are not desired, they only make you suspect; and criticism would be an act of treason. To some extent one can understand that; there is so much to be done that the people who have to shoulder the work cannot waste time on debating decisions already taken. All the same, one loses one's well-meant desire to ask questions, to speak one's thoughts, and the silence grows, the curtain begins to appear. Either you praise, or you keep silent: there is no other way. And so mistrust is sown. Wiska certainly has a sense of humor; but when others show humor also, she immediately suspects even that. A pity. It is unfruitful.

August 30, 1948

Alone in the city.

The impression of a destruction past recall, which had dominated the first two days of my visit here, is beginning gradually to change. Over an excellent coffee, which I am just now drinking, I get the feeling that this could be a good place to live and work in. The people no longer seem, as they did on first impact, to be condemned persons; on the contrary, their faces are happy and alert, much happier than in my own native city. The former main streets look lively and gay, although the houses that should in fact form these streets are not there, either not at all or only as virtually complete ruins; but what lies above eye level seems of lesser significance: one sees shopwindows, swarms of pedestrians, streetcars, automobiles, mainly of elderly vintage, stalls of fruit and flowers. Above all, one sees unmistakably that a beginning has been made, a huge amount of work has already been done, areas cleared of debris; the air is full of noise and dust, but it is also full of the future, once one has learned at last to see the past as past.

Warsaw had a population of one million three hundred thousand. Today it is six hundred thousand—that is to say, less than a half. The severest shortage is housing.

Supper with a young Pole, whose address we had been given, and his sister. Dancing included. The restaurant is underground. A youngish man, somewhat drunk, sees we are foreigners and comes over. Naturally I cannot understand a word; he curses and rages, but not against us. Gestures of shooting, gestures of hanging. His friends seize him bodily and carry him out, so that he will not go on talking when the music stops—

"What did he say?"

"*Pas maintenant,*" replies our Pole.

"Please," the sister says in English. "Come—"

She means to the dance floor; forced to it by this little incident, I find it easy after all, and we go on dancing for hours.

August 31, 1948

A stop in the old city to rest, and it is as if you were the only person left on earth, the last. Grass growing in the alleys, elderberries already sprouting through the empty windows, and when I plod up the hills of rubble to look around, pigeons fly up. What am I looking for? One knows it all already. Weeds on the cellar vaults, rubble, moss on the steps, puddles, weathering, crumbling, rust, façades like empty masks, it is all no different from Berlin, Munich, Frankfurt, Hamburg. But this city had been the first of them. This is where the decisive bombs fell: the first, nine years ago today. A nun in a white coif walks by, a child at either hand, one does not know from where they came or where they are going. Silence: one might be either dead or stone deaf. Everywhere a silence as unrevealing as before an excavation. History as the consciousness of the living. This is where the Polish rebellion of accursed memory was stamped out in blood and ashes, here the fighting continued till all hope was lost, the last fighters escaped through the sewers, the wounded were left behind, the wounded were shot dead. And now one is standing there oneself, hands in pockets, and one faces the same choice as everywhere: whether to bear witness to those who were silenced, or to be silent oneself. I hear a whistle, the chuff of a little locomotive; from a sleep-enchanted street comes a train with a line of clattering wagons, all loaded with rubble, and disappears into another sleep-enchanted alley. Slowly the pigeons return.

September 1, 1948

Conversation with our Swiss envoy. How refreshing to be able to say what one thinks, impulsively and without reserve, and to know that the other is doing the same, never mind whether one agrees with him or not.

I had already visited the ghetto on my first day. There is now nothing of it left to be seen. Its history, which I have been investigating for a year in connection with my new play, I know from the official report of the officer, Josef Stroop, who carried out its destruction. The statements of a Polish eyewitness whom I today discovered, and the numerous photographs taken by Germans, confirm the details of that report, which, beneath a tasteful heading in hand-painted Gothic letters, first pays tribute to the impeccable cooperation of the Wehrmacht and then goes on to describe how, through the tireless efforts of all concerned working in a spirit of loyal comradeship, they succeeded in destroying a total of 56,065 Jews resisting transportation to the gas chambers (March and April 1943).

In the evening a gala reception by the Polish head of state, though I did not see him. I had left my black shoes in Breslau. Huge staircases and endless carpets, wine-red, at every double door two soldiers are posted; they salute. What should I do? Naturally nothing; just keep on walking along the lovely soft carpets until I come to the next double doors and am again saluted. I am not used to such things. A playwright, says François, must get to know everything—halls, people, chandeliers, dress suits, music, evening gowns, mayonnaise, languages, slivovitz, parquet flooring, caviar. . . . That previous acquaintance of mine who feels unable to talk about culture with people like Gide is now urgently desirous of doing so with me. He has already been drinking, and so he too prefers to relapse into German. The tables could again be by Rubens. We misunderstood each other in Breslau, he feels, and he is unhappy about it. There is dancing later. The Poles, both male and female, are magnificent. But the acquaintance will not leave me in peace; with the black coffee he turns up again. Living in Berlin, he says, one can bear no more. His eyes are swimming. Again we are standing in a corner, cups in hand. I must try to understand him, he says, a man in his position, what else can he do? People with convictions should not drink, otherwise their convictions slip out of place, like a mask when one sweats. . . . The young

Mexican painter, who crossed the ocean dressed only in a wind-breaker, has bought himself a European shirt for the occasion. He is quite aware that in the evening it is usual to wear a white shirt and a tie to go with it; but this bright-green one suits his earth-colored Aztec face splendidly. A pity we have no common language. Every time we meet he nods with shining eyes, silent, fraternal to all. His face has something magnificently innocent about it, something unfathomed, an uncramped confidence. I cannot help feasting my eyes on him as he sits there in his open windbreaker, his bright-green shirt, silently smiling, content, always pleased— What about? . . .

A man with convictions finds an answer for everything. Convictions are the best form of protection against the living truth.

A meeting of architects among ourselves. Ostrowski explains the overall plan. Tomorrow and the next day are to be spent on building sites, some of which I have already visited on my own. What happens to the debris? Part of it they use as building material, a sort of brick of compressed rubble, and some is used to reinforce the banks of the Weichsel, where there are soft patches, marsh, danger of flooding. There are also places in the city to be banked up: the new streets and parks will be at a higher level than before, particularly where there are public gardens and high-rise buildings, which need strong and deep rather than broad foundations; somewhat like pile dwellings.

"How much debris is there in Warsaw?" I ask.

"Twenty thousand cubic meters."

"That s nothing," says a German voice. "Berlin has—"

A number of the young Poles engaged in the reconstruction work had studied in Switzerland, where they had been interned. So they had the same teachers as I. Everyone shows pictures of his own work. Cocktails in a studio. A Belgian architect shows factories; a young Mexican shows a fairy-tale skyscraper, a theater, a science institute; an Englishman describes a new town for miners; by comparison, my swimming pool is modest, but it also arouses interest. Expertise revealing itself for once as a blessing; we meet on the same level, at least while asking questions; the discussion has substance.

September 2, 1948

A woman interpreter from Geneva has just been saying that she tried yesterday evening to visit the ghetto, but was stopped by two policemen. Why? It was dusk. But what was there to steal anyway? She found out only after much talk: the memorial standing in that wasteland of death is even today not safe from anti-Semitic daubings. She herself is Jewish.

When one talks of peace, what does one mean? What is usually meant is only the respite achieved by the destruction of an enemy. An American peace or a Russian peace. I favor neither the one nor the other, but peace meaning nonwar. If we want to be honest about the words we use, we have every reason to doubt whether peace is a respectable word at all, a word that means something within the bounds of possibility. And what has so far proved impossible, what has never yet been achieved—why should our own generation in particular, which is not exactly a model of moral purpose, succeed with it? The only special thing about our own present generation, the thing that distinguished it from all foregoing generations, is its basic position: no earlier time has possessed the technical means of carrying out total destruction; war has always until now been an incomplete act of murder within a limited area—even in the great religious wars, so-called, it invariably petered out before God succeeded in demolishing the heretical party completely. There was no lack of mad desire, but people did not have the technical means. Now, however, there are means enough to satisfy everybody. That is the new, the decisive point about our position. Our century can no longer wage war without standing in danger of wiping itself out. The question whether peace in its real sense, peace with the opponent, is possible at all is becoming more and more a question of whether human existence as a whole is possible at all.

September 3, 1948

Professional commitments prevent my accepting a generous invitation to tour the whole of Poland. I am already dreaming about my site overseer!

Reconstruction.

Of vital importance is of course the law, passed immediately after the war ended, making all land in Warsaw state property. And what indeed could the individual landowner do with his piles of rubble if the community did not intervene to provide the streets for them, the sewage, the light, the water, the transport? *Tabula rasa*—with the abolition of private ownership the precondition for genuine town planning is achieved. For the first time ever modern town planning has been given a real chance, after having been taught everywhere for whole decades past. The modern doctrine of town planning arose out of the stone jungles of the nineteenth century, which destroyed the old faces of so many towns without giving them new ones. The doctrine, everywhere recognized as valid, was, however, helpless in the face of vested interests, a game of patience played by men in chains, who knew after years of study exactly what needed to be done to restore our cities, yet saw their knowledge condemned to remain an academic dream, their activities confined to a patient process of respectable patchwork, a lost battle against property rights. Warsaw has been given a free hand. To judge by the designs, the basic provisions of which have already been worked out, there is every hope that this unique chance of building a city of our century will be grasped and effected. The danger of all planning—uniformity, a lack of individuality —should, incidentally, be minimal; each of the larger projects, especially the state ones, will be thrown open to competition, so the city will not be built by a state department but will bear the hallmarks of many individual architects. Among these are many who are still young, many who spent the war years abroad, in France, in England, or in Switzerland. Their architectural outlook, by no means alien to ours, is modern in the sense that the contemporaneity of their task and the contemporaneity of their materials are not susceptible to borrowed ideas, but invite their own solutions, a clear and unencumbered expression of their own inherent properties. With it they show much imagination, in most cases a human scale of values, much feeling for cubic rhythms. It is to be hoped it will all turn out as the models show it now! A colleague who conducted me over the shell of a new ministry building is himself not ecstatic that ministries are being built before hospitals are provided; unfortunately the state has taken over not only the land but also the bad habits of its former owners. But, as I said, the planning is exhilarating. The state has made it possible, but has not yet carried it through; if the authorities become selfish, the whole thing can be spoiled at any time. Most exhilarating of all is the pride of the people working on it, this awareness of a whole generation that they are building their own capital city. It is worth giving one's all for it; there are few experts, and the amount to be done is colossal, yet all are borne along by the unspoken feeling that their creations will go down in history; the streets they are designing will influence the work and life of people yet unborn. And so each of them, quite without personal vanity, has something of that healthy self-confidence of the early pioneers—

Wiska takes leave of us, since she has to return to her professional duties; very friendly, although in her eyes we must undoubtedly belong among those whom it had not been worthwhile inviting here.

Final evening, in some saloon or other. Couples dancing, cheerful, in between eating smoked fish, bread and butter, and gherkins, and drinking schnapps. Three men, very down at heel, playing piano, violin, flute. A single pair dancing a mazurka, indescribably beautiful, she with flowing hair, blissful, an enjoyment free of euphoria, childlike. What an astonishing flair for bodily expression they possess, what expertness in love play, unprudish, yet never sordid! A gracefulness on both sides which, because it is quite general in application, never looks as if it were stripping bare. One feels the strength within them, not a brutish thing, but young, a direct, unquestioning delight in living, in dancing, eating, chatting, or singing. And not only in their leisure hours. In the streets too, during the day, their faces are happier than ours at home, opener, livelier, more lovable, more loving. The dancing by night, the bridgebuilding by day, between them there is no dividing line; behind everything that human sagacity devises and provides or destroys there is something preternaturally blind which no destruction can deter, an unquestioning will to live, which needs no justification, which blossoms of its own accord. In strange cities one often gets the sudden feeling that all these many unknown people are a single being, an entity that the death of individuals can wound but not kill; new towns rise up, new crusts replace the old that have been destroyed, and the desire to live adapts to its surroundings whatever their state, it settles in, begins again with bridges, ships, cranes, and, as long as there are no houses, goes dancing in cellars as here. We overrate our cities by regarding them as the vessels of our lives. Life can only end when the earth grows cold or when the light of Eros is extinguished.

Letzigraben

Samples of glass, samples of plaster, samples of ashtrays, samples of fittings, samples of coatings, all waiting for a decision, and things decided long ago are now arriving daily. Today it is the fitter with the railings for the pavilion, all in tangible form, just as you designed it, pitiless; whether you like it or not, there it is, and no amount of second thoughts, however good, can now change it. How easy it is to pass judgment on a finished object! Even when it pleases you there is something antagonizing, almost frightening, about it; it is iron and stone, final, and there is nothing more you can do about it. But often too a feeling of liberation. The original conception, forgotten perhaps in the work of years, returns here and there to view. The startling feeling: this is your work, seen from the outside. It is your face —and you are completely powerless to disguise that face:

The fitter arrives with your railing.
The painter is spreading your paint.
The plumber is soldering your design.
Etc.

Postscript to the journey

Possibly the strongest impression of our whole Polish journey, stemming particularly from the speeches in Breslau, was the feeling, hard to pin down in detail, that the tension between East and West (to make use for once of that oversimplifying formula) is not first and foremost a conflict between two social systems. Among the speakers were Germans, Englishmen, and

Americans who expressed enthusiastic and unconditional approval of the Eastern system; the audience, which was of course mainly a Slavic one, was gratified by these speeches, but did not show the same sympathy as when the speaker was a colored person, a Negro from America, a Madagascan, a young man from Indonesia. The names of comrades mentioned in the speeches aroused no reaction when they were German, English, American, or even French names; but all other names, Slav, Argentinian, Mexican, Spanish, brought storms of applause. A sympathizer from Vienna, whose sensible differentiations impressed me, reaped only sparse and very uncertain applause, although his conclusions were completely in line. The same with Anna Seghers, who humbly declared that she had come in order to learn; the only sign of approval she received was when she mentioned the name of Neruda. It was hardly any different with the Americans, whose castigation of the criminal conditions in their own country was of course always sure of applause; but their total identification with the Eastern system was received rather as the oath of a renegade is received: with satisfaction, but also with reserve, for after all he is still one of them—valuable because he curses his own people, but that is about all. And in fact it was the colored people who spoke best—at least while I was in the hall; spoke not only the best French and the best English, as my knowledgeable companion asserted, but also best in the sense that what they said was vital and real. Their aim in testifying against the injustice meted out to their races—an injustice contrary to all the large talk of freedom and human rights—is an undeniably worthy one, and they were perhaps the only people present who really wanted nothing more than they said: they were genuine people, not just political chess players. In their case one could really feel that their journey across the ocean had been worthwhile; one had not already read what they had to say a thousand times before in the newspapers. At the same time one felt sorry for them; did the frenetic applause each of them reaped really express concern for the oppressed? For minutes on end the whole audience stood on its feet, delighted with all this weighty evidence against the Americans, the British, the bosses of the world generally. The standing ovation continued long after one Negro speaker had sat down, quite close to us; smiling, animated, solitary, he returned to his breast pocket the curt message he had brought across the ocean, but with an embarrassed shake of his head declined to rise again and acknowledge the applause. Did he perhaps suspect that they were not really thinking of the same thing? An Englishman ventured to remind his audience that there were enslaved people in other continents, transgressions of human rights to be fought against in other camps as well. As if anyone cared about human rights! Intellectuals are often reproached with being naïve; thank God, it is not the naïve the devil finds it easiest to get through to. But what is the real issue? It is concerned not primarily with social revolution, but with a change in the world leadership; it is a revolt of people who, because of the contempt the ruling nations have shown toward them, feel themselves to be a single family. Rise up against the whites! The whites being: the Anglo-Saxons, the Germans, who have screwed racial contempt up to the point of systematically exterminating whole nations, the French, who have been admired and envied long enough as the intellectual center of the world, the Scandinavians for the economic role they play on the high seas, less so the Italians. A revolt of peoples; but the driving force is not the revolutionary device that is printed on the flags: even under another flag the threat would still remain.

The systematic exterminations that in Poland, where the Slav spirit had most closely intermingled with the West, had taken on the character of a veritable industry, only to become if possible even more brutal as they moved east—these have turned out to be a catastrophic burden not only for Germany, but for the whole of Europe as well.

Additionally, one often has the feeling that the nations that survive the bloodshed of another war will on no account be the nations of our European West—

Actors

The vital difference between an actor and any other artist, so it seems to me, is that the actor has no other instrument beyond himself, his own physical form. . . . A painter, a sculptor, a writer, a musician—I do not suggest that these are any less obsessed with themselves (we are all of us vain). But when in company with others they are not primarily painters, writers, musicians, but just people. They come without brushes, chisels, typewriters, pianos—that is to say, without their instruments. The actor, whether he will or not, cannot leave his instrument at home. A sculptor tells us what he thinks of flying or of love; we listen. But when an actor does the same, we look. And he knows we are looking. If that writer over there proves to be a stutterer, it is no reflection on his writing; but if an actor cannot move well, cannot bring to life the anecdote he is telling, how can we believe in his acting abilities? Thus—except perhaps if the house were to fall down—the actor can never wholly escape his talent; his shell is his curse, that being his effect on others, which first astonishes and then eventually, the more he inevitably dominates the company by means of his inseparable powers, bores. The musician too could dominate us—but only if he brought his orchestra with him.

Actors, we are told, can speak only of the theater. This is correct: of the theater, not about the theater. Usually they speak of people, whom they either love or hate, or of roles, in the way a woman speaks maybe of a new coat. Basically, however—and this is why they quickly establish contact and then gradually lose it—they always speak of themselves; to them the theater is always their new coat.

It is no accident that I am speaking here about actors and not actresses: it is among the men that the player's vanity about his physical appearance is most noticeable. A woman is theatrical by nature. If, in addition, she has a talent that might even allow her to make a profession of acting, a woman does not in consequence become unconvincing, but simply more feminine. Or to put it another way: the more feminine she is, the more I can believe in her as an actress. The theater, as one well knows, is completely erotic, but in a feminine way, and the fact that the men in it are so often given to sexual perversions or have to accept them in order to get on is likewise well known, and it is not an incidental but a significant factor. Why is it that an actor, a male one, unless he is outstanding and therefore beyond the reach of comparison, becomes an embarrassment after he attains a certain age? An elderly craftsman may perhaps be slow and clumsy, but he is never embarrassing. We feel sorry for the actor. He, of course, notices it himself and feels the urge to try his hand at directing; he is relieved when there are children around to bear witness to his manliness; now and again, half in fun, he dreams of taking an ordinary job; he loves to go on stage dressed in a black suit and to read poems, and more and more he tends to prefer working on the radio—where he also does not need to wear a costume.

Contramasculinity: the apparent selflessness of the female, who allows every man who comes her way to shape her; her lack of resistance, her limitlessness, that softness and pliancy which basically never take seriously the shape the man gives her. She is always capable of being molded to new shapes: this is what a man describes as the harlot in her, a basic element of the female character that he can never fathom. One might also call it playacting. Playing at being somebody different, at dressing up. When a man wraps himself in a costume, is he not in fact taking a step in the direction of perversion, femininity, contramasculinity?

There is no art without Eros. There is eroticism in its widest sense in the very urge to live and the urge to demonstrate one's existence. Acting and dancing—that is to say, representation by means of the body—these are surely the most direct ways of giving shape to this urge, seen most clearly and in its least translated form in natural eroticism, which likewise expresses itself through the body and through the voice. Other artists, who are obeying the same urge to demonstrate their existence, do so more indirectly; they do it on paper or on canvas or stone; they are obliged to translate it, in a way that, though it does not hinder, does make more difficult that insidious mingling of an artistic with a natural urge; they transfer it outside their own physical being; they sublimate it—because, besides the erotic urge to demonstrate their existence, they are equally dominated by another urge: the intellectual one—the urge to know.

An actor can perhaps be stupid and great at the same time; a writer, I fear, cannot combine the two.

In this connection it is not surprising that the intellectual urge plays only a minor role among actors; in fact it is actively despised. The worst thing they can say, about a director for instance, is that he is literary. By that they mean bloodless, inartistic. And the contempt they are thereby expressing often has a touch of hate in it, they are merciless as only people who feel insulted can be. What has happened? Often the director has only made the mistake of not falling in love with them; a real mistake. What does one expect of an actor to whom one has not shown a personal sympathy? Statements of an impartial kind—well, yes, they will be listened to, maybe even understood; but they will never convince. Actors are not carpenters (meaning no reflection on carpenters!). Actors can only be led if you arouse in them the desire to please you personally. The erotic desire. That is usually the only aerial they have, a wonderful one certainly, a lively and extremely sensitive one, but it is grounded in their private selves—which is the reason why the atmosphere around them as they work is seldom the cool and impartial atmosphere of a workshop; it is and remains the atmosphere of a boudoir.

One must fall in love with them!

Otherwise they are unbearable.

The moment an actor takes off his make-up he is waiting for your praise. Praise him whatever happens—leave your criticisms for the day after tomorrow! Criticism at the moment he comes from the stage is just cruel. The actor, unlike other artists, is at one with his work, and in a completely physical sense. He cannot tear out his failures, crumple them up, and throw them away; his work, successful or unsuccessful, sticks to him. Nothing is easier to understand than his greed to know at once how he was this evening. He cannot see his own work. That in itself is monstrous. Dependent as he is on the views of those who have seen it, our silence can destroy him. The actor is something like a painter who has become blind. Even when things have gone right and we are sitting together after a performance, genuinely pleased, I am always conscious of a feeling of melancholy; the intoxication dies, and his work lives on only in our memory. It is a soft wax; he himself can wipe it all out within a month.

Something may still linger for years, even decades; but where? He cannot take it out of a folder or see it again in a gallery. His gallery is people; his touching delight in meeting old acquaintances, colleagues, or members of the audience, in hearing where old So-and-so is now and what old What's-his-name is doing, in telling about the occasion when he made his first appearance as Mortimer, in hearing that a former female lead has now got married for the fifth time—all these conversations, which seem mere gossip to us, so boring after a while—it is all so easy to understand when one sees that what he is really doing is looking for traces of his work, for people who once saw it. . . .

Why are there so many great actresses, so few great woman writers? . . . The erotic urge that lies at the bottom of all art has a feminine and a masculine character. Feminine is the urge to be; masculine the urge to do. Interpretative art always has more of the feminine about it.

A male actor who one day ceases to appear on stage gives the impression of having failed in his career—not so the actress who one day decides she has had enough and leaves to devote her time to her children. For him it was a profession; she talks of her roles as if they were honeymoons. . . .

Social contempt for actors even in centuries of great theater: deriving, in part at least, from an instinctive uneasiness toward the unmanly nature of all acting, aggravated by the fact that men were obliged to play the female roles as well. It might be worth investigating to what extent the actress has been responsible for the fact that the barrier, if not entirely lifted, is now less rigid. That people feel differently about actors and actresses can be seen in the reaction of any postman, landlady, or gasman: for them an actor is always a second-rate person unless, through long acquaintance with him perhaps, they have learned better, or have previously been influenced by his fame, a picture in the newspaper. An actor, *but* a nice fellow! An actress they find easier to accept, even if she is a bitch.

I do not share the general fear that the theater is being usurped by the film. For several reasons, one of them being the actor's essential quality, that erotic quality which can never find its full outlet in films. The erotic urge to live and to demonstrate one's existence will always call for the physical participation of an audience. Filming an actor—whose image we can then see at any time, perhaps when he himself is lying in bed—might add to his purse and to his fame, but it cannot replace the moment when he plays on the stage and is seen doing so—neither for him nor for us. If the theater dies, Eros will die with it.

Frankfurt, November 1948

Meeting with Thornton Wilder, the man who reawoke my youthful love for the theater after it had lain dormant for a full decade—and that to such a degree that I shall probably remain enslaved to it for the rest of my life . . . Peter Suhrkamp, introducing us, does not neglect to mention that I come from Zurich (where Wilder, incidentally, wrote *Our Town*) and am also occupied in writing plays.

"Oh," says Wilder, "dialect plays?"

Trial shots are not of course meant to be on target. We sit down to lunch. A young man from Hamburg is also there. Rather bashfully I nibble a roll; what will the man I have so long admired have to say? A gentleman, his kindness, wit, compendious knowledge, cordiality, graceful conversation, openness, a man of the world with the sparkling eyes of a child, a humanist, the wit and the brilliance chastely disguising a core of pure earnestness, an American, therefore very direct, a puritan, therefore very courteous—and all the other things I imagine one lauds Wilder for. At the moment we are just eating our soup. I am full to bursting with the desire to get to know one of the world's teachers, greedily silent. Then, perhaps because my bashfulness is all too apparent, the man from Hamburg says to me:

"You know, what really surprises me is that as a creative person (brr!) you can work at all in your narrow-minded Switzerland—"

What now?

(The son of a night watchman spends a thousand days of his earthly existence telling his neighbors that his father, whom one so seldom sees by day, is not a chicken thief, as they always maintain, but a night watchman. And it is true chickens are always being stolen, so the child has no easy task. How praiseworthy, people say, that as the child of a chicken thief you are not a chicken thief yourself! After a thousand days of this the boy has had enough, leaves home in order to get to know people other than these tiresome neighbors, and makes a pilgrimage to a sage whom he has long admired. Oh, yes, he finds him all right, makes a bow and waits in silence, until one of those very neighbors comes along and says: How praiseworthy that as the child of a chicken thief you are not a chicken thief yourself! The poor boy replies: My father is not a chicken thief. He has to say it, it has to be said, though God knows, he is sick enough of the sound of it. Says the polite neighbor: I do not know your father, it is just that people say he is a chicken thief. Says the boy: You worry about your own chicken thieves. For it is irritating—after all, he has come here to listen to the sage. But what does the sage do? He is surprised, having obviously missed the beginning of this unedifying conversation, and obviously did not expect others to start talking before he did; he is surprised to hear the night watchman's son say something so rude as: You worry about your own chicken thieves! Says the polite neighbor: I acknowledge you of course as an honorable exception. Says the boy: I can do without your acknowledgment, thank you. It is true, says the other, we do have chicken thieves of our own. Says the boy: We all know that. It is just, the neighbor says, that with us chicken thieves are the exception rather than the rule. Says the boy: We have been talking about that for a thousand days and more. Oh, says the other, how can you talk about it at all when you have never known starvation? Says the boy: Your starvation is no excuse for abusing my father. Only people who have known what it is to starve, says the other, only they . . . Meanwhile, a valuable hour having been lost in this way, the sage wipes his speechless mouth, truly unused to taking part in a long scene in which he has nothing to say besides the puritanical interjection:

"Very interesting."

It is only when he is outside that Wilder says, shaking the head that in one hour might have imparted so many precious things:

"This young man—no . . . !

He means of course the night watchman's son, who has spent a thousand days plus this one hour in being as vexed as it is possible to be vexed. A rocket cannot be reignited after it has fallen in the water, as the boy well knows. . . . How right you are! says the other now, and suddenly wipes away a completely unbidden tear: We are all chicken thieves, all of us—)

That was my meeting with Thornton Wilder.

Arabesque

"I don't know," said Don Juan, after a passionate argument in which he had been a casual listener, "I don't know what you have against the church. In a city that shall be nameless I once had a sweetheart, one of my first, a very young girl, who taught me more about love than anyone before. She was so uninhibited, so wild, so innocent that one really forgot all sense of shame, an artist of incomparable talent. I have seldom seen a person who could live so physically, who was so at one with her feelings as she. . . . No need to say anything more about that," he added, helping himself to a cigarette. "But then, when I was already slumbering, she woke me up: she was horrified, truly horrified, that I had not said my prayers before going to sleep. Do you never? she asked. Never? But one must, one really must! . . . And you don't go to confession either?"

Hamburg, November 1948

What is meant by culture (one of the great and urgent questions which, though always in my thoughts, very soon brings me to the limit of my capacities)—culture, art, politics . . . At any rate, one thing is clear: culture cannot be reduced in meaning simply to art; a nation has no right to think itself cultured just because it possesses a few symphonies.

As our generation, born in this century but brought up in the spirit of the last, has learned only too well, particularly in the Second World War, people imbued with this sort of culture, connoisseurs who can converse intelligently and reverently about

Bach, Handel, Mozart, Beethoven, and Bruckner, can equally well turn out to be butchers; both beneath the same skin. The sort of attitude that marks out this type of person we might define as "aesthetic culture." Its hallmark, always clearly visible, is detachment: it sets a clear dividing line between culture and politics—or between talent and character, between reading and living, between the concert hall and the street. It is a mental outlook that allows its possessors to think the highest thoughts (for to make the balloon rise they simply throw earthly gravity overboard), but does not prevent the lowest; it is a culture that strictly ignores present obligations and places itself entirely at the service of eternity. Culture in this sense is a false deity which, while apparently content with our artistic or scientific offerings, drinks the blood of our brothers behind our backs. Culture as a form of moral schizophrenia—and this, in our era, is in fact its usual form. How frequently, when we start talking about Germany, does someone come up with the names of Goethe, Stifter, Hölderlin, and all the rest, always with the suggestion of genius as an alibi—

People with the same education as my own, speaking the same words that I do, loving the same books, the same music, the same paintings, are by no means immune from the danger of turning into monsters and doing things we would not have thought possible among the people of our own day, apart from a few pathological exceptions. If they are not immune, why should I be so confident of my own immunity?

Winston Churchill, in a recent speech about the German conqueror von Rundstedt, offered the advice that we should be prepared at last to let bygones be bygones. Even if the purpose of such an amnesty is easy to see, the phrase used to describe it sums up most succinctly just what it is that dismays me. It is unfortunately the case that by the time we are ready to be shocked by these "bygones" and to learn from them, they have already been obscured by new misdeeds, and these allow us to forget in our anger—that welcome, feverish anger which is stirred up with such suspicious alacrity—what is cause and what effect. Not only in Germany, but here in Switzerland as well, we like to talk of today as if there had been no yesterday

231

preceding it. Let bygones be bygones! I find this particularly obscene when one invokes Goethe to dress it up, with talk of Faust's creative sleep, the healing powers of oblivion, etc. Only those who have truly taken the lesson to heart are entitled to say that, and only they. Though we may think we know what these "bygones" were—in fact only too well (as we all like to say)—I have met very few people who have really taken their lesson to heart and in such a way that, if it were a classical tragedy, the chorus would come in to cry: Enough! All we say is: So now we know. But when one stands on the place where it happened, one knows that we most certainly do *not* know; our memory does not encompass the inconceivable, and that is just as well. But sometime, I believe, the full horror of it should strike through to us, otherwise there will be no way forward.

What, we say, has art to do with politics? And by politics we do not mean things that concern the polis; the problems of how men, who cannot survive by themselves, can live together; the problems of a social order which initiates a culture or civilization, safeguards it even when it does not basically form it, and even at times destroys it. What we mean by politics is simply low, vulgar, everyday affairs, with which the intellectual person, the glorious cultural ambassador, should not dirty his hands. The cultural ambassador, the cultural creator. It is remarkable how many Germans (particularly Germans) strive so anxiously and unremittingly to be intellectuals; and above all *how* they strive: by talking of literature, of music, of philosophy. And that is all. Remarkable too how frightened they are of being considered philistines; one can hardly meet a German without hearing this word in the very first sentences he speaks. Philistine being understood as meaning the opposite of intellectual. Were they to have seen Gottfried Keller in the street or in his office or even at a shooting contest, I am convinced that most of those who make use of this fatal word would have categorized him as a philistine, as the opposite of an intellectual, of a cultural ambassador, a cultural creator, a being miles removed from the elite. There is in fact, in our ideas on culture, a not insignificant difference between the German attitude and the Swiss, and it is in this area perhaps that the Swiss are most independent from the German mode of thought. The feeling, essential to all nations, of possessing a culture of its own can hardly be said in our case to derive from the fact that we have artists among us; we do not at any rate feel that the talents of a Jeremias Gotthelf (to take just one example) are sufficient excuse for the practice of selling children in his country, a monstrous practice from a social point of view. By culture we mean primarily our democratic achievements, our communal outlook, rather than the artistic or scientific masterpieces of an individual citizen. Even if for the Swiss artist the air of his homeland seems often rather dry, this disadvantage, however much it affects the artist personally, is still only the sorry reverse side of a way of life that, despised by most Germans as philistine, has as a whole our full approval—and precisely for the reason that it is the opposite of that "aesthetic culture" which has led —as was indeed inevitable—to a lethal catastrophe.

"Of course he was a swine," somebody says, "but a person of his talent—you even admit that yourself!—and anyway, I ask you, what has art to do with politics?"

To that there is only one reply:

There is unfortunately no such thing as a human being who practices nothing but art—and if one day, in order to be free to practice his art, he signs something that for instance sends others to the gallows—former friends perhaps, at any rate people who have been no threat to him—then my interest in his talent is only partial, even if he assures me that he does not "on principle" interfere in politics and that he is "only" an artist, a "cultural creator."

A person who does not concern himself with politics has already made the political choice he is so anxious to spare himself: he is serving the ruling party.

In this category belongs also the literary concept of partisanship which, as we are told everywhere, has nothing to do with literature—partisanship as an interpretation of conditions that, since it does not conform to the reader's own interpretation, must be dubbed a "distortion" and therefore cannot be regarded as pure literature—for we regard literature as pure only when we are not conscious of its partisanship as such, when the interpretation, which of course is always present, agrees with our own because it has become ours; then we come to that state of pure enjoyment that arises from the feeling that our own view is the only possible, true, and absolute one. . . .

The unholy fear of being considered a philistine, the misunderstanding inherent in that very fear, the anxious desire to seek refuge in the eternal in order to escape responsibility for what is happening on this earth, the countless unconsidered metaphysical distortions—are these things not more of a danger to culture than all the philistines together?

Letzigraben

Planting trees, all fine, rather large specimens over seven meters tall, which have in consequence to be transplanted with large root clumps: willows of all kinds, maples, planes, ashes and alders, poplars, oaks, acacias, beeches, and a few pines, whose dark tones we need to provide contrasting accents. A delightful job, but unfortunately in the fog the bare stems make a very meager impression, and it is difficult to imagine how it will look in summer, the greenness, denseness, or sparseness of the various trees; I have to rely entirely on my horticultural adviser, who identifies the trees as they arrive, and on my own imagination.

Back to the tree nurseries in the afternoon.

We are confining ourselves at the moment to the basic groups, about four hundred trees and nearly a thousand bushes; the remainder we will then plant in the spring, according to the effect and what remains of our budget; we still need birches and larches.

Café Odeon

Another Italian film that affects us as if we were seeing all these things for the first time. Once again that unabashed courage in using one's own nation to point out human failings. But without the embarrassment of self-castigation. And once again with the result that acknowledgment of these weaknesses, presented without excuse, never for a moment tempts even a foreign audience to look down on this nation—on the contrary in fact: there is no European people that fills us at present with such confidence as Italy. Precisely because it can look at itself with a critical eye. A further impression, which speaks for this film: I am quite convinced that, if fascism had not been precluded through the fortunate circumstance that it came on us as a threat to our sovereignty, we Swiss would also have failed in exactly the same way, if not worse, at any rate in the German-speaking part of Switzerland.

Letzigraben

A wintry morning, the ground covered in hoarfrost, the sun a red ball behind a metallic haze, the brittle branches of our trees, tender and graceful, as if sketched in India ink on silk, gray with a violet shimmer, and beneath our shoes as we cross the brown field a sound as of breaking glass . . .

Next week the première.

I am very happy, or at least I know that one day this period of my life, in which two such different projects are coming to fruition at the same time, will seem to have been happy. Construction workers here, actors there. The reality is the tension between. Best of all will always be the play rehearsals; one is alone with the people who are working on it, and as always the finished product will be rather desolate, uncanny; finished things cease to be a shelter for the spirit; but work in progress is a delight, whatever its nature—now one sees the warm breath of the workingmen, a silver vapor vanishing as it appears. . . .

1949

New Year's Day 1949

A sympathetic atmosphere—how much we depend on that! We realize it as soon as sympathy once enjoyed is withdrawn. Then it is as if we had no air beneath our wings.

Question:

Is this sympathy which gives us the feeling of being able to fly nothing more than an amiable fraud, a considerate abstention from criticism? If so, is not its opposite—a lack of sympathy—a more valid atmosphere to work in, the only really valid one?

Its infectious nature: within a whole group a single sympathetic attitude is enough, and when this is withdrawn, the whole group withdraws it, though the group as such has nothing really to withdraw.

(Those suspicious eyes looking the other way.)

Of course one can shrug one's shoulders, turn to others among whom sympathy is to be found, or win it in new fields—but that does not lessen the shock: how lost one feels when sympathy is withdrawn!

Lost: without a guardian angel.

Sympathy not as abstention from criticism. But: sympathy is patient, with the patience of hope; it does not judge us on a single gesture, which may be unseemly, impertinent, clumsy, vain, inconsiderate, self-satisfied; it always gives us another chance. . . . Not like the person who feels no sympathy for us: he keeps the account straight, gives nothing in advance, is vigilant and just, and that is terrible. Is his view of us the more correct one? He is treating us as Polonius treated the players, according to their deserts. As Hamlet said: God's bodykins, man, much better; use every man after his desert and who shall 'scape whipping?

To look at it from the other side:

When we ourselves feel no sympathy for someone, consider him as jurors, impartially—how untrustworthy, disreputable, moody a person looks when he feels he does not have our approval and has nobody to speak for him but himself!

This feeling of being deprived of air, so that one's voice fails to carry, each word falling to the ground and disintegrating; and, when one takes one's leave, this feeling of having said too much (and indeed every word was too much), the feeling of departing in shreds, of bleeding.

There is an unconscious, unquestioned assumption without which it would be impossible to write a single sentence: the assumption that somewhere, however far away, one is protected by a feeling of sympathy. Is this the beginning of narcissism?

Memories of a French film that depicts how a man (Michel Simon) suddenly loses the sympathy he had enjoyed in his district for years. Though he himself has in no way changed, suspicion suddenly falls on him—or one could just as well say: his guardian angel suddenly deserts him, and now he sees what this means. He sees his luggage, everything he owns, on the street, he sees all his neighbors standing in doorways or gaping through windows: all of them think he is a murderer. Someone trips him up, he tries to defend himself, but nobody comes to his aid; others are playing soccer with his belongings, he is suddenly like a bull in the arena, and they are after his blood; half in fun, yet half in deadly earnest, they drive him up on a roof, from which in the end he falls to his death—

The mystery of hatred.

(Anti-Semitism.)

Account of a friend who has several times been wrongly arrested, a young doctor, a sensitive man with a lively conscience, arrested and led away by four policemen: through a street lined with people who, torn between curiosity and disgust, push forward and recoil at the same time; when he declares that he is a doctor on his way to a patient, the policemen's last doubts vanish, and they are convinced they have caught him at last, the child murderer they were seeking—

Guardian angel: sympathy—we need it at all times. In our childhood we have it, otherwise we should long ago have been run over in the street; we grow up with it, we rely on it—and yet there is only a hair's breadth protecting and dividing us from the monstrous, hopeless situation in which nothing speaks for us, nothing we ourselves can do or say. . . .

Zurich, January 8, 1949

First night in the Schauspielhaus, Zurich: *Als der Krieg zu Ende war*. Director: Kurt Horwitz. Leading roles: Brigitte Horney, Walter Richter, Robert Freitag. Stage settings: Caspar Neher.

A slight scuffle in the foyer.

Letzigraben

With Brecht at the building site. I had to fetch him from his writing desk, as he bade me, since during working hours he does not answer the telephone. As always when he sees the prospect of increasing his factual knowledge, he is at once eager to start. Abandoning the scene in his typewriter in the middle, he puts on his shoes; on the bed lie sketches of stage settings for Berlin. These would interest me, but he wants to see my building—theater can be left for rainy days. Of all the people I have so far shown over a building site Brecht is by far the most rewarding, thirsty for knowledge, a skillful questioner. Experts easily overlook the big, the essential questions; laymen listen, accept answers to questions that they never even thought of; particularly unrewarding are the literary fraternity, who seek refuge from technicalities, even before they have grasped them, in meditation: mood-mongers, shaking the cocktail of their wit or introspection. Brecht has an extraordinary eye, his intelligence is a magnet that attracts problems in such a way that they show even through solutions already made. How a diving-board tower is constructed, for instance, how its architectural form derives from its static purpose; but not just that: also how the form itself must not only serve its purpose but also represent it to the eye—to explain such things to Brecht is a real pleasure, a mutual one. We trudge around for more than two hours, up and down, in and out and around; in addition there is that something that distinguishes, unmistakably, the creative person from the expert—a kinship, the knowledge, born of experience, that in the beginning there is nothing. . . . Experts, when they see a drawing for instance, take it from Dürer or Rembrandt or Picasso onward; the creative being, in whatever sphere he works, is aware of the empty paper behind.

Reviews

Goethe's advice is never to reply to a reviewer, unless he has asserted in his review that one has stolen twelve silver spoons— but modern reviewers hardly go that far. . . . So really there is only one thing left: to keep silent and go on, as long as one still has the urge; to become one's own critic, avoid stealing silver spoons, and to hell with them. But to be grateful when a review, whether favorable or unfavorable, is serious in tone and has the decency not to assume that the author himself has no doubts or misgivings about his work. There are such reviews, more perhaps than our feelings let us acknowledge; a person who passes us the salt at the table is not of any less account than the one who spits in our soup, but the latter gets more of our attention—and unfortunately knows it, even if we don't reply to him.

Nothing easier than to fashion a potato to look like a pear, to take a bite, and then complain in front of everybody that it doesn't taste like a pear, not in the least!

It is usually true that the uneasiness our reviewers feel has some justification somewhere. But where exactly? For many, it seems, the first explanation for their uneasiness that occurs to them is good enough; in their justified uneasiness they feel anything they say is justified, and the more human their uneasiness, the more rooted in personal feelings, all the greater their lust to sniff out artistic deficiencies, all the more unselective too;

one can feel how delighted they are that the third act is wrong —I could not have done them a greater favor.

It is difficult to be a reviewer; besides the technical difficulties inherent in any form of work, which need not be gone into now, I am thinking particularly of the human difficulties. Reviews I myself once wrote as a student I cannot today look at without blushing, though it is less their ignorance that shames me than the general tone; meant to be witty, they are a mixture of impudence and condescension, though at the time, I well remember, I was suffering from an inferiority complex. Reviewing was for me a necessity, a solace, but only for myself. There doubtless are people who feel hurt by imperfection, genuinely hurt, they cannot help losing their temper, banging the table and cursing until the walls shake. That is all right. But most people, the large majority in fact, do not lose their temper; they just become malicious, witty, impudent, condescending. Malicious when they blame; fraternal when they praise—and that is the other thing that annoys me about those student reviews of mine: their ingratiating manner. Nothing is more difficult than to praise. Even the words soon take on a general aspect: they could be used equally well to praise something completely different, or even its complete opposite. It does not necessarily imply begrudgment or carping if a critic avoids writing words of praise; serious praise can hardly in fact be conveyed except indirectly, through the names used in making comparisons, for example, and more especially in the level of the critical approach. Direct praise is rarely convincing, and however fervently someone may say "This is the best poem," he is still saying nothing about the poem, and one finds oneself asking by what right he holds the sword that is delivering the accolade. One cannot quite avoid the feeling, particularly when someone is doling out praise, that he has rather an exaggerated opinion of himself. But above all, looking back years later on those reviews of my own, I realize that in almost all cases I had in fact been praising myself, praising the things that matched my own strivings and sanctified them by success. It was this that I (not infrequently through jumping to conclusions) had been underlining with my words of praise. . . .
It is difficult to be a reviewer.

There are many experts, very estimable experts, but only very few people who have found fulfillment in their lives, and perhaps it is only these who would possess the precious gift of criticism. Not that they would necessarily have done things better themselves—that is a childish argument. Criticism is a talent in itself. But people who have known fulfillment, never mind where or in what sphere they have found it, do not feel a need to protect themselves against all creative things encountered in their own lifetime.

Pointing out artistic flaws is usually, I believe, an evasion. There are very few people whose uneasiness is really based on artistic considerations. This can be seen in the fact that these same people seldom feel the need to bring up artistic questions when the same author's message is pleasant, harmless, or even flattering. The play whose message they find congenial they always label the better play, better by far.

If you want to say uncomfortable things, you ought really to be a consummate artist—so as to give them no way of diverting their anger.

Pointing out artistic flaws.
Somebody tells me that I have committed a grave injustice against my neighbor, and I answer: Sir, you have a gap between your teeth. And, if he has no gap between his teeth, I will perhaps, in order to avoid having to listen to this uncomfortable person, find he has a fly button undone. Sir, I say, your fly is undone. And when he has done the button up? Then I say: Sir, you seem to me to stink of tobacco, and that I cannot bear, it makes me feel sick— And when one day he comes back and no longer stinks of tobacco, has indeed perhaps never stunk of it, and once more starts to speak of my act of injustice? Then I say: Sir, you keep saying the same old things; that is boring, we know it all already. . . .

Praise and blame—
With praise that seems to us misplaced or vapid we do not need to concern ourselves; we can quickly brush it aside, and

that we do. But to brush aside blame because we find it misplaced or vapid, that is not so easy, there is always something suspect about it. Blame sticks.

In certain circumstances one should be able to read: What Mr. What's-his-name is trying to do I feel to be a grave mistake, but nevertheless what he set out to do he has done well. But instead of that one reads: Mr. What's-his-name is incapable of writing a real play. A real play being a play that the critic considers worth trying to do. Reviews of this sort, of which there are not a few about, are not malicious, simply unprofitable.

An actor plays Romeo, and a female reviewer whom it has pleased God to make a Lesbian writes about him in the press. She might write: Mr. Asterisk's Romeo leaves me cold. There is nothing wrong with that. But what in fact she does write is something more impersonal, more unqualified: The Romeo is lacking in masculine appeal—

What I am trying to say: every reviewer has the sacred right to express his feelings. It is our right to recognize them simply as that—not that that is much comfort! But at certain moments —not when one is sure of oneself, but when one is venturesome or desperate—how grateful one would be for a standard of judgment that is unconditional!

The criticism of creative people? Creative people, I think, are particularly prejudiced, but their judgment has one precious advantage: we know from their own work the nature of their particular prejudice, and above all there is always something fraternal about their judgment. It does not force us into a morass of self-justification, as reviewers can so easily do.

Goethe says one should not reply; he does not say one should not listen. Perhaps it is good for us to spend two or three weeks wallowing in our rage, if only for the purpose of showing us the true state of our fancied enlightenment. Really helpful criticism comes from only four or five individuals, among them close friends and complete strangers who have no idea how helpful they have been. Similar in effect to the criticism of creative people is, in my experience, the criticism of intelligent, nonliterary women; it is personal, decided, sisterly. The sort of criticism that helps is that which helps one not to waste time, which encourages self-criticism, the only sort that is of use for future work.

Basel, Shrove Tuesday 1949

Morning tattoo; huge bright lanterns emerge, always rocking slightly, onto the market square; from all the alleys one can hear the drumming of the masked figures: it is like jungle signals, the drumming has something pent up, something stuttering about it, the windowpanes shiver and titter, the air is rent by the monotonous shrilling of pipes. Then all of a sudden there they are, cohorts of superhuman masks, birds, goblins, cabbages, always in groups, each with a slanting pipe between his lips; the whole group moving as one, monstrous on account of its very diversity, its uniformity—the demon seen not as an individual, but as a race . . .

In the evening a masked ball.

The whole affair, justly famed, reminds me of a custom that is said to exist in China: once a year the whole clan comes together and sits down in a circle; everybody stuffs his ears with mud, and then they tell one another the truth, that is to say, they blurt out scandals, they mock, curse, abuse one another until their breath gives out, everyone admitting his adulteries, his underhand dealings, his trickeries, his addictions, his fears, confessing it all at the top of his voice until he is hoarse. Then, when no one has any strength left to go on, they pick the mud out of their ears, smile, bow gracefully, accompany one another home, invite one another to tea, and live together for a further year in a seemly manner, peaceful, courteous, well mannered. . . .

Stuttgart, April 29, 1949

Guest performance of the Zurich Schauspielhaus with *Als der Krieg zu Ende war.* An icy silence at the beginning; we had reckoned on a scandal and are surprised by its absence; discussions with many people, a particularly valuable conversation, unfortunately interrupted, with a young woman who had herself experienced the Russian occupation in a very personal way. But even when he meets with approval a basic question remains for the writer of a historical work when he comes face to face with people who lived through it all. What if a novelist, specializing in the Thirty Years' War for instance, were to be called on to justify himself to the Swedish officers, one of whom he has described, and at the same time to the women of Bohemia, the Spanish royal court, the citizens of the Netherlands, the German peasants, the men broken on the wheel, the starving, the hanged and their hangmen, both of whom had been there and could hardly be expected to agree on the way in which events are described. Basically their question to him would always be the same: what gives the author the right to tell his story? The only answer would be: the right is his by virtue of the fact that he is an author. But what if he were not, or at any rate not a good enough one? Then they would have every right to fly at his throat, these women of Bohemia, Swedish officers, citizens of the Netherlands, Spanish hangmen; and he could not complain. . . .

All-night party.

Early morning in the woods above the city, tree trunks and fresh new green, the first rays of the sun glittering in spiders' webs, birds twittering, the fragrance of buds, grass drenched in dew, the air cool, spring water, bees hovering around blossoming branches, Sunday, the tolling of a distant bell, then the first early walkers who have taken the streetcar up to the heights and politely restrain their surprise at seeing me in my black evening suit and patent-leather shoes, wearing neither coat nor hat; at length someone tells me that the city of Stuttgart, whose guest I may lay claim to be, lies in precisely the opposite direction—

Letzigraben

It is nearly completed. . . . Furniture, curtains, flowers, inscriptions, goldfish: everywhere the finishing touches are being added to the decorations. The people who have the job of carrying them out are in lively spirits: jokes, both good and bad. The janitor's wife wants window boxes on the sills. She shall have them. Today, for technical reasons, I gave orders that the big flag should be hoisted for the first time—it is still there, fluttering in the light breeze, and children from the neighborhood are crowding around the shallow fountain, whose jet I find rather too thin. After work, when our own workers mount their bicycles to ride off home with their empty food sacks, others come along from the factories, stop on the curb, and press their noses to the wire fence. It is all rather like a big charity occasion. Gardeners are watering the freshly planted flowers.

Story

Somebody tells a story that is said to have really happened in the vicinity of Stuttgart. On a small farm there lived a woman whose husband was taken prisoner by the Russians as a young soldier in the First World War. Many years later she still believed he would return, and so she was considered insane; neighbors told how she still kept fresh linen on his bed and, though she had received no news at all from him, was convinced he was still alive; ten, even twenty years after the First World War ended she could still not be persuaded otherwise. Then came the Second World War. The woman survived it. In all matters not concerned with her missing husband she seemed completely sane. Not even the Second World War could rid her of her unspoken delusion, evident only in her behavior, that one day her husband would return. Hundreds of thousands of women were now once again waiting, with or without hope, for the return of their husbands from Russia. Among the first who in fact did return was a very old man whom the neighbors, when he addressed them, recognized to be the husband of this insane woman; he inquired whether his wife was still alive and was told that she had never believed in his death. Only after he had made these inquiries did he venture to approach the house. The neighbors waited until the following morning before going along to see how the woman had coped with this improbable happening. They found her completely calm, unchanged, and it was apparent that she knew nothing of the man who had arrived the previous day. She did not believe a word of what her neighbors told her until subsequent investigations revealed that they had not been making a fool of her. But neither had she been deluded in believing for twenty-eight years that her husband would return: his body was found in the manure pit beside the back entrance.

Letzigraben

Today, Saturday, June 18, the pool was opened to the public. Sunny weather and a great many customers. They are swimming, diving from the springboards. The lawns are full of bodies, some of them bare, some brightly clad, and it is all rather like a genuine festival; a few elderly folk, who of course do not go in the water, stand admiring the many flowers, and the pavilion on the gallows hill, with its blue-and-white curtains, is being besieged. Everything, being unused, is still being treated like a new toy; only the children are splashing about as if it had always been there.

The pool complex, built by the city of Zurich, cost four and a half million francs. It can cater to four thousand two hundred people at a time and has three large basins, for swimmers, non-swimmers, and sporting events, the water being constantly purified by a filter. The complex, the second of its kind to be built by the city, is situated in a district inhabited mainly by workers and employees. It took two years to build. My work on it occupied me for four years.

Café Odeon

A friend, a much-respected one, writes:

"I cannot deny that I consider this forcible attempt to keep wounds open, to which you like so many others apparently feel in duty bound, to be a mistake."

What I consider to be a mistake: to bandage wounds that are full of pus (and they are still full of pus), to forget things that have not yet been exposed, not been understood or overcome—and therefore are not yet past.

But are there so very many on my side?

En route

Apes in the zoo— My impression: they squat on the borderline where boredom begins. All of a sudden they stop, look up at the sky, for a moment showing all the melancholy that distinguishes the human being; but apes cannot go to concerts, to the theater, they cannot yet turn it into art, they delouse themselves, they have not enough reasoning power for science, they play with nuts or with their sex—more is not yet in their reach. But at least they can play. Salamanders do not play; they just lie on their bellies, breathe, and digest; they have not the least idea what boredom is. A man of intelligence, it is sometimes said, cannot be bored. But intelligence is the precondition of boredom! I have recently been reading again about the Greek gods: how bored they all are! They incite others to murder and war just in order to keep themselves amused in their immortality. . . . The gods, unthreatened by an ending, and the salamanders, lying on their bellies breathing—I should not want to change places with either. Our awareness of our mortality is a priceless gift—not mortality itself, which we share with the salamanders, but our awareness of it; it is this that makes us human, turns our existence into an adventure, and preserves us from the total boredom of the gods. . . . Today our six-year-old daughter Ursel asked me in the middle of a game whether I should enjoy dying.

"All people must die," I reply from behind my newspaper, "but nobody enjoys dying."

She considers a while.

"I shall enjoy dying."

"Now?" I say. "Really and truly?"

"Not now, no, not now—"

I lower my paper a little to look at her. She is sitting at the table, mixing water colors.

"But later," she says, painting in silent pleasure, "later I shall enjoy dying."

Kampen (Sylt), July 1949

At last a workroom exactly as one would wish it to be: large and light, comfortable in a sober way, two windows overlooking the mud flats, plenty of room to move, tables on which to spread out papers, drafts old and new, letters and books, sea shells and starfish, chains of dry seaweed—I have already spent three weeks in this nice house—and outside the wind is whistling, the rain drumming on the windowpanes, which quiver as the wind strikes them, clouds scudding across the boundless sky. One sits and watches, dependent wholly on one's own devices. Now and again I swallow a Steinhäger or two; one needs that with so much empty sky. Or I take up the binoculars which are lying on the sill, looking to see whether anyone is trudging across the heath, a postman, some other human being. The clumps of reddish grass tossing in the wind have the fleeting permanence of flames; the whole slope seems ablaze. An occasional British fighter jet howls across the island. Plenty of space. One can feel the space even when one is not looking out on it; when reading or sitting at the typewriter or standing at the little desk, as I am doing now, it does not stop, this whistling of the wind, one still has the feeling of being on the edge of the world. A fruitful feeling; it makes many things easier. Not for a moment yet have I felt boredom. What I can see of the works of man: six houses, scattered wide apart across the distances, each alone, crouched beneath its hood of mouse-colored reeds. Far away one can see the Hindenburg dam to the mainland. And a lighthouse, of course; an inverted clock: the hands standing still, the clouds flying past. My diversion I find, when not in work, in the ebb and flow of the tide; the mud flats covered for a while by gleaming, foaming waves, then once again a waste of slime, gulls stalking through reflecting puddles, such flocks of them that it looks like a field of white narcissuses. A fishing boat lies with slanting mast on the blackish mud, waiting for the next tide. Along the shore a girl with trailing hair rides past on a horse.

Mail:
Two friends, experienced men of letters and of the theater, write to me on this island to give their opinion of my new play (*Graf Öderland*), now in the process of being written. One finds it at any rate better than the earlier plays, although he would like this and that done to it; the other finds it at any rate weaker than the earlier plays. Which is right? Both letters are sensible, objective, understanding. Encouraging me to con-

tinue, encouraging me to give up. So which should I follow? Both together display the wisdom of the oracle, which basically always gives the same advice, the only possible advice, which, obscured in friendly darkness, is:

"Decide for yourself."

Today, in spite of the rain, an hour's walk along the beach, leaning into the prodding wind. The North Sea is green, with some patches of violet. In the distance, somewhere behind the watery horizon, is a silver sheaf of sunlight. On the cliff top the wind is blowing as in the mountains; one has to turn aside to breathe. The basketwork beach chairs are empty. Breakers such as I have never seen before. I take off my shoes, for every now and again an unexpected tongue of water sweeps up, foaming like soapsuds, and then one's feet sink into the trickling sand. On the edges of the watery tongue the froth of the great breakers lies wobbling for a while, then the wind scatters it; dry as cotton wool, it flies away. There remains a hem of broken shells and seaweed, here and there a starfish writhing in its blind existence. A bomb has been washed up too, empty, rusty, and with bent wings.

A not insignificant advantage: in a foreign country one does not feel the obligation, as at home, to have a sense of identity with everything. One does not expect what can never be. That alone gives a foreign land something liberating, refreshing, something festive, and often makes us unfair toward our own home. Wherever it is, there are only a few people to whom one feels akin. The unfairness lies in the fact that abroad I am thankful for these few, at home I am horrified by the number of the others.

Yesterday my charming hostess went away; Thomas Mann is expected in Frankfurt, and, as I read in the papers, his arrival is awaited with much hatred. . . .

(There is, I feel, something grotesque as well as tragic about this: a contemporary German, a world figure to whom fell the task of preserving universal respect for the German language, comes to Germany, but only a few will look him in the face, the others stare at his feet, waiting for him to trip up. What good will that do them? An emigrant has made good; for those who forced him to emigrate that is a sorry realization, and nothing is more understandable than their fierce urge to expose the weaknesses of this man. And who would deny that he has some? That familiar, self-nurtured identification of himself with the aged Goethe, lacking at times in irony—who would take exception to that if Thomas Mann had not written and spoken so many other uncomfortable things? For many of his fellow countrymen, even if they hardly know his work, he has become something of a bugbear; they pine for world respect, he possesses it, but they cannot ally themselves with him without having to admit the truth of many of the disturbing things he has said— and so most of them now content themselves with trying to hack away the respect he has won for himself: as if they could gain anything by that!)

When I return to the house at night I cannot believe my eyes. There it still stands on its little hill as usual, but the whole flat foreground has vanished. The path I trod only a few hours ago no longer exists; the fence of wooden palings stands in the waves, on which the moon is shining, the haystack too. Neighbors say the water will not rise any higher. All the same, it gives one an inkling of Noah's flood. . . .

Home.
The sum total of our customs, good and bad, a certain sense of habit, the common ground of a shared environment—all these things are not valueless. To have played together at the same lakeside does of course create certain bonds; but to take this as proof of compatibility would be a mistake, leading us sooner or later into unfairness, for we see it only as a disappointment, not as a mistake. Home is an indispensable need, but it has nothing to do with countries. Home means human beings whose nature we can perceive and grasp. To that extent it does perhaps have something to do with language, but it certainly does not lie in language alone. Words form bonds only when we find ourselves on the same wavelength. And that does not mean we must necessarily approve (approval is nowhere more common than among people of totally different outlooks misconstruing one another). It is, rather, a question of accessibility, and it is precisely when one meets under different conditions, not misled

by a similarity of habits, that affinities emerge most clearly, most unexpectedly, most felicitously, and most fruitfully.

(The reason for traveling.)

What I am seeking in Germany: affinities in wider scope. The different dimensions are also reflected in the human qualities. Many here in Germany hold their heads rather higher than is proper for them and tend to judge themselves by the greatness of their numbers, a form of greatness on which sheep and lice could equally pride themselves; but when one comes on true individuality, this is always freer than in a small country, uninhibited, undistorted, unconstrained; in identical circumstances it tends to expand more richly. It has, one feels, more scope—and in all directions, including the positive ones.

One swims here with nothing on, which is delightful, and the only surprising thing about it is how natural it seems. Today, when we were lying in a group on the beach, a young couple we knew approached us, both in swimsuits. Recognizing us some thirty paces away, they stopped and did the only apposite thing—took off their swimsuits and, holding them in their left hands, advanced to greet us—

Thoughts on reading:

The number of works we can genuinely admire grows ever fewer, but our genuine admiration for them increases the longer we have been writing ourselves. Admiration in the sense of saying: I could never do that, not if I were to live my life seven times over. Above all, it seems to me, the difference between admiration and respect becomes much clearer—two feelings that are not interchangeable. Respect is what I feel when the author I am reading, though he may have progressed further than I have, is working on the same level; maybe I shall never reach his heights, but he is not in principle beyond my reach—he uses essentially the same tools as I do, though perhaps he has more of them and makes better use of them; I do not deny his superiority, but it is not beyond my power to understand his success. This goes for the great majority of writers and poets, whom one respects and even at times envies, in the same way that sportsmen respect or envy those who have beaten them.

But there are also others—and this is where genuine admiration can be so redeeming—with whom we do not need to compare ourselves, the difference between us being so inexorably apparent: we walk—they fly. . . .

(Trakl, for example.)

From such winged beings the plodder on foot can, I think, learn little that would not be—for him—a mere pose.

Walk to Keitum. The first trees for weeks; what we mean by landscape: a green forgetfulness that we are living on a planet. Out there on the sand dunes one does not forget it for a single moment.

Like everything else we do, self-criticism is a questionable practice. Its attraction lies in the sense it gives me of raising myself above my own deficiencies by identifying them and thus divesting them of their horrifying qualities, which ought to make me change my ways; when others point them out, I am always reminded how horrifying they really are.

An old lady with white hair, once a celebrated actress, well known both in Vienna and in Berlin, now sitting at the window, knitting. I asked her:

"So you knew Kainz?"

"Oh, yes."

"You worked with him?"

"Oh, yes."

For a while she knitted on in silence, unsure whether she wished to talk about her life or not. At any rate she was not interested in handing out mere crumbs. Then, when I had silently resolved to leave the room, she suddenly put down her knitting, having made up her mind to talk, but in a manner befitting so full a lifetime: from beginning to end, calmly, never verbose, but in a wide sweep—and the hours vanished in a twinkling. . . .

"That was my first success," she said after describing in tender detail even the costume she had been wearing before putting it aside, so to speak, in smiling silence. "On the following day a Herr von Hofmannstahl came to see me. What does he want? I asked myself. I was seventeen, a silly girl, I knew nothing at all really. Later on I was often in his home in Rodaun. He showed me a play in which he wanted me to play the title role. He sat at his writing desk, his wife was standing in a corner, and I had to read it aloud. He was always wanting to hear it over again. He himself had a lisp, he placed his tongue wrongly: when he spoke I always had the feeling he was dribbling. Anyway, he wanted me to play Electra. Incidentally I think he liked me very much, rather too much. I remember thinking: What does this old man want of me? At that time he was just above thirty. His moustache always reminded me of a sea lion. Later on I received a lot of letters from him, but unfortunately they were all destroyed in a fire in Düsseldorf—"

On Wedekind:

"A bad actor in his own plays, but incomparable as a ballad singer. His Doctor Schön in *Pandora's Box*—impossible, I assure you. He was passable as the Marquis of Keith. Because it was a portrait of himself. His best role was Jack the Ripper. An actor he was not, but as a writer—"

Later she took up her knitting again, so that the afternoon should not be wasted, but continued to talk about the men and women she had known, unconcerned by their present fame or their dethronement: her love was as constant as that of any mother who hears the world, which is also only people, praising or blaming her children. Her contempt was equally unshakable. . . . Wedekind, Hofmannsthal, Ibsen, Strindberg, Hauptmann, Gorky, one great name after the other, Kainz, Stanislavsky, Reinhardt, Valentin, Duse, Steinrück, Moissi, Jessner, Bassermann—taken all in all it was a great period, and slowly I began to understand her contempt for the puny people she had been to see yesterday.

"What a rabble," she said, "what a rabble."

She even rose to her feet. "Really, what a rabble—"

Lips pressed tight, hard as only an old lady can be, with shaking head, composed, yet unable to grasp how times have changed, she stood at the French window, for a long time speechless. She felt offended, although none of it was any longer her concern, just quite impersonally offended; then at last she adjusted the comb which had come loose in her white hair, turned to me, and asked:

"Or don't you think they're a rabble?"

This same island, which in mist and rain looks dimly spectral, has now suddenly become classical. Air like glass: the distances are distant, but clear and exact, unghostly, bright and finite. So all this can be found in the North too, the blue darkness of the sea, the blazing light that transports us with gratitude for our very existence. A temple, Doric, would not come as a surprise; but it is only a destroyed bunker. And then, all of a sudden, a naked man is standing on top of a sand dune; a young man, hands on hips; and then a young woman, both brown, splendid as on the first day of creation. For a moment they stand there against nothing but sky. Then they walk on across the shining sand, hand in hand, and suddenly they are running, chased by their own high spirits, they disappear behind the clumps of long, dry, waving grass. . . .

Conversation about honesty.

If honesty were to consist simply of saying everything openly, it would be very easy to be honest, but valueless, unbearable, destructive, virtue maintained at the expense of others. But where does falsehood begin? I should say: where we pretend to be honest in the sense of having no secrets.

To be honest means to be solitary.

A visit, at last, to the barracks, constantly visible in the distance. A transit camp for Silesian refugees. Dirty linen hanging in the sun, children, tin plates, people without jobs, a rabbit hutch full of German *Volksgenossen*, isolated like medieval pest-houses. The state alone takes care of their needs. People never speak of them. The only thing I have so far heard said about them: They've stolen another chicken. Nearby there are people in brightly colored beach robes, gleaming limousines, once again with German number plates. . . . I find myself thinking of that meek Polish farmer who was our host a year ago, now plowing their fields because he has been driven off his own, and keeping an exact diary of his work, even of what he is doing on this very day, his sowings, his harvests—

To whom will he one day be asked to show it?

To these people with their limousines?

Have been reading Wedekind again, a real man of the theater, and Hauptmann. As usual when considering the work of a lifetime: what determines its greatness is not so much the greatness of the creative faculty as the relationship between the creative and the critical faculties. In Hauptmann the creative talent often grows without any support and spreads out into an untidy mess which many lesser men would at once repudiate; judgment trails behind, and the gardener's snippers cannot keep pace. But one can see the danger of the opposite approach: the critical faculty is too alert, too hasty, tyrannical, and in consequence it stifles the tender shoots of creativity, which always need a certain amount of protection in the early stages. To find a fruitful relationship, a balance between these two faculties as they exist in one—this is the constant, most intimate problem of every artist, solvable only in the light of his own experience and a careful consideration of his own limitations. In this task he stands completely alone. All advice we give to an artist is invariably of help only to his critical faculty. (Leaving aside the fact that whoever offers advice is fundamentally only advising himself.) So there may be times when an artist is right to shun his friends' advice and risk disappointing them with an inferior piece of work; it may be that this work, while arousing regret among his friends, is for him of more value than the better work they had hoped for—not more valuable as a work, but of more value to his creative processes and necessary for the restoration of his productive balance. How little are genuine artists concerned with their artistic prestige! Their primary concern is not the masterpiece itself, but the ability to create, to remain alive, even when this may often push them down below heights previously reached.

Swimming in the breakers. Today was high tide, and the breakwaters, with their stakes thickly clad in blue-black mussel shells, were not visible, so blood was soon flowing. But otherwise it is a bliss beyond compare—almost beyond compare—springing around in the foam as the waves rear up and then collapse; they come in often like crumbling avalanches, and in the evening sun it is as if one were bathing in pure brass or nickel.

The gulls:

How they sail along the cliff, riding on the upcurrents, their wings held almost stiff, swift as arrows, then suddenly, as if shot from a gun, they drop down on the water, snatch their prey, and fly up before the next wave—

Teatime conversation in a spick-and-span country house, style of the good old thirties, with painted tiles, farmhouse chests, engravings, cast-iron banisters, Berlin porcelain, camel-hair rugs, pedigreed dogs.

"Switzerland did not suffer at all."

"No," I say.

"It would not have done you Swiss any harm," the lady says, "particularly the Swiss. Suffering is good for you, you know—"

We are sitting in a spick-and-span garden, which in the good old thirties, as I later heard, had played host to many high-ranking uniforms, both brown and black; the view is splendid; only far away on the horizon can one see the barracks of those Silesian refugees, those innocent victims of treacherous foreign powers.

Thoughts on writing:

Years ago as an architect I visited one of those factories in which our celebrated clocks and watches are made; no impression gained in a factory was ever more devastating, yet in no conversation have I ever succeeded in reconstructing that experience, one of the most vivid of my life, in such a way that it came through to the listener as well. Put into words, it always remains insignificant or unreal, real only to the person concerned, indescribable as all personal experiences are—or, to put it better, every experience basically defies description as long as we try to express it through the actual example that has impressed us. I can express what I want to say only by means of an example that is as remote from me as it is from the listener, that is to say, an invented one. Essentially only fiction—things altered, transformed, shaped—can convey impressions—and that is the reason why every artistic failure is always linked with a stifling feeling of loneliness.

Walk along the sand dunes to List, then back via the bird sanctuary, Luftwaffe installations everywhere.

At nine in the evening the sun is still shining, dusk lasts until midnight, giving way almost imperceptibly to moonlight. One does not feel like sleep. The plovers too are still flocking on the heath. A smell of salt, seaweed, hay. The pools on the mud flats gleam in the moonlight like fragments of glass. The lighthouse, spotlighting my warm pile of hay at every third breath, seems touchingly industrious in all this huge stillness. Another light is flashing out on the Danish coast, but it is very tiny. In a fenced field two horses are grazing. Often one finds oneself holding one's breath, as if at any moment something unbelievable might occur. But it is nothing: just a horse shaking itself. A fraught, pent-up silence, such as must precede the arrival of an angel—

At one moment a shooting star.

Reminiscence

That teatime conversation with the brown lady—among the many things that occur to me in this connection is the little memory of my last days of military service, April 1945 in Graubünden. I often went up to the border to talk to the German guards; they were all of an older generation, ten men who were not Nazi supporters and with them two brown shirts. One of the ten, a man with an unusually kind face and almost childlike eyes, came from Rothenburg. His view of the situation: We poor Germans, the way we are always being overtaken by another war! We contemplated the evening landscape and talked about spring, birds, the weather. He was a family man, a Catholic, his son had been killed in Russia. We arranged that on the day the Americans captured Rothenburg I should remove a certain stone from the wall. For they were allowed on the border only when they were on duty. They were grateful for both tobacco and news. . . . During the day I was posted in the woods above, from which one could survey the whole valley through a stereotelescope. Every morning at twilight I saw the forced laborers marching to work, watched them rubbing their hands before they at last took up their shovels, the German guards standing beside them with slung rifles and frozen feet, while I myself was already bathed in sunshine. There was never much to report; now and again a field-gray limousine, hastening from Italy to Austria, hour-long convoys during the night, in the daytime a female farmworker in the fields. I can clearly recall the flat images the stereotelescope conveyed, quite without depth, the gesticulating speakers reminding one of silent films, a puff of smoke from a pipe. The slaves were given their first meal at about ten o'clock. . . . In the evening, when I was free, I would go down to the border again and crouch on a rock until somebody saw me and came along. One of them was from Berlin; he told me, rather overexuberantly, about his relations in Switzerland, where there was certainly no shortage of bacon and butter. And whipped cream! They couldn't unfortunately cross the border yet, he said, for "those two" kept a constant eye on them. This man was also touchingly naïve. For years they had been guarding these foreign slaves, who also had wives and children, they didn't enjoy guarding them (that I can believe without any hesitation) and in consequence they felt it very unjust that they themselves were in danger of being taken prisoner—after all, they had committed no crimes. I considered it expedient to listen, not to speak. In doing so I heard a lot about "those two," who, even at this stage of the war, would still kill anyone who made a bleat. Just once did I ask what they would do with "those two" when it was all over.

One of them said:

"May the devil take them—"

So there we were; I never saw the devil, only the men: each with a rifle and a belt full of cartridges . . . and a whistle—shots I never heard, the valley was quiet, peaceful, uncanny, we peered through our stereotelescope and at ten o'clock the slaves were once more given their meal. Berlin was stormed, Goebbels silenced, but all we heard was the dripping of melting snow and an occasional plop as a whole cake of it slid down from the fir branches; all we saw was the valley, the German guards walking up and down, rocks bathed in sunshine, wire entanglements, the overgrown frontier road. To report: border crossings by all sorts of people taking their chance during the night. With the first morning sun they would walk down the valley, to reach our post about midday, limping, half frozen, betraying signs of ill treatment. Most of them were French, but once there were two Russians. Every day the number increased. Once it was a very young German army lieutenant. I should have liked to speak to him; a handsome, intelligent face, a youngster from a good stable. But there were already enough curious people surrounding him. Above all I remember two young lads from Belfort, who had been abducted three years previously; nineteen-year-olds. They had come from Stuttgart by a very roundabout route, both still dressed in the clothes they had been wearing at the time in Belfort; one of them was a delicate lad, a child of the proletariat, the other from a nobler house, a bold and hardened gangster who had already been caught twice trying to escape. His final gesture was a wave in the direction of the valley: Deutschland, he shouted, adieu! And spat in a wide arc. On the day a man from the Waffen-SS arrived I was unfortunately on leave; my friend, whose word I trust, described him as a deeply shocked man, at any rate he talked a lot, and my comrades were able to describe with striking unanimity what it looked like when a Ukrainian village was totally destroyed. At that time we had already learned a lot; now at last here was a man talking who had actually been there. . . . One morning, sitting at the stereotelescope, I saw something I could not at first believe: on the road on which we had so far seen only German sentries and an occasional old peasant woman, whole columns of forced laborers were now coming into view, marching without a guard. I focused the telescope on the bridge: the German guards were engaged in removing the barbed wire. The column passed over the bridge, that bridge that during the past years so many individuals had longed to cross and not a few had actually tried to cross, until in most cases they had been struck down by salvos. But this column had now really crossed the bridge, and although there was nobody on our side of it, they were waving their caps and scarves. I seized the telephone and reported: Peace. That was unfortunately somewhat premature, but in fact more and more columns continued to arrive. When I was relieved I went down to the border. Many were singing, the French in particular. There were women there too, a young Dutchwoman. Among them prisoners of war, faces from all nations. We had of course bought up all the cigarettes available in the little inn, and these we distributed while stocks lasted; since they had no matches, it happened naturally enough that one was again and again able to see an individual face close to. Most of them felt the need to say something.

"*Ik—finf Jahr!*" (Me—five years!)

Others tried to show how many children they had. One man with a shaved head, whose language I could not even guess, embraced and kissed me, as once a Greek peasant had kissed me, weeping with joy. . . . Beside them stood the German guards, the one from Rothenburg silent, the one from Berlin waving affably and saying:

"Have a good journey, good luck, have a good journey!"

Shortly after that we were transferred. On the Italian border things were no less lively. On the Ofen Pass we erected barracks for the refugees, while others went out on patrol. They seldom returned alone. With particular clarity I remember a German in civilian clothes, miserable, hungry, tired, for there was still much snow in the mountains, crusted and frozen in the night, soft during the day, so that one sank in down to one's hips. We sat him down before the stove that warmed our little barracks room. Eating his soup, of which he had much need, he assured us that he wanted only to return home, to Cologne, where he had a wife and children to look after, and it was all very understandable, very deserving of sympathy, except that it was not our task to decide whether our little country should let him in or not. We waited more than two hours. Our corporal, a windbag of the first water, gave him cigarettes, at first singly, then a whole pack, combining it with a glorification of our own kindheartedness which I found quite sickening. Ultimately I put in a word in an attempt to stop this chatterbox, but my effort was unfortunately in vain, for the poor German came to his aid with a stream of eager flattery, as if he believed the corporal could have some influence on the decision still to be made. They were two of a kind. However, an illustrated periodical which happened to be lying on the table put an end to this pitiful conversation. Could he have a look at it? the German asked politely, it was weeks since he had last seen a newspaper. It was an old number, with a picture of Mussolini's corpse, looking like an upturned statue. He contemplated it in silence, then turned the page. Some horrifying pictures of Warsaw. The man was very upset, pushed the periodical away, and tried to keep silent. But after a while, when I had given up expecting it, he said:

"If your papers print pictures like that, it's no wonder people hate us."

I could think of nothing to reply to that.

"I don't believe it," he said in a more conciliatory tone. "Germans don't do things like that. I was in the army myself. No," he declared with a vigorous shake of his head and in the tone of one who alone was in a position to know, "the way they finished off the Jews in Riga and afterward in Russia, I saw that with my own eyes, but this—no, I just don't believe it. We're not monsters."

I did not keep a diary in those days, but I did write down that sentence. Eventually the order came through that the man must be sent back. He turned very pale. As I collected my helmet and rifle—for the duty of escorting him had fallen to me—he understandably enough cursed our country, its inhumanity and so on. The path was narrow; he marched in front, I behind. We spoke little. There were many questions I should have liked to ask, but our circumstances made it impossible. I had the feeling there were three of us: he and I and the loaded rifle. I walked about ten meters behind him. He had his coat collar turned up, his hands in his trouser pockets. A sunny afternoon; I thought intermittently of the woods around Riga and I took him to be a man of experience, one who had shot people; I on the other hand had so far shot only at cardboard targets. His obvious air of condescension toward me was probably located somewhere in this region; I and the rifle together made a rather ridiculous picture, as I could feel myself. We had about an hour to walk. First through a gorge, in which the snow looked like porcelain; the man was shivering like a dog. Later through open woods; sunshine, ski tracks, silence, a frozen waterfall, tracks of hares, a deep-blue sky, beneath it the bright gold of rocks steeped in sunshine. Once we smoked a cigarette together. He assured me that he would be able to make it somewhere else, indeed this very night. He had a narrow, somewhat crooked face with pale eyes, which were as alert as they were undecided. I was glad that it was not he wearing the uniform. Eventually we moved on; he was smiling. I don't think I am mistaken when I describe it as a smile of base contempt. It was as if he felt my uncertainty; I did not know what he might do next: all I was sure of was that he took me for a fool. And indeed

I had anything but the feeling of being his superior. The weapon belonged by rights to him; it was only stupid chance that had reversed our roles. But nothing happened. At the border he asked merely what time it was. . . .

"Four o'clock," I said.

"Oh, well," he said—

Neither of us spoke even a word in farewell; as I stood there adjusting my cap over my ears, he went off down the slope on the other side. It was a narrow little pass, a completely deserted spot. I waited there for another hour or so. In our section at least, in which all who arrived had to pass through this gorge, he was not seen again. But there were other ways across. Our barracks were soon full to overflowing; those who arrived in a state of exhaustion were taken down to Zernez by truck, mainly women and children; the others went on foot, one small group after another. Here too there were several who sang as they walked. The war was over, the capitulation signed. Almost all to whom I was able to speak had one feeling in common: a longing for the things in life that are so often held in contempt: home, family, work. It was precisely because of these encounters that I felt at that time quite soberly confident that peace was a possibility. My final job was to keep watch over a group of Germans, customs officials in uniform. They were complaining bitterly about the Italian partisans, who had taken all their watches from them. Others were grumbling about their feet and our lack of organization, since we were obliged to keep them waiting outside in the rain. Among them, since he was also German, we put a man in civilian clothes. A taciturn person, he kept his thoughts for a long time to himself; but eventually he burst out, calling them a stupid mob, bloodhounds, ending with a reminder of how they themselves had treated the Italians. He turned out later to have been a deserter. It was a grisly situation, for it was by no means certain whether the whole lot of them might not eventually have to be sent back across the border. The more silent the men in uniform became, the more openly the other man let fly at them. Luckily, they did not have to be sent back. Once they were home, the man said, he would know what to do with them; and, as they marched off, he remained demonstratively apart. I had to accompany them for a few miles. The man came from Munich; during the march he took me even further into his confidence. But back home, he assured me, back home that lot would soon be sorted out. It was not my task to interfere. I accompanied them to the next picket point, silent, but not indifferent—

Westerland

Reading the newspapers again:
  "Germans to Be Rearmed—?"
  (By America.)

Kampen, August 1949

What we experience is either anticipation or memory. Their point of intersection, the present, can in itself barely be experienced: that is why one seldom succeeds in describing a landscape while one is looking at it. True, I am always trying to do so; the result is always the same: stilted. There is also no real compulsion behind it. As long as it is all in front of my eyes, why should I describe it? This is the time for seeing.

To overstate it somewhat: a person mounting the scaffold experiences fear of the ax, not the ax itself. And when he is pardoned on the scaffold, we can hardly conclude that the man has experienced nothing. No individual has ever experienced his own death; but every individual experiences the fear of death, the anticipation of it—
  "We who experienced the war—"
  (Apart from anything else that might be said about this frequently heard statement, it is comical that a man should boast of his experience, rather than show us what that experience has made of him—or what he has made out of his experience.)
  A confusion between two ideas: experiencing and being present.
  By far the greater part of what people experience lies on the plane of anticipation; the other plane of experience, memory, is much smaller. If that were not so, there would be no poets, only reporters, and above all there would be no readers. What is a

reader in fact doing when he opens a book? He is abandoning his position of being present, since it does not satisfy him, and moving onto the plane of his anticipation: in order to experience something.

Hamburg, September 1949

Left the island of Sylt by boat in the early hours, fog over the sandbanks, later the bright blueness of an open sea. A few hours with no land in sight. Toward evening we sail up the river Elbe. Procession of ships steaming out, each with a trail of brown smoke. Gulls, buoys, lighthouses. And then, the nearer we come to the harbor, a tangle of cranes, tugs, cutters, masts of all shapes and sizes, dredgers, a floating ruin of rust, yachts, sleek and jaunty, tackle, in the background factories and sheds without number, chimneys, gasometers, all with the same coating of oily black, whether iron or stone or wood. A human world: freight trains, bridges, streetcars, locks, trucks, airplanes, a milky way of electric lamps . . . Later a storm over the Alster lake in the center of the city, looking like the last fireworks display of summer, thunderclaps in plenty, often quite close, deafening, an old avenue of trees tossing and rustling, rain whipping like flags across roofs and terraces and lake; over the streets it hangs like a white mist, a veil of sprinklers; close by stand the ruins of a villa, gleaming in the darkness like all the other villas; but then, as a flash of lightning illumines it, one sees that it no longer has any floors, and the façade looks like a black mask; the exuberant gurgling of an overflowing gutter.

En route

What is nationalistic? It is when I put the demands my nation makes of me before all other demands and recognize no other criterion but the advantage of my tribe; when I pay lip service to, and even advocate, the moral principles (for example, Christian ones) of which my nation approves, yet never on any account acknowledge these same principles if directed against my own nation; it is when I am ready to perform any deed, even if according to my own moral principles it is a crime, and perform it proudly, or at any rate obediently (always a good Hottentot); when I acknowledge nothing higher than my own instincts and look on these instincts, reflected a million times in my fellow nationals, as a thing of the spirit, a spiritual aim to which it is praiseworthy, even virtuous, to sacrifice even my conscience. In short, it is when I am a nihilist: without the courage that goes with it.

Jealousy

If the unhappy man who visited me yesterday—his mistress has gone off with another man—if this man could be quite certain that no words, kisses, acts of tenderness, embraces of any other man could come up to his own, would he not take things rather more calmly?

Jealousy as the fear of comparisons.

What could I have said to him? One can share grief, but not jealousy. I listen and think: What exactly do you want? You are claiming the right to victory without a fight, desperate that there should be any question of a fight. You speak of faithfulness, but know very well that it is not her faithfulness you want, it is her love. You speak of betrayal, and yet she is quite open and honest when she writes that she has gone away with "him." What exactly do you want, my friend?

One wants to be loved.

Only in fits of jealousy do we at times forget that love cannot be had on demand, forget that even our own love, or what we call our love, ceases to be serious as soon as we take it to confer certain rights. . . .

How is it possible that jealousy can often extend to dead people who cannot return, at least not in physical form?

Only because of the fear of comparisons.

Every man knows, moreover, that for the woman herself his jealousy makes him anything but alluring. Not infrequently his jealousy, his obvious fear of comparisons, gives her the first incentive to start looking around, to start making comparisons. She suddenly senses his weakness. Because of his jealousy she actually begins to blossom—he is right in thinking she has never looked more beautiful! Involuntarily she is filled with new hope, feeling that her love must still be capable of finding completely different satisfactions (for why otherwise should he be so fearful?).

One seldom encounters jealousy in men who are very confident of their power and glory or in women who are sure of their seductive charms (so sure in fact that they do not feel the need to give in every time). Yet there is surely cause enough! It is because they have nothing to fear. They do of course know the sense of loss, the burning wounds inseparable from any love, but they do not feel themselves on that account to be ridiculous, scorned, inferior. They put up with it, do not consider it a defeat, any more than death is a defeat, they do not moan about unfaithfulness, and the woman for whom they have all at once become inadequate they do not abuse as a whore, which anyway is usually a false and inaccurate term—

The rape of the Sabine women—what healthy and relatively honest person, man or woman, is not on the side of the robbers? I can think of no single work of art that attempts to excite our compassion for the poor Sabine men.

And virtue?

We can feel sorry for the Sabine men who have to rely on the virtue of their Sabine women, even when that virtue is steadfast. They are their wives' owners, protected by law, insured by church and state against all comparisons, and that should keep them happy—until the robbers appear on the horizon, until the whole world hears how the Sabine women rejoiced when at last their virtue was unable to prevent their falling into the arms of the stronger.

Oh, what fear there is of this rejoicing!

Language itself aids and abets with its talk of horns and cuckolds: it has no better words to offer, and it is no accident that jealousy, bitter though it may taste in reality, is the subject of so many farces. It is always in danger of appearing ridiculous.

Even Kleist, the tragedian, felt obliged to turn to comedy when dealing with Amphitryon, whose rival was after all Zeus himself. It is obvious that jealousy, though it can cause havoc enough, is not in fact a tragic emotion, since somehow it lacks the final quality of greatness—

Othello?

What moves us about Othello is not his jealousy as such, but his mistake: he murders the woman who loves him above all others. If it were not for this mistake, if his jealousy had been well founded and his wife had really been having an affair with the Venetian officer, all Othello's ravings would (without a single word's being altered) inevitably become comic; he would be a cuckold, nothing more, and thus a ridiculous figure, murder and all.

Why, incidentally, a Moor?

The full title of the play is *Othello, The Moor of Venice*. Othello is not primarily a jealous man but a Moor, that is to say, a member of a despised race. His newly won personal success does nothing to assuage his wounded self-esteem. He is respected, yes—but in spite of being a Moor. The in-spite-of remains, and he knows it. His different-colored skin also remains, and he suffers through his feeling of being different. This, it seems to me, is where the tragedy lies, and these are the lines along which it develops. Jealousy has not yet arisen; but behind everything, like a shadow, there stands that feeling of inferiority, and the Moor is after all ambitious, as all of us must inevitably be to the extent that we are ourselves Moors. The only man who divines the nature of his wound is Iago, who is himself a wounded man: his very first words, as far as I can recall, betray his wounded ambition. He knows, better than any other, how to destroy the successful Moor: through his Moor's fear, his fear of inferiority. This is the feeling on which Iago must work if he wants (as he does) to get his revenge. The feeling of inferiority with which we are all most familiar is jealousy, and Shakespeare achieves a tremendous effect by pulling out both stops at once. He identifies the one through the other. The particular, apparently alien fate of a man who has a different skin or a different nose becomes real for us because it culminates in a related emotion with which we are familiar; jealousy typifies the

270

more general fears of inferiority, fears of comparison, fears of being the black sheep—

What if Othello were not a Moor?

It could be tried—to confirm that thus the play collapses, loses its essential symbolism; and to demonstrate that jealous people are all of them Moors.

Café Odeon

Russia now also has the atom bomb.

More on jealousy

I myself once experienced an excess of jealousy. It was horrible. I bought myself a weapon and, after a ten-hour walk, fired some practice shots. Up till then I had shot only with rifles and howitzers; compared with them there was something dashing, exciting, personal about a revolver, something sporting. But all the same I was very much in earnest. It was November, full moon, fields covered in mist. At midnight, before the inns closed, I got myself drunk in a village, then walked on until I was so exhausted that I vomited. That was at dawn. I was already feeling somewhat easier, easier than I had been in all the preceding weeks during which I had often kept watch throughout the evenings. I washed myself in a cold spring in the open fields. I was aware of the ridiculousness of the whole situation, but all the same, though in later years one may smile rather cheaply, it was anything but a joke at the time. Sober in all senses of the word, too weary to strike attitudes, I once more slipped the safety catch on my tested weapon, walked on down the twilit road until I saw something that was alive—a crow, perched on a mast carrying a power cable. I fired. The crow, flying up, abandoned the insulators, one of which (to judge by the tinkling sound) I had hit, and landed after circling once on a small, leafless pear tree, where it calmly settled, as if the whole business had nothing at all to do with it. It was now closer to me than before. I fired. The crow, flying up again, tumbled to the ground. I had hit it, then. As I approached, it fluttered its wings wildly and flew at least a hundred yards as if nothing had happened before it once more tumbled to earth in a meadow adjoining a marsh. I tramped along after it. Barbed wire, ditches, detours. My shoes were solid lumps of mud, my trousers soaked through by the time I at last had the poor creature, which was still fluttering around on the ground, in such a position that I could pin down its muddied wings with my foot and give it my third and last bullet. On the road I saw the first solitary cyclist, a workman with a rucksack on his back. And that was the end of the affair. As I abandoned the dead crow, which, held by the wing tips, revealed a surprisingly large span, to its lifeless state and trudged back to the road, I did in fact immediately find myself thinking again about the affair, but it already seemed to be very far away, no longer topical, a memory. I did not know the man she had all of a sudden preferred to me; I only knew that he was considerably older. . . . The next time, I could imagine, he might be considerably younger. . . . At any rate he will always have some quality that we cannot in any way argue about, and always, when the time comes, the pain will be devilish.

When the time comes: when the look in two eyes, the lighting up of a familiar face, which for years you took to mean you, when all this suddenly belongs to another; in exactly the same way. Her hand, ruffling that other's hair: you have known it. Only a lighthearted impulse, a playful gesture, but you knew it. In this hand lay things shared and familiar, beyond words, and suddenly you see its playful movements from the outside and feel that for this hand of hers it makes no difference whose hair it is ruffling, that everything you felt to be your very own can be done without you; in exactly the same way. Although you know from your own experience how interchangeable the love partner is, you are appalled. And not just because for you it has ended. What appals you is a suspicion concerning all that had been, a mocking sense of loneliness: it is as if it had never been you with whom she had lain (already you are thinking of her without a name) but only your hair, your sex, which all of a sudden revolts you. It is as if, every time she uttered your name, she had betrayed you. . . .

On the other hand you know exactly:

Neither is she the only possible partner of your love. If she had never come along, you would have found love with another. And there is something else you know, which concerns nobody else, only yourself: I mean your dreams, which push interchangeability to the verge of complete facelessness, and, if you are not completely deceitful, you will not deny that all the things you experienced together and felt as a symbol of your utter togetherness could have happened without her; in exactly the same way. That is to say, within the range of your possibilities. Perhaps after all it is not this interchangeability that gives you such a devilish jab the moment her hand grasps that other head of hair but, on the contrary, the fear that for her hand there may indeed be a difference. There is no question of it: you are not interchangeable, you and he. Sex, which is common to all, has many provinces, and you are one of them. You cannot go beyond your limits, but she can. She certainly cannot go beyond her limits either, but beyond yours she can go; as you can go beyond hers. Surely you knew that we are all limited? It is a bitter recognition, even when unspoken, kept to oneself. Now you have the feeling—like all whose limits have been overstepped and thus, so to speak, identified—the feeling that she has put you in the pillory. Thus it is not only grief that remains, but also rage, the anger of shame which often makes a jealous man mean, revengeful, and stupid, the fear of being inferior. All of a sudden you yourself no longer believe that she ever really loved you. But she really did love you. You! It is just that you are not, as I have already said, all that is possible in love. . . .

But nor is he!

Nor is she!

Nobody is.

This is something we must learn to accept, I believe, if we are not to become ridiculous, deceitful, not to stifle all that love really is—

Arles, October 1949

Avignon, Nîmes, Arles—one sticks to the monuments, very fine, but at some point one sits down, orders wine, and watches the street: cities as the face of our human existence. In strange cities, where one is not protected by habit, one feels it more blatantly: above all when the language being spoken around one is not one's own. . . . What is it all for? . . . I light a cigarette. Never mind which city it is, one sits before the riddle of an anthill. Do not ask what for: they are walking to and fro just because they are alive. They are just living. Fine. Though many of them are not living very finely, living maybe in alleyways that stink perpetually of drains, but *they* can't smell it, one gets used to everything. At any rate they are living, they walk or sit, they chat together, a man has just come from hunting in La Camargue, he leans his gun against the wall, orders coffee, and tells of the mosquitoes that plagued him. Would I care to be this huntsman? Or any other citizen of Arles—that undoubtedly much-respected gentleman on the left, for example? I don't give a damn for his reputation, for a reputation of any kind in Arles. Funny. Why should a reputation anywhere else seem more worth having, more significant? . . . The waiter brings us our wine, *vin du pays*—culture, beginning as agriculture and then after a few millennia packed with history: a town like this or others, buses, stores full of bright bottles (a sight that always tempts me to stop and look), wines, liqueurs, bottles of all conceivable kinds, the felicitating plenty of unnecessary things. Countries of wine, of leisure, of culture, leisure and good living as the indispensable precondition of all culture. A shop full of vegetables and fish, a shop full of sprightly liquor, a shop full of books, *voilà*, this is our direction: from necessity to play, from the material to the spiritual, from the animal to the human, from existence to awareness. . . . But how narrow is the climatic zone in which this species to which we belong has been able to flourish! A few coasts, a few river courses. Once established, it was then of course able to spread; it conquered areas where it would never have emerged by itself, where the natural climate permits no culture, or at least does not favor it; but our species gets it going. Against the natural climate. It makes facilities for itself in places where nature has not provided them. By engineering. Pont du Gard. By erecting a favorable world outside nature: cities . . . Entering them by rail, particularly when it is night and the tracks are glistening in the rain, one sees a flickering of lights from a hundred thousand windows; entering harbors such as Genoa or Marseilles or Hamburg, a fabulous world of man-made contraptions, chimneys and warehouses and cranes: how unbelievable is the shape of a human city, how puzzling and unnatural, how artificial and idle and bold, how dismaying when life has deserted it and only the shell remains, its crust—rather like those arenas we visited yesterday and today. . . . A German sculptor, angry about a certain place up north, recently said to me: What can you expect? The Romans were never here! I shall send him a picture postcard of this arena in Nîmes. Here they were, those Romans, and is he not right? Even if they were not great artists, we owe these legionaries all it is possible to owe technicians: who clear forests, bridge rivers, irrigate the land, organize leisure, plant vines, enlarge the space in which human beings can flourish—

Leisure!

Concerning these arenas, what most excites my wonder is the gigantic effort our species makes in order to keep itself amused, in order not to be driven to desperation by the leisure it has won for itself. What bastions it has built against boredom! And how industriously arched, how unhumorous, how massive, how Roman! Rome, seen from Athens, is rather like Russia seen from Paris. . . . We sat for an hour on the top step. Nothing but stone and stillness and sunshine; the sky of Provence, now at last displaying the deep blue for which it is famous. I called to mind those twenty thousand legionaries as they sat here in this arena, cheering a fistfight, a species that with forty thousand feet had walked many thousands of miles, with forty thousand hands had arched a hundred bridges, and to crown it all had arched this arena—an indescribable amount of work to ensure that the species might, at least for a few hours, get what it wants: to see someone bashing someone else on the snout. . . . Sometimes I imagine it must be terrible to be part of this species; even when I occasionally look in the other direction, down on the teeming alleyways, the balconies with their gray washing on the line, the yards, the windows full of darkness, the carts in the streets, the boxes, the gesticulating vendors, the coming and going, the dogs, the garbage, the children, the torn curtains, the cats, the scolding of a woman, the masses of objects—

"Just look at it," the angel says. "This is the way humans live —here and everywhere, today and always."

I look.

"Would you like to be a human being?"

I hesitate.

"If I had never been born," I say politely, "no."

My angel smiles.

"But you have been born."

"I know," I say. "And that's why I hang on so to life—"

I hang on to life, that is true, even if it sometimes appals me and frequently drives me to drink wine in the middle of the day; in the middle of a journey on which I should be congratulating myself. Let him who can take comfort in the picturesque charms of our decaying West. Sometimes I feel I have had enough of this ubiquity of ruins, old and new, the louselike teeming of humans in the stinking refuse of their centuries. Whether it is a Roman arena or a weatherworn medieval palace or a blown-up railway bridge, kaput is kaput. I should like to see something whole, not the remains or the fragments or the beginnings of a whole, but something really whole, as far as the eye can see, not a landscape but a man-made thing, a human world free of damage, crumbling, dilapidation, decay, something without the corroding grimace of dissolution. . . . Not even the children, playing down there in the dirt, radiate hope, that halo of the future; they will go to school and grow up into adults, certainly, but no different from the adults of today; now and again they will sing the Marseillaise, but it will be the fervor and hope of their ancestors: *Le jour de gloire est arrivé!*— We have missed our train, otherwise we should by now be in Marseilles; we have time, Constanze and I, just like those men sitting over there on benches, their arms on the cast-iron armrests, their chins on their arms. What are they doing? Watching the street. It is Thursday. A funeral comes by, a short procession headed by a white priest and an acolyte, a black coach with painted silver, behind it a widow and a little retinue of people keeping patient step. The men opposite rise to their feet as it passes and doff their caps. And somewhere above the roofs a bell is tolling. The mistral rustles the trees. A little while later comes a truck full of youngsters who are celebrating something, we saw them earlier, drunk, bawling; a truck with seven

276

tricolor flags. Gone. The air is like spun glass, brittle and autumnal, bracing, one feels the nearness of the sea. The funeral bell is still tolling. Then a little donkey, slowly pulling a murmuring cart, a two-wheeler, slow as a dream; on a pile of hay sits an ancient, bent woman, looking like history in person, and constantly overtaken by hooting buses. And then, shortly after, two strolling soldiers: two black men—life unburdened by decay, an undamaged present, two children of the future . . .

Sketch

Heinrich Gottlieb Schinz, lawyer, father of four healthy children, the eldest soon to be married, was fifty-six years old when he one day encountered the spirit, as he called it. . . . Schinz, as his name suggests, came of a good family, and his interest in things of the spirit dated back to his early youth: he played the piano and made several journeys abroad while still a student. Paris, Rome, Florence, Sicily. Later London, Berlin, Munich, where he studied for a year, his interests veering between natural science and art history. His career as a lawyer, to some extent imposed on him by his father, who was himself an eminent lawyer, soon brought the usual rewards: marriage and honorary posts, including some of real and not merely social significance—charities for the aged and the sick, preservation of ancient monuments, refugee resettlement, promotion of the arts and so on. . . . His encounter with the spirit did not pass unnoticed, in fact it was for some weeks a topic of streetcar conversation; but the world outside—if one can call a medium-sized city that—saw it merely as a clinical case that, remarkable, puzzling, and disturbing as it undoubtedly was, held no significance for the outside world.

One Sunday morning, when it was snowing, Schinz went for a walk in the woods, as for many years past he had done for the benefit of his health, accompanied by his dog. Having grown up in this district, the home of his family since the days of his grandfather, he knew the woods like the back of his hand. The dog, a mastiff, knew them too. When the familiar clearing failed to materialize his astonishment was considerable, though he took it calmly enough. For a while he just remained standing where he was, the panting dog too; it was snowing, but not so heavily as to have caused Schinz to lose his way. The path was clearly visible, only the clearing was not. The dog had to wait while Schinz lit a cigarillo—something he always did, both in his lawyer's practice and earlier as a major in the army, at moments when he was not sure what to do next. A cigarillo is soothing. It is always possible for trees to disappear, whole clumps, half a forest; but one hardly expects a clearing to disappear. It can happen perhaps in poetry, Schinz told himself, when the poet wants to indicate in a fantastic way the passing of many years or something like that. Schinz was a well-read man. Walking on, so as not to keep the dog standing around, Schinz thought of this and that, smoking his cigarillo; that damned clearing must sooner or later show up. He had once tried his hand at poetry himself; so there was no reason to smile. As I said, he had been interested ever since his youth in things of the spirit. Then there had been his preoccupation with natural science; a pleasant time to look back on, peering through microscopes and so on. Some traces still remained too: not just odd scraps of knowledge, now become somewhat vague, but also in the way he showed his children what wood looks like under a magnifying glass and explained how water rises up from the roots into the branches. Now, however, the children learned such things in school; yet even so, left on his own, Schinz still kept the magnifying glass. And then art history with Wölfflin, back in Munich. Also a pleasant memory for Schinz; in the society for the promotion of the arts he was often the only one who did not waffle; Wölfflin had taught him that by showing him up in public once, and in fact shortly afterward he gave up the art-history classes. But something of it still remained: Dürer and so on. The world, if one can call a medium-sized city that, was certainly not wrong in regarding Heinrich Gottlieb Schinz as an intellectual man, although—oddly enough—he himself never spoke of the things of the spirit; he avoided this word as if he hated it, got around it in all sorts of ways, often quite wittily, as if it were something indecent; at any rate in its presence he was always very cautious, feeling obscurely that there was something terrible about the spirit, the true spirit,

278

something seismic, not to be called on at will, something catastrophic that could upset all known values, something fatal if
one did not have the extraordinary gifts needed to cope with it—
   The clearing did not show up.
   At five o'clock—Schinz having been expected home for lunch
—dusk began to fall, and soon it was too dark to see a thing.
Schinz sat down on a log, relieved to see traces of human activity around him. A certain nervousness was beginning to creep
up on him. In front of him the dog, panting, somehow uneasy
and confused. Like dogs before an earthquake, Schinz thought
to himself. He had run out of cigarillos. The snow showed no
signs of letting up. Silence; the panting of the dog served only
to make the silence between the tree trunks seem even more
impenetrable. All at once some snow slid from a fir tree, very
close, but making no sound. This is what it must feel like to be
deaf. Then, as well-read people sometimes do, Schinz permitted
himself the whim of regarding his situation from the literary
angle; the dusk, the timelessness, the silence among the trees,
the dog—all this was very poetic, in some way familiar, and even
the fear of having suddenly become deaf was not without its
hidden significance. Of that he was fully aware, as, though not
whistling, he was also aware that his little whim of regarding
his situation from the literary angle was like the whistling of a
boy going down into a dark cellar. He brushed the wet snow
from his hat, having made up his mind to get up and walk on.
But where? The dog, seeing its master taking up a broken
branch, a stick, whined in anticipation that he would throw it,
but ran ahead in vain. Once, quite without thought, he knocked
the stick against a tree. Not to reassure himself that he was not
deaf, but just for something to do. How dull it sounded, how
toneless, though he kept on striking the tree with increasing
force until the stick broke. Never a ringing tone. That was the
snow of course. Like cotton wool. Why should a person suddenly become deaf? He put the dog on the leash. Nothing for
it but to walk on and above all, Schinz told himself, not to work
himself up into a state of alarm. No sense in that. Every wood
ends somewhere, and after all they were still on a visible track.
The dog's growling told him that someone was coming. From
behind. For heaven's sake don't start thinking: Here comes the
spirit. The dog began to bark, and he tightened his hold on the

leash. A man in a loden coat came level with him: a forester per-haps, a woodcutter, a nature lover, a Sunday walker avoiding the crowds—

"Pardon me," said Schinz—

Although his forehead was in a sweat, he was quite calm, glad to hear his own voice asking the way to the town. Having to restrain the barking dog, he was unable to examine the stranger closely.

"You have lost your way?"

"Yes," replied Schinz with a laugh; "that has never happened to me before in my whole life—"

Even Schinz could hear how monstrous that sounded: a man who never in his whole life had lost his way! He added:

"And I know these woods as well as I know myself."

The dog refused to be silenced.

"Where do you want to go?"

"To the town," Schinz said, "where I come from—"

The forester was regarding the dog.

"Where I come from," Schinz repeated, "before night falls—"

The dog, straining as if to leap on a housebreaker, was almost pulling him over, so that he could scarcely speak coherently. It was behaving like a fury, that damned dog, making one realize what a huge beast it was. Luckily the forester showed no fear, merely interest. And anyway all the forester had to say concern-ing the way to the town was something that Schinz might well have asked himself:

"Why don't you just go back?"

"On the track I came—?"

Quite true, Schinz thought.

"Or if you prefer to come with me, I should think the dis-tance is about the same either way. . . ."

Schinz had to make up his mind.

"That's very kind of you—"

"Just as you like."

As they walked along, Schinz having decided to go on, the dog reverted to its former good behavior. The man was indeed a forester. They talked about dogs. All quite matter-of-fact— why should it have been otherwise? Of course they did not talk all the time. There are tracks like this, leading in circles, to give access to all the trees in the forest. Schinz was almost too tired to stand upright, but he was content—what did a few hours matter as long as he came to the town in the end? The thought that he was returning home on a different route, all the literary thoughts full of hidden significance which invaded his mind during the lengthy silences, none of them had substance when the man in the loden coat, who was becoming increasingly hard to see in the darkness, opened his mouth: he certainly did not talk like a spirit. Once he even spoke derogatively about the state, though he was a state employee; some trouble about a syndicate. It was still snowing. At another time they spoke about cellulose, and Schinz let fall some evidence of his scientific training, which might have given the forester wrong ideas, so that he felt constrained to mention his true profession.

"So you're a lawyer?"

"Yes."

"Hm."

"Why shouldn't I be?"

The forester described a case to him: in rather too much detail, so that Schinz now and again attempted to interrupt, as experts do in order to cut things short. It was a very ordinary case. But the forester was not to be diverted from his lengthy explanations.

"No," he contradicted, "the man did not steal, I did not say that, the man was in dire straits, for one day—"

"That's when he stole."

"No."

"But you said—"

"No," the forester repeated with the obstinacy peculiar to certain simple people who think slowly and are not to be intimidated. "I said the man was in dire straits, for one day—"

Schinz was not at his office desk but in the woods; he had no choice but to listen, his large dog on the leash. No telephone to interrupt the conversation, no secretary to come in and give the lawyer a clear excuse for getting to his feet, nothing at all like that; Schinz had to listen. There were still no signs of the town lights. The case was not an absurd one, not at all, but it was in no way unusual, and Schinz could not see why he should have to listen to it in such detail. Now and again, when they came to a fork in the track, the conversation died; Schinz was fully aware that he needed the forester's help, at least as far as the first street lamps. So there was nothing for it but to keep on listening to the story. Not that the man was unwilling to allow expert comment. Schinz could always give his view of the matter; the forester did not cut him short, but neither was he to be cut short himself.

"I understand," he said, quite courteously, "but that's not how it was, though of course you couldn't know that. One day, you see—"

At one point Schinz said:

"Pardon me."

He could not help himself, had to step aside and relieve himself against a tree. The dog sniffed the ground, the forester waited, while the snow fell soundlessly between the trees.

"I'll catch up with you," Schinz called out.

Silence . . . To prolong the pause he not only adjusted his clothing more deliberately than usual, but also removed his hat to shake the snow from it and took off his coat for the same purpose. He searched through all his pockets in the hope of finding another cigarillo. In vain. Having restored himself to order and armed himself, deliberately, with a new topic of conversation, he trudged back to the path; the snow was already deep, his trouser cuffs soaking wet.

"So there you are," Schinz said, relieved and good-humored. "You know, when we were boys, we used to play cops and robbers in this wood. And do you know what once happened to me?"

The forester listened.

"In my shirttails," Schinz concluded. "There I stood in nothing but my shirt and had to walk like that back to town."

They laughed.

"That forester," Schinz said after they had gone a few paces. "It could have been you."

"Maybe."

Silence.

"And then of course," came the forester's voice, "there was more to this story. As I said, the man was in dire straits, he had no choice, as you yourself admit, and one day he did steal the bicycle, and then of course things started to move. One day I was called as a witness—"

That was Schinz's last attempt to evade the story of the bicycle. A petty but long-winded affair, ordinary, muddled, but real . . . When at last they came to the first street lamps it was almost midnight. In the town the snow had not settled, it was very wet, the snowflakes falling past the urban arc lights, a limousine splashing through puddles, not a soul about. Luckily there was still a streetcar, the last, so Schinz had, as he hoped the forester would understand, little time for farewells. Hop inside with the dog! Once inside, Schinz raised his dripping hat, though in the darkness he could no longer see the forester—

"What weather!" he said.

The conductor made no reply, simply gave him two tickets, one for himself and one for the huge dog, which stood outside on the platform, while Schinz would gladly have taken a seat. . . . In the lights it seemed as if none of it had really happened. . . .

Schinz did not carry his door key when just taking his dog for a morning stroll. But of course Bimba had not gone to bed. She was quite beside herself.

"Not even a phone call!" she said.

His one wish was to get to the bathroom before she could ask where he had been. She would not believe him. He yawned, not quite involuntarily, but as an excuse for not speaking.

"Where have you been?"

No answer; he took off his shoes, at bottom pleased to be back at home, annoyed only because he did not want questions now. A vain attempt—Bimba knew him, knew he didn't wish to tell; no conversation, but a hot bath. Bimba turned on the taps, annoyed too, but all the same she fetched a clean towel and laid it down without a word, annoyed by men and their ways: I'm in trouble, leave me alone! The dog too, eating in the kitchen, was dripping wet. The children were already asleep, the maidservant also.

"Why don't you want to eat?" Bimba asked. "I can make some tea, eggs, there's also some cold meat left—"

"No, thank you."

Bimba looked at him.

"Gottlieb, what is the matter?"

"Nothing," he said. "Just tired—"

The bath was ready.

"Thanks," he said—

She gave him a kiss, to find out whether he had been drinking. Not a trace. Schinz returned the kiss, hoping to be left alone with his bath at last.

"You've got a temperature."

"Nonsense," he said.

"I'm sure you've got a temperature!"

"Please," he said, "leave me alone—"

"Why can't you say where you've been all day? I just don't understand. Not even a phone call! I sit here all day long, worrying myself crazy, and you come home at midnight, when we've been waiting for you since lunchtime, and won't even say where you were."

"In the woods!" he shouted.

And banged the door shut. He hoped he had not woken the children. He had been very uncontrolled, very un-Schinzish. The bath lasted three-quarters of an hour. When Schinz came out, rosy, newborn, Bimba was sitting there with reddened eyes.

"What's the matter?"

"Don't touch me," she said.

It was almost two o'clock; how lovely it would be to get some sleep now, if Bimba would only stop crying! A woman of forty-four, with four healthy children, the eldest soon to be married, sobbing with shaking shoulders simply because her husband had taken the liberty of spending one whole Sunday lost in the woods!

"Bimba," he said, stroking her hair, which was still beautiful, "it's Monday tomorrow."

"Go to bed then, if you want."

"I really was in the woods—"

"Let's not start that again," she said, sobbing.

"What?"

"Why are you lying to me?" she said suddenly, her tears gone. "If it's some other woman, why don't you say so?"

Pause.

"It isn't another woman."

Pause.

284

"And even if it were!" he suddenly shouted. "I have been telling lies, yes, yes, lies! All my life I have been telling lies—"

Bimba did not understand a single word Heinrich Gottlieb Schinz said during the next quarter of an hour, pacing back and forth. He was, as she knew, not drunk, but back and forth he went, shouting, and the more she tried to calm him down the louder he became. He was saying things that had no sense in them, that turned everything upside down, everything, leaving not a single belief or word that had been valid the day before, a whole lifetime long, unscathed. Perhaps he really was running a temperature. . . . There was no other explanation Bimba could think of for his unintelligible shouting. She herself said scarcely anything except—just once:

"Gottlieb, I'm not deaf."

Bimba had never seen him like this before.

The next day was a Monday, a working day, the children had to go to school, ate their breakfast standing, with their books under their arms, though Schinz disapproved of such sloppiness. But this morning, as Schinz and his wife Bimba breakfasted together, everything seemed to be in order again. Not a word about the scene during the night. Bimba, in a dressing gown that particularly became her, made toast, as she always did on Mondays, before the fresh bread arrived. Schinz was skimming through the morning paper, leaving it to his fingers to take the top off his egg—in other words, the usual routine, everything back in its accustomed place . . . No question of running a temperature: Schinz had already measured it.

"Thank goodness," Bimba said, "you could have caught your death of cold."

She now believed him about the woods.

"All the same we'll take it again this afternoon," she declared. "Anita has a really bad cold."

(Anita was the dog.)

Monday passed as usual, nothing special in the office, and Schinz felt quite well, so they did not cancel their seats for *Der Rosenkavalier*. After the opera, which brought no surprises, they drank a glass of wine together. Bimba, in a black fur, was particularly gentle with him, instinctively, as one is with a sick person. Schinz noticed it more than she did: a sort of protectiveness, like a mother who does not want people to see that her child has the falling sickness. Since he was feeling in fine shape, it did not annoy him; all the same, he did notice it, and hoped that she would soon drop this rather touching manner. It wasn't like Bimba at all. But he did not want to say anything. If he did, it would have to be something like: Darling, I'm not off my head! Out in the street Schinz bought a newspaper, in his usual way. When he returned to the car, Bimba was already seated behind the steering wheel. She wanted to have a go at driving again. Schinz was silent.

"Otherwise I shall forget how," she said.

On the journey home Schinz did not speak a single word. That was rare for him, but not unknown. All the same Bimba said:

"What is the matter, Gottlieb?"

"Why do you ask?"

"You're so silent."

"Nothing," he said. "Just tired—"

"Steinhofer was in splendid form."

"Very."

"She's become more mature," Bimba said. "Don't you think so?" No answer.

"I thought her splendid."

If things go on like this, Schinz thought, life will be hell. If what goes on? He did not know. But it would be hell for sure. . . . He closed the garage door, while Bimba waited for him at the door, though it was raining.

"Go on in," he called out.

But still she waited. Suddenly at the end of his self-control, he pulled the garage door open again, turned on the light, and opened the car door.

"What's the matter?" Bimba called.

He had forgotten the newspaper.

"Go in," he called.

But Bimba waited for him, even came back a few steps, as if she were afraid Schinz would take the car and drive off again. To the woods, he thought, to my lady love in the woods, taking his time about closing the garage door again. She is waiting there like a nurse, he thought.

That was Monday.

———

The same on Tuesday, Wednesday, Thursday . . . On Thursday Schinz was given a new case, a rather routine one: a charge of theft. Not the theft of a bicycle! Schinz had also immediately thought of that, literary as he was in his way of thinking—he would not have been surprised if it had been the case that the forester had described to him at such length. But after all life is not like that—so witty, so audacious. It was not a bicycle that had been stolen, but an automobile, a Citroën. Schinz listened to the account of it, a long-winded but ordinary affair, muddled, but real. He was prepared to take on the defense in the way he had always done, that is to say, conscientiously; he did nothing differently; he wanted justice done; he presented the case as he saw it—and at once caused a scandal.

(His first scandal.)

Heinrich Gottlieb Schinz, lawyer and son of an eminent lawyer, a well-known and much-respected citizen of a medium-sized town, father of four healthy children who were attending or had once attended high school, Heinrich Gottlieb Schinz stood up in the courtroom that he had graced for three whole decades and declared:

"No, this man did not steal, no more than the gentleman who owns this car. The man was in dire straits, for one day—"

"No, the man did not steal—"

It eventually became a household word, the only one Schinz left behind on this earth. . . . Other little jokes flew about at the time of this first little scandal, but were not general enough in application to endure. A lot of people laughed at them, even Schinz himself—but not Bimba, who first heard of the affair on the telephone, more or less in the tone of "What has gone wrong with your dear husband?" Bimba had been fearing the worst—ever since that outbreak on Sunday night. It was almost a relief to be told the news. If that were all! Embarrassing enough, since of course it got into the newspapers. Schinz read it at breakfast, not indifferent, but also not agitated.

"This is not correct," was all he said.

A very malicious report.

"I will write to them at once," he said, putting down the paper and pouring his coffee. "They must be made to put it right."

Two days later his letter was returned. This *did* upset him. It was breakfast time again. Bimba was still in the bathroom when the mail arrived. He put the envelope in the pocket of his dressing gown, before Bimba came down.

"You know what," Bimba said, "you really ought to see a doctor—"

She said "really ought" because she had been thinking it secretly for weeks past. Schinz noticed more than she did. And what she had been thinking was: A nerve specialist. Oh yes, so as to avoid saying a mental specialist . . . He ate his egg, and half an hour later vomited it up again, but all in such a way that Bimba should not notice.

"Where are you going?"

No reply.

On that morning Schinz went to see a friend who, though not a member of the legal profession, was a true friend, his only one in fact, even though the friendship was rather one-sided; it meant more to Schinz than to the other man. He was a musician. A nice person, who tended to agree too readily. Schinz knew that, when Alexis said you were right, it did not mean very much. It meant only that he felt sympathetic toward you. But this was not the main concern now. Alexis was an emigrant, and that was important; a stranger in the land. As a witness he did not carry much weight; something he had just had to resign himself to. Alexis was content just to be tolerated; he did not enjoy interfering. But a really fine character, one of the few. All Schinz would want Alexis to do would be to read the two texts, the newspaper report and his reply, and then to say whether he found the reply correct or wrong, arrogant, exaggerated. Above all one mustn't exaggerate!

"I need your advice."

Alexis was still in bed.

"I'm having a spot of bother—"

"I know."

"This is what I want—"

The phone rang. Alexis picked it up. Schinz waited, rose rather restlessly, went to the window to smoke a cigarette. . . . Bimba was wanting to know whether her husband was with Alexis. A minute later Schinz left without broaching the matter he had come about, as uncontrolled as a moody youngster, though a man of fifty-six, a doctor of law, director of a society for the promotion of the arts.

Alexis phoned Bimba:

"What's the trouble between you?" he asked.

Bimba sobbed. . . .

So it went on, all rather ridiculous, rather petty, rather exaggerated. Schinz visited the newspaper office; there were social ties, so the people had to receive him—which they did, quite courteously. But they could not convince Schinz that his reply, to stick just to that, was impossible.

"No, this man did not steal—"

The two men looked at each other in silence, as poor Bimba had been silent while Schinz paced to and fro, saying things that made no sense, that turned everything upside down, leaving nothing that had been valid the day before, a whole lifetime long, unscathed. . . .

"All right," said the editor, "let's stick to the point. You insist on our publishing your reply?"

"Yes."

"Well, all I can say is this," the editor said. "I am prepared to do so, but I must warn you of the possible consequences."

Schinz, touched by the man's evident concern, looked through his reply once more, although he knew it almost by heart. The editor considered it his human duty to warn Schinz, and he repeated his warning several times. Schinz did not of course wish to be pig-headed. An affectation of courage? The editor did not consider it courage if Schinz persisted, but madness, though he put it more gently: a *faux pas*. Neither did Schinz consider it courage; there was nothing in the reply that was not his considered opinion. He was putting it forward not in the sense of: I, Heinrich Gottlieb Schinz, am telling you; but quite simply: Why should I conceal what I think? When someone mentioned courage, he felt almost apprehensive; but he himself could see nothing courageous about it.

"As you wish," the editor said.

So this time his reply would remain in the newspaper office.

"And without any cuts?"

"Yes," said Schinz. "It's hardly more than a page and a half."

Schinz, briefcase in his left hand, took his leave in his usual manner, politely, looking them straight in the eye; they were regarding him as if he were going off to the front. . . . It appeared next morning and he read it again at breakfast. At the top of the second page, very prominent, accompanied by a short postscript in which the editor said he must leave it to the readers to make up their own minds about a lawyer with such views. This was the first thing Schinz glanced at before reading his own text, somewhat anxious that they might after all have distorted it. True, they had not; yet it was as if the words, accustomed to being used to express views the exact opposite of his, doggedly refused to convey what he meant to say. Growing paler with every line, Schinz now realized at last that something had happened to him, that he had changed, that what was so self-evident to him contradicted everything around it, finally and irreconcilably. Hence the warning? Now for the first time, as if he had suddenly awakened, he saw the heading they had put above his reply:

"No, this man did not steal. . . ."

In this moment Schinz knew that he was finished; at any rate as a lawyer; at any rate in this city.

The rest was like a bad dream. It can soon be told, I think, the turning point having been that meeting with the forester in the woods, when he went forward instead of back. He had come from his home town, and he had wanted to return to his home town. The dog, lovely Anita, died shortly afterward. Every dog dies someday; Schinz was determined not to read anything into what was a natural occurrence, but it distressed him nonetheless; it was as if he had lost his final witness, his last companion. One day Schinz found himself at the border, not as on previous journeys to Paris, to Rome, Florence, London, Munich, but this time alone, without luggage, somewhat unshaven. He found himself standing in a small bare room, where he had to undress down to his shirt. Schinz hesitated, as if he could not believe it, but the commissioner repeated:

"Down to your shirt."

Every pocket was searched, not roughly, but unmercifully. Schinz had no idea what they were looking for. He had not swum across a river, crept over fields by night; he had come on the railroad. But without luggage. Perhaps it was this that made them suspect him. His passport was in order, even when held up against the brightest of lights. Weapons he did not have, or gold bars, not even pamphlets, nothing had fallen out of his underpants. But he was suspect all the same. Schinz tried to keep calm, to say nothing. The men who were feeling him over also said nothing. The body of an elderly man, that was all they could find. There was nothing even inserted in the soles of his shoes, which, in spite of his sworn assurances, they insisted on splitting apart. Schinz was allowed to get dressed again. The commissioner, carrying his passport, left the bare cell; the police-man remained. Through the half-open door Schinz could see the other travelers closing their examined or unexamined bags, respectable citizens, male and female, fur coats, hatboxes, porters grabbing bright suitcases.

"Be so kind," Schinz said, "as to close the door—"

The policeman kicked it shut.

"Don't panic," he said. "You won't catch the train anyway."

"Why not?"

The policeman was carrying a gun.

"Why not?" Schinz asked—

The policeman could have been his own son.

"Ready?"

It was not the policeman who asked that, but a third person who had opened the door again and did not bother to shut it properly; in and out— Ready? Nothing more than that: Ready? . . . Schinz tried hard not to give way to hatred; they were only doing their duty, he told himself, a wretched duty, putting on a uniform in the middle of the night to wait for trains running late, watching people on their way to the sea or the mountains, examining people who were themselves to blame that such duties were necessary. Schinz tried hard to put on his maltreated shoes and not to hate. An elderly man, looking in this greenish light rather disheveled in trousers held up by suspenders, a shirt with-out a collar, could not, Schinz realized, expect the outward forms to be preserved in the way the gentlemen of the press had done before they picked on that headline:

"No, this man did not steal. . . ."

One very quickly becomes known.

"Sit down," the commissioner said as Schinz, his coat on his arm and once more wearing a tie, stood before his desk. "Please sit down."

Schinz remained standing.

"I should like to remind you," he said, "that my train goes in four minutes."

"That is not my concern."

Pause.

"Stay on your feet, if you prefer."

Schinz sat down; there was no point in antagonizing these people; this was their duty, a wretched duty.

"Schinz, Heinrich Gottlieb—"

"Yes."

"Doctor of law—"

"Yes."

"A lawyer—"

"Yes," said Schinz. All we now need, he thought, is for this oaf to tell me how tall I am.

"Born—"

"Yes!"

Outside he could hear the puffing of the locomotive, ready at any moment to pull out; Schinz bit his lips, while the oaf flicked through his passport as if he had never seen one before.

"Where are you going?"

"Abroad," Schinz said.

"I asked where you were going."

"I have told you: abroad."

Pause.

"I ask you for the last time."

It was all Schinz could do not to hate, to hate them all in the person of this one man sitting there holding his passport, to hate, to hate. . . . Don't lose your nerve, he thought. He told himself: I must get away, I must, I can't bear seeing injustice and keeping quiet about it, reading newspapers that say the opposite of the truth, seeing people who treat me like a poor, sick man, like a child with the falling sickness, knowing how anxiously they are waiting for me to make my next *faux pas*, all this maternal concern that I might drive the car over the curb, this friendly advice not to smoke so much and not to imagine things, this silence as I speak my mind, this unspoken hope that I will

292

go and see a nerve specialist, I can no longer bear it, I must get away! . . . And the train is still there, the puffing locomotive full to bursting with steam. . . .

"Where are you going?"

"What the hell has that got to do with you?"

Schinz had sprung to his feet.

"Please," the commissioner said.

"What the hell," Schinz shouted, "what the hell has that got to do with you?"

Shouting was so un-Schinzish, he saw it every time, regretted it every time, not because the oaf would now punish him, but because it was not his style. . . . Gottlieb, Bimba had said, I am not deaf. But, good God, they're deaf all right. Every one of them. They hear that you are shouting, but not what you are shouting. Yes, that's it. Of course they are deaf, otherwise they would not be able to live with themselves, they would die like his dog, because they had heard and could not say, just like the dog! Thus he was thinking as the commissioner also got to his feet and smiled dryly:

"Very well. You can go."

He had thrown the passport into a drawer, which he locked. He put the key in his hip pocket, showing the wide expanse of his backside. Schinz understood, took up his coat, and went out, but had not got far before the young policeman caught up with him.

"You're to come back."

"Why?"

"You're to come back."

Schinz went back; the commissioner, still standing, was light-ing a pipe, so that he was unable to speak for a while; then he said:

"Close the door like a person with manners."

Schinz gulped. The commissioner was smoking, his mind al-ready on other things. Schinz closed the door like a person with manners. . . . At three in the morning, as the rain was again pouring down, he crossed the border illicitly, Heinrich Gottlieb Schinz, lawyer, a man without papers.

Bimba was in tears.

The children went to school ashamed.

For some nights Schinz found himself sheltering in barns,

never really sleeping, watchful while still near the border. In ways such as this, he thought, Alexis had crossed the border into our country, an emigrant who carries little weight as a witness; and how quickly one becomes an emigrant! One has a fixed abode, as fixed as can possibly be, one has a family tree and a house; then suddenly one is an emigrant. It has happened often enough before. One begins to see things somewhat differently from the way in which they are taught; one cannot prevent the newspapers' writing the opposite of the truth. . . . One day they printed a report to the effect that Schinz had been arrested—on the other side of the border of course. He would, in the official phrase, be deported. Deported! For the family an unimaginable blow. Only Bimba behaved well; she aged, received hardly any visitors. Not that people avoided her—people are not quite as bad as that; but Bimba could not bear them, not even their silence. She did not try to defend everything that Schinz had said or done; that ridiculous quarrel with the newspaper, for instance. But as far as that automobile was concerned, well, the more Bimba thought about it—unaided—the more she felt the man had not really stolen it. Funny how differently one sees things when habitual social contacts begin to fall off. And how they fall off when one sees things differently! Then it is no longer funny— Bimba aged a great deal—

Again there was a commissioner sitting there:

"Schinz, Heinrich Gottlieb?"

Schinz said nothing.

"Doctor of law."

Schinz said nothing.

"Lawyer," said the commissioner, who was this time holding not a passport, but a warrant, and he continued: "Why are you living under an assumed name?"

Schinz said nothing.

"You crossed the border illicitly. Your own country confiscated your papers—"

"That is not true!"

"So you did not cross the border?" the commissioner asked, not without pride in the effective way he was conducting his interrogation. "You are not in this country at all?"

"None of my papers have been confiscated from me."

"Then why do you not have any?"

Schinz, contenting himself for the moment with a short malevolent laugh, drew out a handkerchief, a very unwashed one, such as a man like Schinz could never have carried, except perhaps when he was a boy, a gray and crumpled thing, damp and disgusting; then he said:

"That is a long story—"

Soon he would be unable to remember it himself!

"And so you admit," the commissioner said, "that your name is not Bernauer, but Schinz—Heinrich Gottlieb, lawyer?"

"Yes."

Schinz blew his nose; he needed no reflection in the window to know what he looked like. No money for clean shirts, several nights in third-class waiting rooms, trouser creases gone, several nights in the open, no hot water, soap from public conveniences, a coat that had, so to speak, become his living room—the costume of a suspect was complete. Don't bank on your face to pull you out, the fine features of your face! Forget *Der Rosenkavalier*, forget the society for the promotion of the arts, forget the public monuments; such knowledge only serves to make you even more suspect. A man like you, with a house and a car of your own, why do you leave your home town? Why do you need to call yourself Bernauer? . . . You can sign the statement, the first of many, as soon as it is finished; but there are still a few questions to come.

"Dr. Schinz," said the commissioner, opening the still modest-looking file, and the tone in which he used the title "Doctor" was in no way sneering. In fact, since this apparently ordinary vagrant had now turned out to be an important find, it was entirely respectful: "Dr. Schinz, you have contacts with a man named Becker?"

Schinz hesitated.

"Becker, Alexis, an emigrant."

Schinz said nothing.

"Yes or no?"

Schinz said nothing.

"Very well," the commissioner said with a smile. "Perhaps you will remember if I show you his photograph—"

Schinz could feel himself growing red.

"The photograph is admittedly old," said the commissioner. "Your friend no longer wears a moustache, as far as we know."

Schinz was silent.

"I am not trying to catch you out, Dr. Schinz, you will be given plenty of time for reflection." The commissioner spoke in the almost intimate tone of deadly enemies, both of whom know the rules. "You also probably know a man named Marini. . . ."

"Marini?"

"Francesco Marini."

"No."

"Or Stepanov."

"Stepanov?"

"Ossip Stepanov."

"No."

"Or Espinel."

"No," Schinz said.

"Roderigo Espinel."

"No," Schinz said.

"His name doesn't matter," the commissioner said. "But if you know him you will remember his face—a very striking face which nobody who has seen it ever forgets."

With that he handed over the photograph:

"A ready-made Jesus Christ face."

Schinz turned pale. . . .

"You remember him, Dr. Schinz?"

Schinz was holding the photograph: the forester, the loden coat— They're trying to turn me insane, he thought, they're trying to turn me insane! There he was, standing in his loden coat, a forester in his Sunday best, posing in front of his trees, looking rather embarrassed; it was a bad photograph, an amateur photograph, but distinct. Schinz put it back on the table, his instinctive action rather hasty, as if it were burning his fingers or weighing as heavy as stone. . . .

The commissioner had meanwhile taken a cigarette and lit it. Now he said:

"Do you know this man?"

The cell Schinz was given was quite presentable. It even got some sun through a window placed rather high up, so that he could see nothing of the world except a chimney, and that only when he stood on his bunk. The bunk was hard but clean, not unworthy. At three in the afternoon the sun disappeared; shortly afterward a clock struck outside. Schinz found it something to be thankful for that he did not have only a wall to look at, maybe even a wall in shadow, but the open sky. His cell was apparently on the top floor, for he often heard the fluttering of pigeons, and now and again one flew past the bars. At times Schinz was even quite cheerful: You shouldn't go slipping across borders, he would tell himself then. The cell was small; it reminded him of that well-known monastery in Fiesole. All these reminders! His main anxiety when he was first put in this place: that he would lose his belief in his own innocence. That photograph of the forester, he told himself: that had been a hysterical reaction; he had not really looked at it; he had been startled and had put it down. Startled by a loden coat, of which there were thousands around! The face, Schinz told himself—and rightly—he had not seen at all clearly at the time; it had been dusk and then night. Don't let them turn me insane! And even if it really had been he, he thought another time, what crime have I committed? I saw him, yes, I talked with him, all right, though he did most of the talking. What else? Schinz asked himself, coming suddenly to a halt as he paced to and fro. What has this Marini or this Stepanov or whatever he calls himself to do with me? Then he lay down on his bed. They are trying to turn me insane, he told himself quite calmly, they are trying to turn me insane. Outside he could hear the clucking of hens. In a way rather nice. A window full of sky; the bars in front were not so bad; Schinz had no intention of jumping through the window to his death or flying out over the chimney tops. In time, he thought, there would be a trial. Occasionally he also heard the hooting of cars, but rather far away; beyond the trees, across a yard, or something like that. The whole building (who knows?) had perhaps been a monastery once; on his travels Schinz had visited so many monasteries, had often tried to visualize having to live in such a cell. And then Bimba would arrive, raving about a cloister, and together they went down to view it, to admire the frescoes, slowly making their way out, sunshine on a piazza, a little *ristorante* opposite. The frescoes: Saint Sebastian with arrows in his flesh, children being slaughtered in Bethlehem, a Christophorus, the three familiar crucifixes on Golgotha, a whole series of grim stories, but all of them beautiful. It reminded him of Wölfflin! And so on. Luckily the children were no longer small. Sometimes Schinz would simply stand beside the wall, his arms against the wall, his head in his arms, in order that he should see nothing; with his eyes open. The sky made him desperate. Sleeping did not help. Dreams made everything look so out of proportion. But soon his food would arrive, and then he would know: whether they were wardens or nurses, whether he was in a prison or a madhouse. That was his only real anxiety. To know that nowhere in the world do you rate as a responsible witness. But when he heard their footsteps, he did not raise his head from the wall; the door opened, Schinz remained as he was, the door closed again. Schinz looked: there was a plate, a tin one, but clean, potato soup and bread, a rather comic-looking jar with fresh water. . . . Weeks like years, years like weeks, interrogations covering the same ground over and over again, names Schinz did not know. Now and again he had the feeling that it was all nothing but a dream, but that made no difference; whenever he awoke, he saw the bars across the sky, and every morning, as it turned gray, he could hear the cocks crowing—

At last things began to happen.

One day Schinz saw himself in the middle of a scene familiar from pictures he had seen: standing in shirt and trousers, a tight rope around his wrists. He was not alone. They were standing in a schoolyard, gravel underfoot, chestnut trees flaunting their red-and-white candles. Hours of uncertainty. The soldiers guarding them were wearing a uniform that Schinz had never seen before; history, it seemed, had taken another new turn: the caps were different, the cut of the trousers, different too their manner of holding their rifles. It was already fairly light, but the sun had not yet risen. What struck Schinz (incidentally the only one in his group who spoke German) even more than the unfamiliar uniforms was the janitor's little chicken yard, where for the first time he saw the two familiar cocks he had been hearing every morning. They had not yet begun to crow. . . . On the steps of the gymnasium appeared a man in civilian clothes, a very young boy who was wearing an armband. He read out names from a list:

"Stepanov, Ossip."

"Here."

"Becker, Alexis."

"Here."

"Schinz, Heinrich Gottlieb."

"Here."

The others looked down at the gravel. Soldiers led those whose names had been called across to the gymnasium, which was still brightly lit, though it was now daylight. Condemned men were of course no longer crucified, but hanged. The apparatus was ridiculously simple, almost schoolboyish; three ropes were let down, and to each was attached a rather thin cord with a loop in it. Under them stood hastily nailed wooden stools, each with three steps. Schinz thought: You surely can't mean this seriously! But at the same time he had no hope that it would not happen. Schinz was likewise aware that he would now never know the crime of which he had been found guilty. Somehow, it now hardly seemed to matter; thus far had he come. More time passed. The three condemned men had been placed back to back in such a way that they could neither speak to nor see one another. Schinz could see a table, made of two trestles and a board, and on it an iron stake, two gloves such as welders wear, three small pincers, a Bunsen burner, a piece of wire that showed signs of having often been heated—equipment enough to inflict all the torture one wanted. A man in uniform was speaking to a sort of doctor, who kept shrugging his shoulders. Then, since they obviously could come to no agreement, the man in uniform turned around, holding three photographs in his hand; each of them was again compared with his photograph. Then the boy with the armband came up and showed them to their places. Becker on the left, Stepanov in the middle, Schinz on the right. They had to place the loops around their necks themselves. It really was the forester. He said:

"Why did you betray me?"

Schinz could not find his voice.

"Why did you betray me?"

The forester helped him, unreproaching, in the same way as he had just helped poor Becker—one would think he himself had been hanged countless times already. Schinz looked at him and said:

"I don't understand a word of it."

The forester smiled.

"I did not speak to you, Dr. Schinz, you spoke to me. You asked me the way—"

"No," said Schinz.

"We must bear it."

But Schinz, with that Jesus Christ face before him, could not bear it: he shouted, as if he could thus force himself to awaken, shouted as loud as any man can:

"No! No! No!"

This was the last time Schinz heard the sound of his own voice— Now awake, covered in sweat, feeling his undamaged neck with his own hand, he did not realize it at once. Bimba was stroking his forehead, Bimba was old, Bimba was smiling, a doctor was standing at the foot of the bed. Bimba was moving her lips, but she did not utter a word, the doctor was also moving his lips, but not a word could be heard. Schinz was deaf. When he realized it, he closed his eyes; as if, when he next opened them, everything would be different again. But nothing was different, they were still moving their lips. As he tried to say that he could no longer hear them, he realized that he was also dumb.

Schinz lived on a further seven years after these events without ever again leaving his home town. At the age of sixty-three he died a natural death. He was still regarded with respect. His curious *faux pas* had not been forgotten, but it was forgiven; though deaf and dumb, he continued to be greeted with civility when met on the street; for, as I have already said, the outside world—though not Bimba—saw the whole thing merely as a clinical case that, remarkable and disturbing as it undoubtedly was, held no significance for the outside world.

In the office

Last week brought me, without any effort on my part—and I have often made efforts along these lines, though never with success—two new commissions: for a country cottage and for a small open-air swimming pool.

Café Odeon

The question of chance: what comes our way without our preknowledge, with no conscious use of will power. Even the chance that brings two people together is often seen as an act of providence, though, as we know, this chance can be a ridiculous one: a man has taken the wrong hat, returns to the cloakroom, and in his slight confusion makes matters worse by treading on a young lady's toe, which distresses both so much that they speak to each other: the result is a marriage with three to five children. One day each of them will wonder how different life might have been if he had not picked up the wrong hat.

For most people who are not believers this sort of thing is probably the only kind of miracle they are prepared to acknowledge. And people who keep a diary—do they not also believe in chance, something that raises the questions and supplies the images? Does not everyone who describes something he has experienced believe basically that whatever happens to him has some sort of relevance? In order to explain the power of chance and thus to make its existence bearable it should hardly be necessary for us to call on God; enough, surely, just to tell ourselves that at all times of our lives, wherever we may be, a totality exists. But for myself, whatever I am doing, it is not this totality that determines my behavior, but only those parts of it I can see and hear. This is my potential, of all the rest I am unaware. I am not tuned in to it, at any rate not now—later maybe. The amazing and startling thing about every chance happening is that it brings us face to face with ourselves; chance shows me the things for which I now have an eye, which I am at this moment attuned to hear. If it were not for this simple trust that nothing can occur that is not relevant to us, and that nothing can change us if we have not ourselves changed, how could we even cross the street without wandering into insanity? Of course it is conceivable that we do not see and hear everything our potential allows us, in other words, there may be many chance happenings that we fail to see or hear, though they are relevant to us; but we experience none that are *not* relevant to us. In the final count it is always the most fitting thing that befalls us.

301